Julie King's Everyday Photoshop® for Photographers

JULIE KING

McGraw-Hill/Osborne

New York Chicago San Francisco
Lisbon London Madrid Mexico City
Milan New Delhi San Juan
Seoul Singapore Sydney Toronto

McGraw-Hill/Osborne
2100 Powell Street, 10th Floor
Emeryville, California 94608
U.S.A.

To arrange bulk purchase discounts for sales promotions, premiums, or fund-raisers, please contact **McGraw-Hill**/Osborne at the above address. For information on translations or book distributors outside the U.S.A., please see the International Contact Information page immediately following the index of this book.

Julie King's Everyday Photoshop® for Photographers

1234567890 WCT WCT 01987654

ISBN 0-07-225437-8

Publisher	Brandon A. Nordin
Vice President & Associate Publisher	Scott Rogers
Executive Editor	Jane K. Brownlow
Senior Project Editor	LeeAnn Pickrell
Acquisitions Coordinator	Agatha Kim
Technical Editor	Tim Cooper
Copy Editors	Margaret Berson
	Judy Ziajka
Proofreader	Stefany Otis
Indexer	Karin Arrigoni
Creative Director and Series Design	Scott Jackson
Composition	Peter Grame
Cover Design	Pattie Lee

This book was composed with QuarkXPress™.

About the Author

Photographer Julie Adair King is the author of several popular books about digital imaging and photography. Her most recent titles include *Shoot Like a Pro! Digital Photography Techniques, Digital Photography For Dummies, Photo Retouching and Restoration For Dummies, Adobe PhotoDeluxe For Dummies,* and *Easy Web Graphics.* A graduate of Purdue University, King established her own company, Julie King Creative, in 1988, in Indianapolis, Indiana.

Acknowledgments

I am deeply grateful to all the hard-working people at McGraw-Hill/Osborne who helped make this book possible, including Jane Brownlow, Roger Stewart, Katie Conley, Agatha Kim, Judy Ziajka, Margaret Berson, Scott Jackson, Peter Grame, and, most especially, the always patient and understanding LeeAnn Pickrell. Much thanks also to technical editor Tim Cooper for sharing his experience and to Danielle Jatlow and Margot Maley Hutchison at Waterside Productions for providing wise counsel and constant support.

Finally, I could not have written this book—or any other, for that matter—without my incredible family and friends. Thanks for lending a willing ear when I need to share (okay, vent), for encouragement when the days get long, and for the hugs and laughter that remind me always of the important things in life.

CONTENTS AT A GLANCE

CONTENTS

PART III | Exposure and Color Techniques

PART IV | Retouching Techniques

PART V | Photographer's Guide to Output

INTRODUCTION

At last count, Adobe Photoshop offered more than 50 tools, more than 500 menu commands, and 19 palettes packing scads of other controls. By my calculations, that means if you spent just two hours a day learning about each feature, it would take the better part of a year to acquaint yourself with everything this granddaddy of the digital imaging world has to offer.

I'm going to take a wild guess, though, and assume that you don't have two spare hours in your day—and if you *did,* you'd rather spend it doing something else, like, say, taking pictures. I'll go further out on a limb and assume that because the title of this book intrigued you enough to give it a look, your primary interest is using Photoshop to retouch and enhance the photos you do find time to snap.

If both assumptions are correct, I have good news for you. Over the years, I've studied and written about each and every Photoshop feature, and I can tell you with absolute certainty that you can safely ignore all but a few dozen.

Don't get me wrong—Photoshop is an amazing program, and each of its tools is a testament to the genius of Adobe's software engineers. The truth, though, is that a good many Photoshop features are designed for people who use the program for original digital artistry and special-effects work, not for the kind of image retouching and subtle photo enhancement that most photographers want to do.

It was this realization that led to *Everyday Photoshop for Photographers.* This book cuts through the maze of Photoshop menus, tools, and filters and focuses on the core techniques that photographers need to be successful in the digital darkroom. So instead of spending hours honing Photoshop skills you'll never use, you can concentrate on techniques that will serve you well every day.

How Is This Photoshop Book Different?

Most Photoshop books fall into two camps. You can buy doorstop-size tomes that provide encyclopedic detail about even the most obscure program features, leaving no room for any practical guidance about how to implement the really useful tools. At the other end of the spectrum, many books are *too* lightweight. They emphasize special-effects filters that you could easily figure out on your own, for example. Or they show you how to do offbeat projects such as giving yourself a nose job, ignoring topics that are critical to any serious photographer—monitor-to-printer color matching and safeguarding digital files, to name just two.

In fairness, these books are what they are because they're meant to appeal to all Photoshop users, who have a wide variety of interests. *Everyday Photoshop,* on the other hand, is geared specifically to photographers who simply want to harness the program's power to solve common picture problems and then prepare the finished product for print or the Web.

Whether you're a professional photographer, a serious hobbyist, or just starting to discover digital imaging, you'll get the step-by-step guidance you need to tackle these and other everyday projects:

- Crop to a better composition or specific frame size
- Brighten underexposed images, restore lost shadow detail, and repair blown highlights
- Tweak color balance, saturation, and contrast
- Remove red-eye, cover up other small blemishes, and patch over larger defects
- Fix lens distortion and manipulate focus
- Replace a distracting background
- Convert color photos to stunning black-and-white images
- Set up your digital studio for improved color consistency

Because producing a great photo is pointless if it goes no further than your computer, this book also provides in-depth information about how to output your files, whether you're having them professionally printed, doing the job on your own photo printer, or sharing them via the Internet. Along the way, you'll also find the background information you need to make sense of important digital imaging concepts, such as resolution, color management, bit depth, and file formats.

Expert Techniques Made Easy

As you explore this book, you'll find that I've opted not to cover simple, automated correction filters. Like most quick fixes in life, these don't produce very good results and can even harm your images. (And if you do want to investigate the one-click filters, you don't need my help.) Instead, I've focused on expert-level techniques, which take a little longer to understand at first but give you much more control and flexibility, making your life easier in the long run.

The point is, don't be intimidated if you encounter unfamiliar jargon or seemingly complex instructions when you first flip through this book. When you try the techniques, you'll find that they're actually fairly simple, and I'll break down all the technical mumbo-jumbo for you.

To make things even easier to digest, each chapter includes sample projects that give you hands-on experience—the best way to learn any new skill. You can download low-resolution copies of the images used in the projects free of charge from the McGraw-Hill/Osborne Publishing web site: www.osborne.com. Find and click the Free Code link, and then navigate to the link for *Everyday Photoshop for Photographers*. (I probably don't need to mention this since you're a fellow photographer, but do note that the pictures are all copyrighted and not available for any use other than working with this book.)

Version Notes, Operating Systems, and Other Details

Everyday Photoshop for Photographers covers Photoshop Version 7.0 and Photoshop CS (Creative Suite). When information applies to only one version, you see a little icon next to the text. If you use an earlier version of the program, you'll find that many of the instructions apply to your software as well; many core Photoshop components haven't changed much over the past few releases.

This book covers both Windows and Macintosh systems, too. Although most illustrations feature the Windows operating system, I provide Mac-specific information when the two versions are significantly different. Keyboard shortcuts— keys you can press to quickly invoke certain functions—are provided for both Windows and Mac as well.

When you see an instruction such as "Choose Filter | Sharpen | Unsharp Mask," it's your cue to click through a series of commands accessible via the program menus. In this case, you would click Filter on the menu bar, click Sharpen to unfurl a submenu, and then click Unsharp Mask to open the Unsharp Mask dialog box.

Finally, although you don't need any experience with Photoshop to use this book, if you're brand new to computers as well, you may find it helpful to invest in a beginner's book about your operating system. So that I can devote as much space as possible to Photoshop-related information, I don't go into great detail about basic computer operations.

How to Get the Most from This Book

Many techniques in the second half of this book build on fundamentals presented in the first half. So I recommend that you use the same approach to this book as you would reading a mystery novel: start at the beginning and work your way through to the end. At the least, exploring the chapters on customizing tools (Chapter 5), creating selection outlines (Chapters 6 and 7), and using layers (Chapter 8) will enable you to have a much stronger foothold when you tackle projects in later chapters.

However, if you're like some of the fine women in my book club, who can't resist reading the ending first, that's perfectly acceptable, too. I've provided lots of cross-references throughout each chapter so you can easily flip to the chapter that offers more help should you get hung up on a particular step.

Whichever direction you go, don't try to absorb everything at once. And don't feel stupid if you can't make sense of things on the first, second, or even third read, either. Even when you whittle down the list of Photoshop features to the photography-related set covered in this book, some tools and techniques can be pretty darned confusing at first.

I promise, though, that if you spend just a few minutes with *Everyday Photoshop* each week, you'll quickly acquire the skills you need to turn problem pictures into good pictures—and make good pictures even better. Before long, you'll not only be able to correct any photographic flaw with expert results, but also have the experience you need to get the job done quickly. Then you can spend less time staring at your computer monitor and more time doing what we photographers love best: enjoying the view through the camera lens!

Photoshop Road Map

1

Many parts of the Photoshop workspace follow established rules of the computing road: You open a Photoshop menu just as you do in any program, and the program windows adhere to the standard Windows or Macintosh design. But a few components work in ways that aren't obvious, so this chapter gives you the lowdown, explaining how to manipulate the Photoshop tools, palettes, and other controls. You'll also find information that will help you customize your new digital studio.

In This Chapter:

Getting Familiar with Photoshop

Figure 1.1 labels the main elements of the Photoshop CS window, which looks virtually identical to its predecessor. The one significant change is that the File Browser is now accessible via a button on the options bar as opposed to being stuck in the palette well. (You can read more about the File Browser in Chapter 3.)

The next several sections provide details on working with these program elements, with the exception of the menu bar, which I won't discuss for fear of insulting your intelligence. (But do remember that when you see a phrase such as "choose Filter | Sharpen | Unsharp Mask" in this book, it means that you're supposed to select a series of items from the menus. In this case, you click the Filter menu, click Sharpen to display a submenu, and then click Unsharp Mask in that secondary menu.)

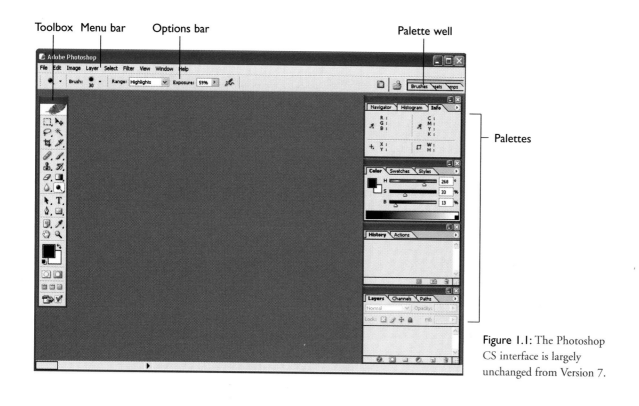

Figure 1.1: The Photoshop CS interface is largely unchanged from Version 7.

Selecting Tools

The primary Photoshop editing tools are clustered in the top two-thirds of the toolbox, shown in Figure 1.2. (If you don't see the toolbox, choose Window | Tools.)

To activate a tool, just click its icon. Note, though, that some slots in the toolbox are occupied by more than one tool. For example, the Brush and Pencil tools share the same slot, as illustrated in Figure 1.3. Multi-tool slots are marked with a little black triangle. If you position your cursor over the triangle and then hold down the left mouse button, Photoshop displays a flyout menu containing icons for all tools in the slot, as shown in the figure. Click the tool that you want to use. The icon for the selected tool takes center stage in the toolbox, and the flyout menu disappears.

Time Saver

You also can select tools with the keyboard shortcuts laid out in the upcoming Speed Keys table. Some tools that share a toolbox slot also share a keyboard shortcut. Your first key press activates whichever tool is currently visible in the toolbox; press SHIFT plus the shortcut key repeatedly to cycle through the other tools that share the shortcut. (If the SHIFT-key thing doesn't work, see the section "General Preferences" later in this chapter.)

Figure 1.2: To select an editing tool, click its toolbox icon.

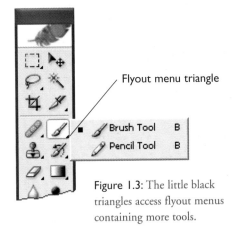

Flyout menu triangle

Figure 1.3: The little black triangles access flyout menus containing more tools.

SPEED KEYS: Selecting the Editing Tools from the Keyboard

Tool	Shortcut*	Tool	Shortcut*
Rectangular and Elliptical Marquees	M	Move	V
Lasso, Polygonal Lasso, Magnetic Lasso	L	Magic Wand	W
Crop	C	Slice, Slice Select	K
Healing Brush, Patch	J	Brush, Pencil	B
Clone Stamp, Pattern Stamp	S	History Brush, Art History Brush	Y
Eraser, Background Eraser, Magic Eraser	E	Gradient, Paint Bucket	G
Blur, Sharpen, Smudge	R	Dodge, Burn, Sponge	O
Path Selection, Direct Selection	A	Type, Type Mask	T
Pen, Freeform Pen	P	Shape (six tools)	U
Notes, Audio Annotation	N	Eyedropper, Color Sampler, Measure	I
Hand	H	Zoom	Z

*Press SHIFT plus the shortcut key to cycle through tools that share a shortcut.

If you're a Mac user and can't get certain Photoshop keyboard shortcuts to work, you need to tweak your operating system controls. Otherwise, some shortcuts invoke system-related actions instead of Photoshop actions.

- In OS 9, open the Keyboard control panel, click the Function Keys button, and uncheck Enable Hot Function Keys.
- In OS X, choose System Preferences from the Apple menu to open the System Preferences window. Click the Show All icon and then the Keyboard and Mouse icon. Click the Keyboard Shortcuts button and disable conflicting shortcuts. Click Show All again, click the Exposé icon, and disable Exposé shortcuts, too.

Setting Tool Options

One of the features that makes Photoshop such a powerful program is the flexibility built into its editing tools. Depending on the tool, you can customize its performance in a number of ways:

- **Options bar** The main tool controls live on the options bar, shown in Figure 1.4. To hide and display the options bar, choose Window | Options.

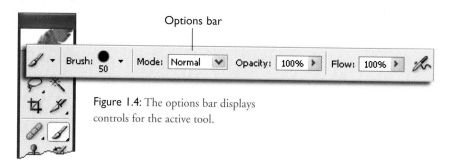

Options bar

Figure 1.4: The options bar displays controls for the active tool.

- **Toolbox color controls**
Just underneath the editing tools in the toolbox, you see four controls that establish the colors produced by certain tools. Figure 1.5 points you to these controls; Chapter 5 has details.

- **Keyboard modifiers** You can affect the behavior of some tools by pressing certain keys. For example, if you press SHIFT while painting with the Brush tool, you limit the tool to creating a line that's perfectly horizontal or vertical. Look for the Tool Tricks boxes throughout this book to learn the really useful keyboard controls, or *modifiers*, as Photoshop geeks like to call them.

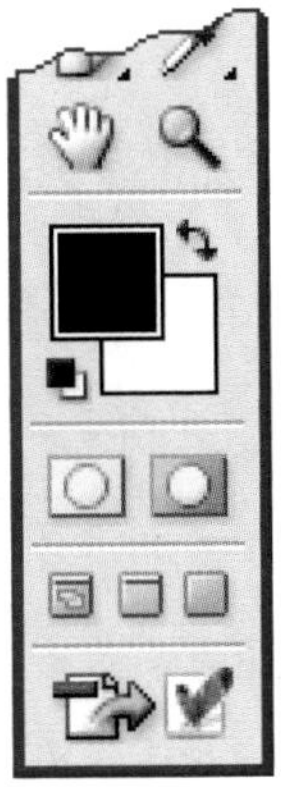

Color controls

Figure 1.5: The large swatches indicate the current foreground and background colors.

Working with Palettes

When you first install Photoshop, several palettes appear open on-screen, and other palettes peek their noses out of the palette well, labeled in Figure 1.6. (Don't see the palette well? Check your monitor display settings. The palettes don't appear unless the screen resolution is set to 1024 x 768 or higher.)

To open a docked palette, click its tab, shown in Figure 1.6, or choose its name from the Window menu. To display a free-floating palette, choose its name from the Window menu. You also can open some palettes by using the keyboard shortcuts listed in the upcoming Speed Keys table.

In addition to the controls you normally see in a palette, you can display a palette menu that offers related

Palette well   Palette tab

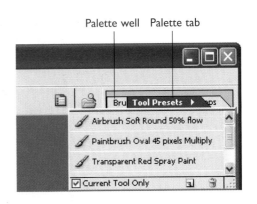

Figure 1.6: Click a tab to display a palette that's docked in the palette well.

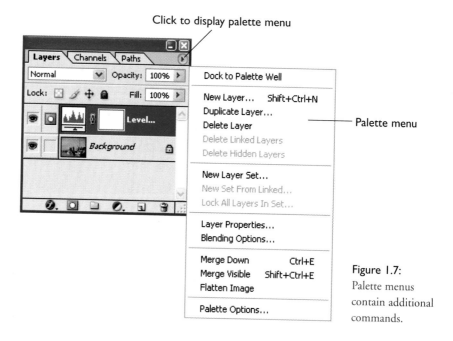

Click to display palette menu

Palette menu

Figure 1.7:
Palette menus
contain additional
commands.

SPEED KEYS:
Hiding and
Displaying Palettes

Palette	Shortcut*
Brushes	F5
Color	F6
Layers	F7
Info	F8
Actions	F9

*Mac users must disable
system keyboard shortcuts.

commands. Click the arrow in the top-right corner of the palette to display the menu, as shown in Figure 1.7.

The next few sections provide a few more tips on working with palettes in general. Later chapters detail specific controls in important palettes.

Working with Palette Windows

By default, the free-floating palettes are grouped in palette windows. Figure 1.8 shows the Windows version of a palette window that houses the Layers, Channels, and Paths palettes. The Mac version is identical except for the minimize and close buttons, which follow the OS 9 and OS X standards. Familiarize yourself with the following palette-window maneuvers:

- **Choosing a palette** To switch among the palettes in the palette window, click the palette tabs.
- **Moving a palette window** To relocate a palette window, drag the bar that runs across the top of the window. Officially, that bar is called the *title bar,* but in this case, there's no actual title.
- **Resizing a palette window** Drag the lower-right corner of the window to adjust the window size.
- **Collapsing a palette window** When you click the Minimize button, labeled in Figure 1.8, the palette remains open, but with just the top

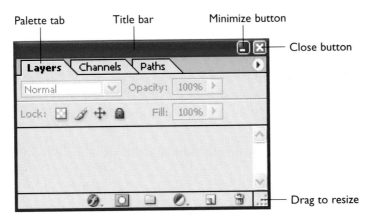

Figure 1.8: You can group palettes in free-floating windows.

part of the window showing. Click the button again to restore the palette to its original size.

- **Closing a palette window** Click the Close button, labeled in Figure 1.8, to close the palette window.

Rearranging Palettes

If the default arrangement of palettes doesn't suit you, you can reorganize the palettes as follows:

- **Turn a docked palette into a floating palette** Drag the palette by its tab out of the well.
- **Dock a floating palette** Open the palette menu and choose Dock to Palette Well.
- **Separate a palette in a palette window into an individual, free-floating palette** Drag the palette by its tab out of the palette window.
- **Reorganize palette groupings** To alter the original grouping of palettes in palette windows, just drag the palette tabs from window to window. For example, you can move the Actions palette into the window that holds the Layers, Channels, and Paths palettes. Using this technique, you can combine your most frequently used palettes into a single palette window, which cuts down on screen clutter.

Preserving Palette Positions

If you rearrange or reorganize your palettes, tell Photoshop that you want it to retain the changes before you close the program. In Windows and OS 9, choose Edit | Preferences | General. In OS X, choose Photoshop | Preferences | General. Select the Save Palette Locations box and click OK. To return to the original, default palette setup, choose Window | Workspace | Reset Palette Locations.

Choosing Program Preferences

The Preferences dialog box, shown in Figure 1.9, gives you access to additional options for tweaking Photoshop's appearance and performance. Open the dialog box via the Preferences | General command, which appears at the bottom of the Edit menu if you're running Photoshop on a Windows computer or a Mac with OS 9. If you're working with OS X, look for the command on the Photoshop menu.

The Preferences dialog box is a multi-panel affair, with each panel housing different options. You can select a panel from the drop-down list, labeled in the figure, or cycle through the panels by clicking the Prev and Next buttons.

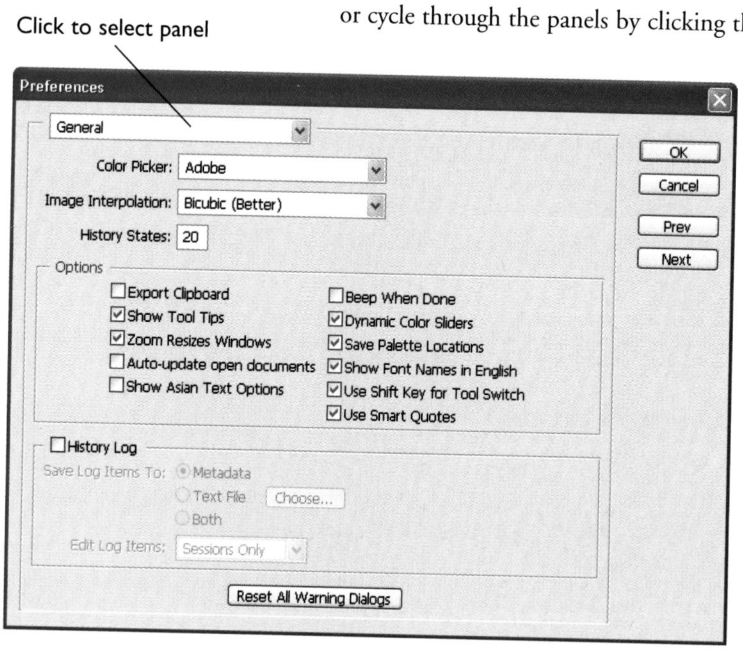

Click to select panel

I could devote a whole chapter to each panel, but frankly, that would not only put us both to sleep, but would also be a waste of time and paper. In most cases, the default settings established by Adobe will serve you well, and many options don't come into play at all for everyday photo-editing tasks. So the next several sections discuss those settings that you may want to adjust before you start working with Photoshop. I mention certain other options throughout the book, and you can read about the remaining ones in the Photoshop Help system if you're interested.

Figure 1.9: Set basic program options via the Preferences dialog box.

General Preferences

Figure 1.9 shows my settings for the options on the General panel of the CS Preferences dialog box, which is slightly different than Version 7. A few items warrant explanation:

- **Color Picker** A *color picker* is a tool that you use to select paint colors. Stick with the default setting, Adobe; it's more sophisticated than the alternative, which is the color picker provided by your computer's operating system (Windows or Mac).

- **Redo Key** This option specifies what keyboard shortcuts invoke the Edit | Undo and Edit | Redo commands. While working with this book, use the default option, which sets CTRL-Z (Windows) or ⌘-Z (Mac) as the shortcut for toggling between Undo and Redo. Otherwise, my instructions related to those commands won't work.

- **History States** This setting controls the number of edits the program enables you to undo. You can raise the value higher than the default (20), but doing so increases the demand on your computer's resources. See Chapter 4 for more about undoing edits and other ways to protect yourself from mistakes.

- **Use System Shortcut Keys (Mac OS X only)** Turn this one off. Otherwise, some keyboard shortcuts perform an OS X system function rather than a Photoshop function.

- **Use Shift Key for Tool Switch** This option determines how you cycle through tools that share a keyboard shortcut. If you select the check box, you press SHIFT plus the tool shortcut to switch tools; otherwise, every press of the shortcut key by itself toggles the tools. So that we're on the same page, so to speak, select this option while working with this book.

- **History Log** Photoshop CS offers an option that logs the changes that you make to an image and preserves the log either as part of the image file or as a separate text file. The feature is designed for users whose jobs require them to keep careful track of what changes are made to a photo. If you fall into that category, read the Help system information about the feature to decide which of the tracking options makes the most sense for your situation. Otherwise, keep the option turned off. Storing the tracking information in the image file increases file size and can strain the program's performance.

Remember

To open the Preferences dialog box with the General panel at the forefront, press CTRL-K (Windows) or ⌘-K (Mac).

PART I | INTO THE DIGITAL DARKROOM

Remember

Photoshop stores your preferences data in a file named Adobe Photoshop 7.0 Prefs or Adobe Photoshop CS Prefs. If Photoshop starts behaving strangely, the file may be corrupt. Close Photoshop and use your system's file-searching function to locate and delete the file (location depends on your operating system). When you relaunch Photoshop, it creates a new preferences file, and your problems may be solved. Unfortunately, all the preferences return to the defaults, so you need to redo any changes that you made to those settings.

File Handling Preferences

Options on the File Handling tab of the Preferences dialog box, shown in Figure 1.10, affect how Photoshop saves and opens image files, topics you can explore in Chapters 3 and 4. You may want to adjust the following options, depending on how you will be working with the program.

CS **Ignore EXIF Profile Tag**

Today's digital cameras store certain bits of extra information in picture files. This data, called *EXIF metadata,* includes such details as the model of camera, color profile, shutter speed, and other capture settings. The Ignore EXIF Profile Tag option in Photoshop CS relates to the color-profile information.

Giving a recommendation on this option is tricky because the best choice depends upon your camera. Every camera designates a color profile in metadata, but many models don't report the profile accurately. Instead, they simply assign a tag for the sRGB profile, which you can explore in Chapter 14. As a result, you may not retain all the colors your camera actually captured.

My advice is that unless you're sure that your camera tags color space information correctly, turn this option on. That way, Photoshop ignores the EXIF profile data.

v.7 For Photoshop 7 users, Adobe offers a free plug-in that provides the same result as enabling the Ignore EXIF Profile Tag option. Look for the plug-in in the Downloads section of the Support area of the Adobe Web site (www.adobe.com).

CS **Enable Large Document Format (.psb)**

Normally, Photoshop does not allow you to save a file larger than 2 gigabytes (GB). That limit far exceeds what most users need, but some photographers may on occasion need

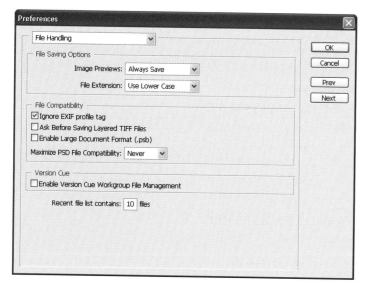

Figure 1.10: These options affect how Photoshop opens and saves your images.

to create larger files. For those huge projects, Photoshop CS offers a new large-document format, which carries the file extension .psb. If you want to save files in this format, enable this option. You probably won't be able to open the file in any program *other* than Photoshop CS, however.

Maximize PSD File Compatibility

The Maximize PSD File Compatibility option affects files that you save in Photoshop's native file format, PSD. In Photoshop 7, the option name is slightly different: Always Maximize Compatibility for Photoshop (PSD) Files.

Either way, if you select the check box, the program saves files with extra data that ensures that they can be opened in earlier versions of Photoshop. Because that extra data bloats file sizes, I recommend turning this option off. If you need to share a PSD file with someone who's using an older incarnation of Photoshop, you can turn on the option before saving the file.

| v.7 | ### Enable Workgroup Functionality |

Photoshop 7 provides the Enable Workgroup Functionality option for users who collaborate on images with co-workers in a workgroup setting. Among other things, the feature enables you to control who can make changes to a file stored on a workgroup server. If you're part of a team that uses Photoshop in this fashion, ask your workgroup administrator when and how to implement the feature. Otherwise, turn it off.

| CS | ### Enable Version Cue Workgroup File Management |

Version Cue is a new, updated version of the workgroup features found in Version 7. Again, check with your workgroup poobah to find out what settings to use. If you're not part of a workgroup, turn the option off. Note that Version Cue features aren't available unless you own the entire Creative Suite.

Display & Cursors Preferences

Figure 1.11 shows my recommended settings on the Display & Cursors panel of the Preferences dialog box. Three settings deserve comment:

- **Color Channels in Color** Photoshop enables you to view the individual color channels that make up a digital image, a topic you can

Figure 1.11: Change tool cursor styles here.

explore in Chapter 2. If you turn this option on, Photoshop displays a tint over the channel image to remind you what color channel you're viewing. Nice idea, but the tint hinders your ability to evaluate the channel contents, so turn this option off.

■ **Painting Cursors** When you work with tools that feature customizable brushes, you can choose from three cursor styles: Standard, Precise, and Brush Size, illustrated in Figure 1.12. Brush Size is the best choice. With this option selected, your cursor reflects the size and shape of your brush.

■ **Other Cursors** These options affect the brushless tools. Precise gives you the best indication of what area your tool is about to alter.

Tool Tricks

While working with a tool that has a customizable brush, press the CAPS LOCK key to toggle between the Brush Size and Precise cursor styles. (For this trick to work, you must select Brush Size on the Display & Cursors panel of the Preferences dialog box.) Turn off CAPS LOCK before you use other keyboard shortcuts, though, or the shortcuts may not work correctly.

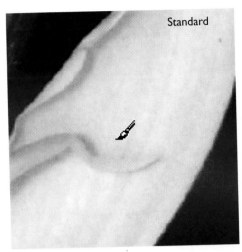

Standard

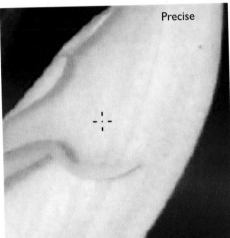

Precise

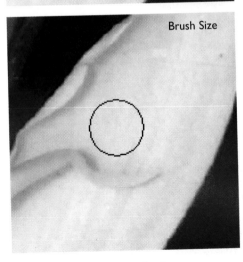

Brush Size

Figure 1.12: You can customize the appearance of tool cursors.

Plug-Ins & Scratch Disks

To flex its muscles, Photoshop requires plenty of RAM (system memory). But RAM alone isn't enough. As you run the program, it uses empty space on your computer's hard drive as a temporary data-storage tank. Computer folk refer to that temporary storage space as the *scratch disk*.

On computers that have a single, nonpartitioned drive, Photoshop automatically sets that drive as the primary scratch disk. If your computer has multiple hard drives or a single hard drive that is partitioned into several virtual drives, visit the Plug-Ins & Scratch Disks panel of the Preferences dialog box, shown in Figure 1.13. Here, you can designate the order in which you want Photoshop to access your drives for its scratch disk needs. Select the drive that has the greatest amount of free space from the First drop-down list, select the next-roomiest drive from the Second drop-down list, and so on.

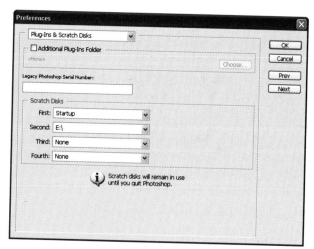

Figure 1.13: Specify which hard drive you want Photoshop to use as the scratch disk.

Regardless of how many drives your system boasts, make sure that you give Photoshop substantial scratch disk space. If the program acts squirrelly or displays a message saying that the scratch disk is full, delete unneeded files from your hard drive.

Memory & Image Cache

By default, Photoshop helps itself to as much as 50 percent of your available RAM. If the program gets bogged down when you work on large image files, you may want to allow it to consume even more memory.

In Windows and Mac OS X, you make this change from inside Photoshop, using the Memory & Image Cache panel of the Preferences dialog box. Try bumping up the value in the Memory Usage section of the panel by 10 or 20 percent. You must close and reopen the program for this change to take effect.

In Mac OS 9, you assign RAM to individual programs via an operating system control. After closing Photoshop, locate the Photoshop program icon at the Finder level. Click the icon and choose File | Get Info | Memory. In the resulting dialog box, try raising both the Minimum and Preferred values.

Watch Out!

Don't feed Photoshop *all* your computer's RAM, or the computer won't be able to run the operating system itself or the other programs that normally run in the background while you're working. For safety's sake, limit Photoshop's memory allocation to 75 percent of the available RAM.

Viewing Pictures

Every open image in Photoshop appears inside its own window, as shown in Figure 1.14. You get the standard Windows or Mac controls for closing, minimizing, and restoring windows, as well as scroll bars for scrolling the image display.

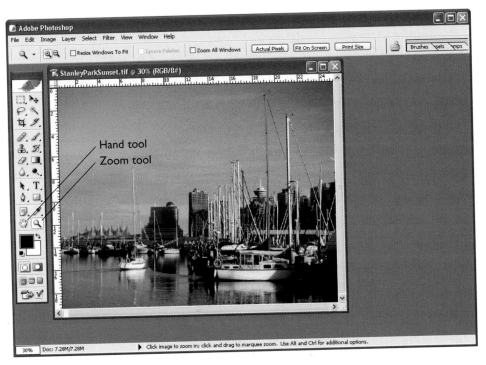

Figure 1.14: Every open image appears inside its own window.

Use these tactics to get a closer look at your photo or pull out for a wider view:

- Click the Zoom tool, labeled in Figure 1.14, and click the image. Keep clicking to zoom in further. To zoom out, ALT-click (Windows) or OPTION-click (Mac).
- Use the keyboard shortcuts listed in the upcoming Speed Keys table.
- Choose Window | Navigator to open the Navigator palette, shown in Figure 1.15. Drag the zoom slider to the right to zoom in, drag the slider left to zoom out. Alternatively, click the zoom-in and zoom-out buttons at each end of the slider.

To scroll the image display, select the Hand tool, labeled in Figure 1.14. Then drag in the image window. If the Navigator palette is open, you can also drag the box that appears on the image thumbnail. Just drag the box over the area you want to see.

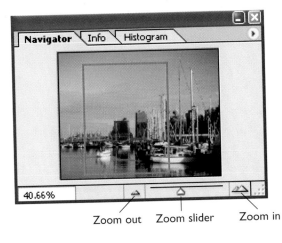

Zoom out   Zoom slider   Zoom in

Figure 1.15: The Navigator palette offers one way to scroll and zoom the image.

Tool Tricks

Press H to select the Hand tool. Or press the spacebar to temporarily switch to the Hand tool while any editing tool is active. Release the spacebar to go back to the editing tool you were using.

SPEED KEYS: Zooming the Image Display		
Action	Windows	Mac
Zoom in	CTRL-+ (plus)	⌘-+ (plus)
Zoom out	CTRL-- (minus)	⌘-- (minus)
Fit entire image	CTRL-0 (zero)	⌘-0 (zero)
Display actual pixels*	ALT-CTRL-0 (zero)	OPTION-⌘-0 (zero)

*Matches one image pixel to one screen pixel;
see Chapter 2 for details.

Displaying Rulers and Guides

You can display rulers across the top and left side of the image window, as shown in Figure 1.16. To hide and display the rulers quickly, press CTRL-R (Windows) or ⌘-R (Mac). Or, if you're feeling overwhelmed by all these short-cuts, choose View | Rulers. Specify the rulers' unit of measurement as follows:

- In Windows, right-click a ruler, which displays a pop-up menu of options.
- On a Mac, CTRL-click a ruler to get the pop-up menu.

Figure 1.16: The rulers come in handy for positioning photo elements.

- Alternatively, on either platform, double-click a ruler to open the Rulers and Units panel of the Preferences dialog box. Select the unit that you want to use from the Rulers drop-down list.

By dragging outward from a ruler, you create a guide, as shown in Figure 1.16. Guides are helpful for checking alignment and positioning of picture elements. Use these techniques to manipulate guides:

- **Reposition a guide** Select the Move tool, labeled in Figure 1.16. Place it over the guide until the cursor changes into a two-headed arrow and drag to move the guide.
- **Prevent guides from moving** Choose View | Lock Guides.
- **Delete a guide** Select the Move tool and then drag the guide back to the ruler from whence it came. To delete all guides, choose View | Clear Guides.
- **Hide and display guides** Press CTRL-; (Windows) or ⌘-; (Mac) or choose View | Show | Guides.
- **Change the guide color and style** Head for the Preferences dialog box, introduced earlier in this chapter. Options for customizing guides appear on the Guides, Grid & Slices panel.

Displaying the Grid

If you choose View | Show | Grid, Photoshop displays a grid of dotted lines over your image, as shown in Figure 1.17. I use this feature primarily when I'm trying to correct convergence distortion, a subject covered in Chapter 13. The gridlines serve as a useful guide for getting things back into proper vertical alignment. As with the guides, you can customize the grid on the Guides, Grid & Slices panel of the Preferences dialog box.

Figure 1.17: Turn on the grid for guidance when correcting convergence problems.

Pixels, Channels, and Other Digital Mysteries

2

In This Chapter:

- ☐ Digital photo fundamentals

- ☐ How pixels affect print quality and on-screen size

- ☐ A look at RGB, CMYK, and other digital color schemes

- ☐ Introduction to color channels and alpha channels

- ☐ Bit-depth primer: How high should you go?

When most people begin to pursue photography, they're interested in exploring the creative promise of the medium, not the mechanical and chemical processes that make it possible. But as any good photographer knows, you need to learn the science behind your camera to exploit its artistic capabilities fully. You can't manipulate depth of field and exposure, for example, without understanding aperture and shutter. In the same way, familiarizing yourself with the technical aspects of digital imaging enables you to take better advantage of Photoshop and avoid missteps that lower the quality of your photos. This chapter gives you this background information, explaining such concepts as resolution, color models, channels, and bit depth.

Figure 2.1: When you
enlarge a digital image, the
pixels become visible, and
picture quality goes down.

From Tiny Pixels Come Great Pictures

All computer-generated art falls into one of two categories:

■ *Bitmap* images are made up of tiny colored squares called *pixels,* which is short for *picture element.* The computer software translates—maps—your picture onto a rectangular grid of pixels, much the same way that a mosaic artist ren-  ders a scene using colored tiles. All digital photos, whether from a scanner or digital camera, are created in this fashion. Figure 2.1 gives you a close-up look at the grid-based nature of bitmap images, which are more commonly referred to as simply *digital images.*

■ *Vector* graphics are composed of line segments that can be defined by mathematical formulas—*vectors,* in the official nerd handbook. Realistically reproducing a photograph out of lines is impossible, which is why the vector approach is reserved for simple graphics such as the one in Figure 2.2.

Watch Out!

Figures 2.1 and 2.2 illustrate one other critical difference between bitmap and vector art. When you enlarge a bitmap image, the pixels grow in size, and picture quality goes down, as shown by the insets in Figure 2.1. A vector graphic retains its original quality at any size, as shown by the insets in Figure 2.2.

Photoshop enables you to work with both pixels and vectors. However, the vector-based tools rarely come into play for most photography work, which is why this is the last you'll hear of them in this book.

How Many Pixels Do You Need?

Every digital image contains a specific number of pixels. The term *pixel dimensions* refers to the number of horizontal and vertical pixels in the image. If you multiply the two values, you get the total number of pixels. For example, a 1280 x 960–pixel

Figure 2.2: Vector graphics can be scaled to any size without degradation, but are suited to simple artwork only.

image contains 1,228,800 pixels, or approximately 1.2 *megapixels*. (One megapixel equals one million pixels.)

A photo's pixel count affects print quality, on-screen display size, and file size. The next three sections discuss these issues.

Pixels and Print Quality

Before printing a photo from Photoshop, you specify the image *output resolution*. This value determines how many pixels are spread across each linear inch of your print, which has a major impact on print quality. For quality that equals traditional photographic prints, you typically need between 200 and 300 pixels per linear inch, or *ppi,* depending on the printer. A few printers produce optimum results when fed more than 300 ppi, so check your manual for the manufacturer's recommendations.

Figures 2.3 and 2.4 illustrate the relationship of ppi to print quality. The first image has pixel dimensions of 750 x 900, resulting in an output resolution of 300 ppi at the print size, 2.5 x 3 inches (750 pixels divided by 2.5 inches equals 300 pixels per inch; 900 divided by 3 also equals 300). Compare this image with its 125 x 150–pixel counterpart in Figure 2.4, which has an output resolution of just 50 ppi. The low-resolution image appears blocky, due to the larger pixels, and curved and diagonal lines have a stair-stepped appearance. (Some photo gurus refer to this stair-stepping as *jaggies.*)

750 × 900 pixels, output at 300 ppi

Figure 2.3: For good prints, you need between 200 and 300 pixels per inch (ppi).

Photoshop enables you to add pixels to an image—a process called *resampling*—to increase the output resolution. Unfortunately, resampling doesn't improve print quality, as illustrated by Figure 2.5. Starting with the 50-ppi image in Figure 2.4, I increased the pixel count to bring the output resolution up to 300 ppi. The resulting image isn't any better than the low-resolution original, and in fact looks slightly worse.

Watch Out!

The moral of this story is that you should calculate your pixel needs *before* you scan or shoot a picture. To find your pixel sweet spot, divide the desired print size by the desired output resolution. (The following table shows the required pixel dimensions to print an image at traditional frame sizes at 200 ppi.) If possible, capture more pixels than you think you will need to allow yourself the flexibility to crop the photo and print the remaining image area at a decent size. You can always dump excess pixels if necessary; see Chapter 15 for details.

125 × 150 pixels, output at 50 ppi

Figure 2.4: A lack of pixels causes lousy print quality.

50 ppi resampled to 300 ppi

Figure 2.5: Adding pixels to a low-resolution image doesn't improve picture quality.

Pixel Requirements for 200 ppi Output		
Print Size (Inches)	Pixel Dimensions	Megapixels
3 1/2 × 5	700 × 1000	<1
4 × 6	800 × 1200	1
5 × 7	1000 × 1400	1.5
8 × 10	1600 × 2000	3.2
11 × 14	2200 × 2800	6

Remember

Don't confuse ppi (image pixels per inch) with *dpi*, which stands for *dots per inch* and measures how many dots of ink, dye, or toner a printer can lay down per inch. Although many people use ppi and dpi interchangeably, the two are *not* the same; many printers use several dots to reproduce one image pixel.

Pixels and Screen Display Size

When you display a photo on a computer monitor, television, or other screen device, the pixel dimensions determine how large the photo appears.

Like digital images, display devices are pixel-based beasts. The pixels generated by a display vary in size and number depending on the device resolution. For example, you can probably set your computer monitor to several resolution settings: 800 × 600, 1024 × 768, 1280 × 960, and so on. At a resolution of 800 × 600, you get 800 horizontal pixels and 600 vertical pixels. When you increase the resolution, the computer crams more pixels into the same display area, which means that the pixels get smaller.

To project your photos, the device uses one display pixel to reproduce one image pixel. Therefore, if you display an 800 × 600–pixel image on a monitor that's set to a resolution of 800 × 600, your photo fills the screen, as shown in Figure 2.6. Change the monitor resolution to 1600 × 1200, and that same 800 × 600–pixel image occupies one quarter of the screen, as shown in Figure 2.7. (The lower part of the image is hidden by the Windows taskbar, which I left visible in both figures.)

800 × 600 image pixels, 800 × 600 screen resolution

800 × 600 image pixels, 1600 × 1200 screen resolution

Figure 2.6: An 800 × 600–pixel image fills the screen when the monitor resolution is set to 800 × 600.

Figure 2.7: The same image fills just one-fourth of the screen when the monitor resolution is increased to 1600 × 1200.

PART **|** INTO THE DIGITAL DARKROOM

Remember

Given that the pixel requirements for screen and print are so different, how do you create an image that serves both purposes? Always shoot or scan your original according to the print requirements. Then duplicate the image and eliminate pixels as needed to create a screen version of the photo. You can safely toss excess pixels without harming image quality, but adding pixels does not improve quality.

As for the quality of an on-screen photo, pixel count is irrelevant. I know that you've likely heard people referring to screen images in terms of pixels per inch, which may lead you to believe that ppi affects screen quality as it does print quality. But a display device has no way to read the output resolution (ppi) that you establish in Photoshop; the only thing that matters is the total number of pixels.

The bottom line is that you need far fewer pixels for images destined for the screen than you do for pictures you plan to print. For most images, in fact, you need to dump some pixels to properly size them for the screen; Chapter 15 shows you how.

Pixels and File Size

For every image pixel, the computer must store a certain amount of data. More pixels mean more data—and larger image files. As a point of comparison, the 750 x 900–pixel image featured in Figure 2.3 has a file size of 1.94MB, while the file size of the 125 x 150–pixel version in Figure 2.4 is a mere 68.1K (1MB, or megabyte, equals 1024K, or kilobytes).

Watch Out!

Large file sizes are problematic for several reasons. On a Web page, large image files increase the time needed to download the page. Large files also take longer to transmit via e-mail, slow down Photoshop, and put more strain on your computer's resources. And of course, the larger the file, the more storage space it consumes on your computer's hard drive or removable storage media.

If you're preparing a photo for print output at a large size, you can't do much about file size because you need a hefty pixel supply for good print quality. For Web use, however, always strip files to their minimum pixel requirements to ensure the fastest downloads.

How Many Pixels Do You Have?

Photoshop gives you several ways to check pixel dimensions:

- In the File Browser, click a photo thumbnail to display image details on the Metadata tab, as shown in Figure 2.8. The Width and Height values indicate the pixel dimensions. If you turn on Details view for the thumbnail area of the browser, the pixel dimensions also appear with the thumbnail, as shown in the figure.

To switch to this display in Photoshop CS, choose the Details option from the View menu inside the browser (not from the program View menu). In Version 7.0, change the view via the File Browser's palette menu or the View By pop-up menu at the bottom of the palette. (The name of the pop-up menu changes to reflect the selected view.)

■ After opening an image, choose Image | Image Size to open the Image Size dialog box, shown in Figure 2.9. The Pixel Dimensions area at the top of the dialog box lists the pixel count.

■ You can display the pixel count for the active image in the status bar, which appears at the location shown in Figure 2.9 in Windows. (Choose View | Status Bar to toggle the status bar on and off.) On a Mac, the status bar is always present at the bottom of the image

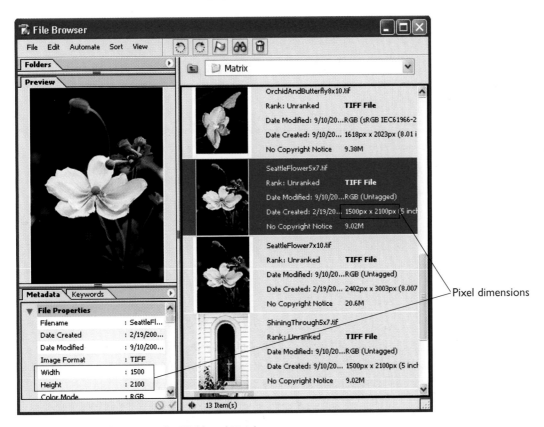

Figure 2.8: In the File Browser, the Width and Height items on the Metadata tab indicate the pixel dimensions.

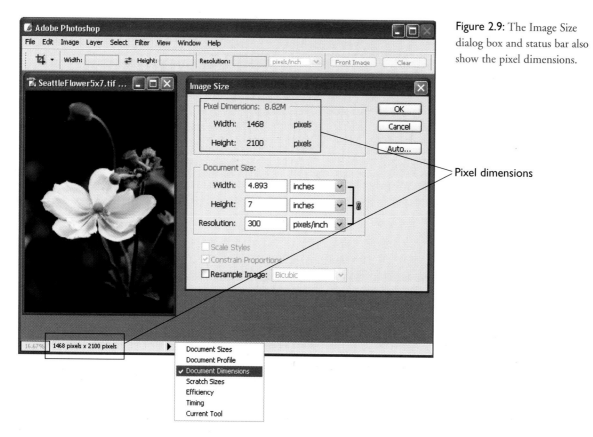

Figure 2.9: The Image Size
dialog box and status bar also
show the pixel dimensions.

window. Select Document Dimensions from the status bar pop-up
menu, as shown in the figure, to set the status bar to display the
pixel dimensions. You also must set the ruler's unit of measurement
to pixels; see Chapter 1 to find out how.

Color as Math

I have this rule about math: Avoid it whenever possible. The part of my brain
that's supposed to handle numeric processes just doesn't function properly, and
even simple calculations require major effort. I think that sometime around third
grade, my mathematically oriented brain cells became overloaded and fried themselves out—probably as a result of one of those "story problems" that asked you to
figure out the square root of the sum of the diameters of the wheels of two trains
of different lengths traveling in opposite directions at different speeds and . . .

I confess this math aversion so that when I say that I regret having to bring numbers into a discussion, you know that (1) I'm sincere, and (2) there's no way to get around dealing with math when it comes to digital color. Trust me, I've tried.

Computers and digital-imaging devices—scanners, digital cameras, monitors, and printers—can't perceive colors the way we humans do. Unlike our brains, theirs understand numbers only. That means that every color must be translated into numeric code.

Here's an analogy that may help you understand this number-based approach to color. You probably learned in kindergarten that you can mix red, yellow, and blue paint to create other colors. Yellow and blue make green, for example. If you were so inclined, you could describe green in terms of its red-yellow-blue mix. Instead of *green,* you could say "0 percent red, 50 percent yellow, and 50 percent blue." Digital color works just like that, except that the formulas involve primary components other than red, yellow, and blue.

Imaging scientists have developed several color-coding schemes, known as color *models* or color *spaces.* Each model uses a different set of primary components, and each can represent a specific spectrum, or *gamut,* of colors. Why not one universal code? Because that would be too easy, silly. (Okay, the real reason is that no one space adequately serves all color-production needs.)

The good news is that Photoshop handles all this color coding for you; you don't have to type long strings of numbers to specify the color of each pixel in your image. But you do need a passing familiarity with the major color models to understand some important Photoshop techniques and tools. The next five sections tell you what you need to know.

Color from Light: RGB

The human eye provides the basis for the primary digital imaging color model, RGB, which stands for *red-green-blue.* Your eye contains three light receptors, each corresponding to one of these primary colors. As you gaze on a scenic vista or just inspect your own navel, the red receptor measures red light, the blue receptor measures blue light, and the green receptor measures green light. Your brain adds those three values together to produce all the colors you see.

RGB

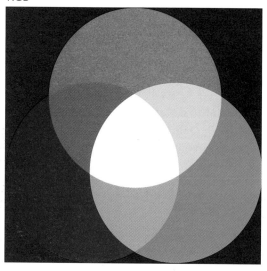

Figure 2.10: In the RGB model, full-strength red, green, and blue produces white.

Digital cameras, scanners, and other displays are called *RGB* devices because they produce color by mixing red, green, and blue light. In the RGB color space, light is measured on a scale of 0 to 255, with 0 representing the complete absence of light and 255 indicating maximum brightness.

To understand RGB, imagine that you are standing in a pitch-black room and you have three colored spotlights at your disposal: one red, one green, and one blue. If you set all three beams to maximum brightness and then position them so that their beams overlap slightly, as illustrated in Figure 2.10, the overlapping area becomes white. Where no light falls, blackness remains. It stands to reason, then, that an equal mix of red, green, and blue at any value other than 0 (black) or 255 (white) produces a shade of gray.

Variation on the Theme: HSB

Like RGB, the HSB color model is light based. But with HSB, the primary components are hue, saturation, and brightness.

- Hue values range from 0 to 359, corresponding to a 360-degree *color wheel,* which you can see in Figure 2.11.
- Saturation values can range from 0 to 100 percent. At 100 percent saturation, you get a "pure" color—that is, it contains only a single hue. At 0 saturation, you get white, gray, or black, depending on the Brightness value.
- Brightness values also run from 0 to 100 percent. No matter what the hue or saturation, 0 percent brightness produces black.

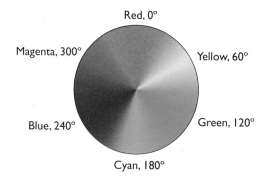

Figure 2.11: Hue values represent positions on a 360-degree color wheel.

Saturation and Brightness   Hue

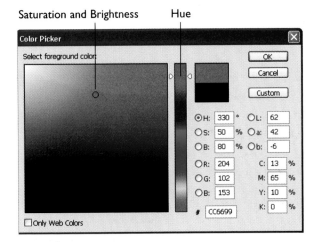

Figure 2.12: The HSB model comes in handy for visually selecting colors in the Photoshop Color Picker.

You can't create an HSB image; this color model is primarily used to simplify the job of selecting paint colors in image-editing and graphics programs. In Photoshop, for example, you can set the Color Picker dialog box to HSB mode, as shown in Figure 2.12. You then select a hue in the vertical color bar and drag inside the large color box to adjust the saturation and brightness. This setup is the most intuitive for those of us raised in the red-yellow-blue paint-mixing world. (Chapter 5 details the Color Picker.) Some Photoshop filters are also based on the HSB model.

Print Formulas: CMY and CMYK

While scanners, digital cameras, and display devices mix colors using red, green, and blue light, a printer creates colors by mixing cyan, magenta, and yellow inks, which leads us to the CMY color model.

CMY values range from 0 to 100 percent and represent ink coverage on the paper. Figure 2.13 shows the result of blending 100 percent cyan, magenta, and yellow. Blending two colors produces a darker color. When you mix all three colors at full strength, black ensues (well, sort of; more on that momentarily). Zero percent coverage of all three inks produces white, assuming that you're printing on white paper.

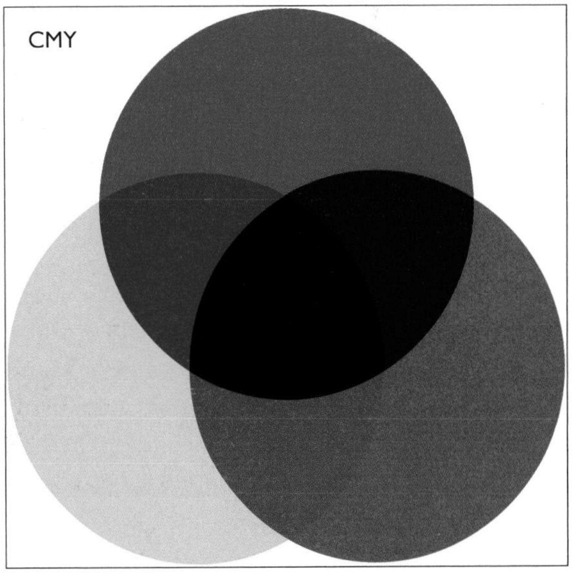

CMY

Figure 2.13: The print color model, CMY, is based on cyan, magenta, and yellow inks.

When you compare Figure 2.13 to Figure 2.10, you may notice that both illustrations feature the same eight colors. This fact may lead you to assume that you can create the same colors with either model. Unfortunately, that's not the case. You can't reproduce in CMY the most vivid hues that you can create with RGB because of the inherent differences in the two processes: CMY color is a result of light reflecting off ink-coated paper, and RGB color is pure, projected light. Colors in Figures 2.10 and 2.13 *appear* to be the same because they are both output in the CMY space. On-screen, the colors in the RGB illustration are much more vibrant.

Put another way, CMY has a much smaller gamut than RGB, which is the core problem with getting screen and printed colors to match. Chapter 14 discusses ways of getting the two as close as possible, but you should never expect absolute color matching when going from screen to print.

Now for the promised follow-up on the issue of black in the CMY color model: Because inks are impure, it's difficult to achieve true blacks by blending cyan, magenta, and yellow. For that reason, most printers add black ink. Black is called the *key* color, so printers that use the four-ink setup are called CMYK devices. (The illustration in Figure 2.13 was printed on a CMYK printer, which is why the black area appears to be true black.)

CIE Lab: The Theoretical Model

Unlike RGB, HSB, and CMYK, the CIE Lab color model—Lab, for short—wasn't developed around the color mechanics of any device. Instead, Lab aims to define in numerical terms every color that the human eye can perceive. Lab is based on three components. The first, lightness (the *L* in Lab), is akin to the brightness value in the HSB model. The other two variables, *a* and *b,* indicate how much of the color falls in the green-to-red spectrum and the blue-to-yellow spectrum, respectively.

If all that sounds way too complicated for your taste, I'm right there with you. Not only is working the Lab color space something only an engineer could love, it can be an exercise in futility. What's the point of creating colors that you can't print or display? Lab does have one purpose for everyday Photoshop projects, however. The lightness data can provide a great basis for converting a full-color image to black and white, as discussed in Chapter 11.

Grayscale: Not Just Black and White

The final entry in the color model hit parade, Grayscale, is childishly simple compared to all the others. This color model incorporates a single component, brightness. Brightness values range from 0 to 255, just as in the RGB model. A value of zero produces black, 255 produces white, and everything else generates gray.

Given that you can produce the same grays in RGB, why the need for Grayscale? Because a Grayscale image file, which needs to store data for only one color component, is much smaller than an RGB file, which must track three color components. Compare the RGB and Grayscale images in Figure 2.14, for example. Both have the same pixel count, and yet the Grayscale image is one-third the file size of the full-color version. (To find out how to convert an RGB image to the Grayscale mode, see Chapter 11.)

Image Channels: Surfing for Data

A digital-image file contains one or more *channels,* which you can think of as containers for holding different types of image data. At minimum, an image contains

4.6MB   1.5MB

Figure 2.14: A full-color image (left) has a much larger file size than a Grayscale image (right).

one channel for each component used in the image color space:

- RGB images have three channels: one each for the red, green, and blue brightness values.
- CMYK images have four channels: one each for the cyan, magenta, yellow, and black values.
- Lab images have three channels: one for the lightness data, one for the *a* spectrum data, and one for the *b* spectrum data.
- Grayscale images have just one channel that contains the brightness values for the entire photo.

You can view the contents of the individual channels in Photoshop by displaying the Channels palette, shown in Figure 2.15. To display and edit an individual channel in the image window, click the channel's name in the palette. Click the RGB channel at the top of the palette to return to normal, full-color view.

Figure 2.16 shows the color channels for an RGB image. As you can see, a channel is really a self-contained grayscale image. If that seems odd, understand that the channels simply reflect pixel brightness, or lack thereof. White areas in a channel image indicate high brightness values for that color component. For example, the green portions of the totem appear very light in the Green channel, and the sky areas appear bright in the Blue channel. The white eye areas appear bright in all three channels; remember, in RGB, white is produced by mixing high-intensity red, green, and blue light.

Figure 2.15: The Channels palette gives you access to the individual color channels in an image.

Other than being a cool exercise, what's the point of surfing the color channels? Here are just two ways channels play a role in everyday Photoshop projects:

- When you want to create a grayscale version of a color image, lifting the information from a single color channel may produce better results than the standard conversion route, which combines the brightness values from all three channels. Chapter 11 explains this technique.

RGB composite

Red channel

Green channel

Blue channel

Figure 2.16: An RGB image contains three color channels.

- One channel—usually the Blue channel in an RGB image—is often "noisier" than the other channels. Noise gives an image a speckled look, as shown in the sky area of the Blue channel in Figure 2.16. If you apply a sharpening filter to the entire image, you emphasize that noise. Applying the filter only to the noise-free channels enables you to achieve the benefits of sharpening without the downside. See Chapter 13 for more about sharpening.

In addition to manipulating color channels, you can add new channels, called *alpha channels,* to store selection outlines, discussed in Chapter 7. If you are preparing artwork for output on a commercial press, you can create *spot-color channels* to specify the spot-color ink plates. That channel feature is beyond the scope of this book, but the Photoshop help system provides details if you need them.

When to Shift Color Spaces

Most of your images will start life as RGB images because that's the color model used by digital cameras and scanners. Photoshop enables you to convert an RGB image to the CMYK, Grayscale, or Lab color model. Just select the color model you want from the Image | Mode menu. (Again, HSB is just a theoretical color model; you can't create images in HSB.)

Watch Out!

However, don't do so unless you have good reason—for example, if a client needs a CMYK file for output on a commercial press. When you change color models, Photoshop translates the original colors into the new color space, permanently altering the color data. You can lose detail in the process. Note, too, that after you convert to the Grayscale mode, you can't get back your original, full-color image. Always save a copy of your original image before you perform the conversion.

Bit Depth: How High Should You Go?

Bit depth refers to how many units of computer data—*bits*—are used to represent each pixel in a digital image. Most scanners enable you to specify bit depth when you scan an image. My scanner, for example, offers 24-bit and 42-bit scanning. Some digital cameras also offer a choice of bit depth.

Scanner and camera bit-depth options usually reflect bits per pixel. But you also can assess bit depth on a per-channel basis. For example, a 24-bit RGB image has 8 bits each for the Red, Green, and Blue channels. Photoshop further simplifies things by grouping everything into two categories:

- An image with 8 or fewer bits per channel is treated as an 8-bits-per-channel image.

- An image with more than 8 bits per channel is treated as a 16-bits-per-channel image, or a *high-bit image* in Photoshop lingo.

For most images, 8 bits per channel is plenty. Theoretically, more bits provide more editing flexibility because you have more original data to manipulate. When you apply heavy exposure and color corrections to an 8-bit image, you sometimes create breaks in what should be a continuous blend of colors. Figure 2.17 offers an illustration of this defect, known as *banding* or *posterization*. The left image shows how the colors should look; the right image shows the defect. Starting with more bits may—I repeat, *may*—alleviate the problem.

Before you jump on the high-bit wagon, take these other points into consideration:

- 16-bit images have significantly larger file sizes than 8-bit images.
- In Photoshop 7 (and earlier versions), many tools and filters don't work on 16-bit images. Photoshop CS changes all that; you now can do nearly anything to a 16-bit image that you can do to an 8-bit image. But you may not see any difference in your images, which means you're working with needlessly large file sizes.

For every expert who advocates 16-bit editing, an equally qualified person dismisses the idea as overkill. Personally, I don't go the 16-bit route unless I'm facing a tricky exposure or color situation. If so, I start in 16-bit mode, do my exposure and color corrections, and then convert to 8-bit mode before doing any other retouching. Of course, I make a copy of the 16-bit original just for good measure.

To convert a 16-bit image to an 8-bit image, choose Image | Mode | 8 Bits/Channel. Converting an 8-bit original to 16-bit mode has no positive effect; it only increases file size.

Remember

After opening an image in Photoshop, you can determine its bit depth by opening the Image | Mode menu. A check mark appears next to the 8 Bits/Channel or 16 Bits/Channel item to let you know which category applies.

Figure 2.17: A defect known as banding produces abrupt shifts in what should be a smooth gradation of colors.

Open and Organize Your Photo Files

3

Before you can process a roll of film, you have to break open the film canister and extract the negatives. Before you can work on a picture in Photoshop, you have to crack open the digital image file—the virtual canister that holds the picture data.

This chapter explains how to open photo files. You'll also find information on scanning photos, creating a new image canvas, and rotating sideways images to their proper orientation. Of course, being able to open a file assumes that you can *find* the file, which isn't always easy when you have scads of images. To that end, the first section of this chapter shows you how to track down photos in the Photoshop File Browser.

In This Chapter:

- ☐ Image management with the File Browser

- ☐ Tips on searching for photos

- ☐ Ways to open picture files

- ☐ Guide to the Camera Raw file converter

- ☐ Steps for scanning directly into Photoshop

- ☐ How to adjust canvas size and orientation

Using the File Browser

For everyday photography work, the File Browser represents one of the most important differences between Photoshop 7 and CS.

In Version 7, the File Browser enables you to view image thumbnails, organize images into folders, and examine metadata—extra file data that records details such as the date and digital-camera capture settings. But the browser doesn't offer a feature critical to anyone with a large image collection: the ability to search for files by name, date, user-assigned keywords, or other criteria. In CS, the File Browser offers not just a capable search feature but also several other enhancements, including higher-resolution previews.

Although there's not room to discuss all features of the CS File Browser, the next several sections introduce you to the main tools. If you use Version 7, read "File Browser Basics," which covers features common to both versions, but do yourself a favor and also invest in a third-party image-management tool. Programs I recommend include ACDSee (www.acdsee.com), ThumbsPlus (www.cerious.com), and JASC Photo Album (www.jasc.com).

File Browser Basics

Take any of these steps to open the File Browser:

- Choose Window | File Browser.

- In CS, click the File Browser icon, found on the options bar near the palette well, as shown in Figure 3.1. The browser appears inside its own program window, shown in Figure 3.2.

- In Photoshop 7, the browser is presented as a palette, so you can open it by clicking its tab in the palette well. All the Chapter 1 tricks related to palettes apply.

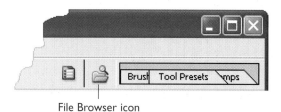

File Browser icon

Figure 3.1: In Photoshop CS, the File Browser has a permanent options bar icon.

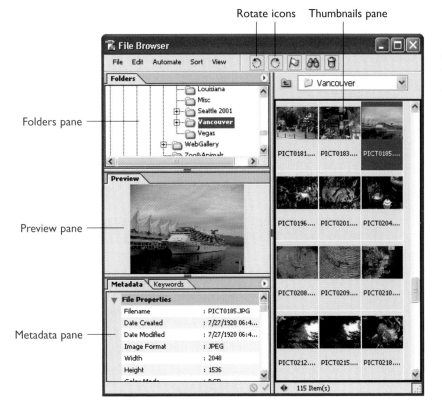

Rotate icons   Thumbnails pane

Folders pane

Preview pane

Metadata pane

Figure 3.2: Click a folder to display thumbnails of the images it contains.

In both versions, the File Browser is divided into four major panes, labeled in Figure 3.2. The basic browser operation is the same, too:

- **Displaying thumbnails** Click a folder in the Folders pane to display thumbnails for images that are stored inside that folder.
- **Displaying a large preview and file metadata** Click a thumbnail to see a larger preview in the Preview pane and display the file metadata in the Metadata pane.

CS In CS, the Metadata pane contains two tabs, Metadata and Keywords. Click the tab you want to display. See the upcoming section "Adding Keywords for Easier Searching" for information on the Keywords tab.

- **Adjusting pane sizes** Drag the pane borders.
- **Rotating thumbnails** To rotate a thumbnail in CS, click one of the Rotate icons, labeled in Figure 3.2. In Version 7, you get a single icon, labeled in Figure 3.3.

Watch Out!

In both versions, Photoshop rotates only the thumbnail, not the image itself, until you open the file. But in CS, you can choose Edit | Apply Rotation from the File Browser menu bar to rotate the image without opening the file. Use caution: This step causes Photoshop to resave the image file, overwriting the original. It's not a great idea to use this option for JPEG originals because each time you alter and save an image in the JPEG format, you lose image quality. (See Chapter 15 for details.) Instead, open the file, rotate it, and save in the PSD or TIFF format or, if you need a JPEG file, save under a different name. That way, you always retain your original at its best quality.

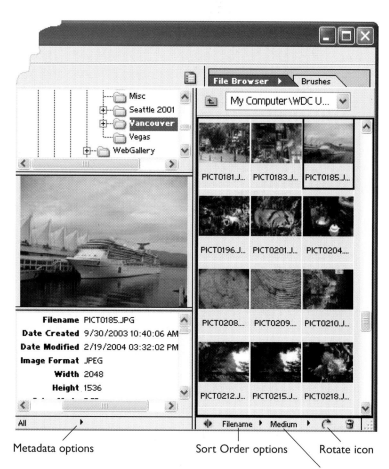

Figure 3.3: In Version 7, change the thumbnail size via the pop-up menu at the bottom of the window.

Customizing the Thumbnails Display

You can customize the thumbnail size, the label information displayed with each thumbnail, and the sort order of the thumbnails.

■ In Version 7, access these options via the Sort Order and Thumbnail options pop-up menus, labeled in Figure 3.3.

■ In CS, choose the options from the View and Sort menus on the File Browser menu bar. To set the thumbnail size produced by the new Custom Size Thumbnail option, see the upcoming section "Setting CS File Browser Preferences."

Customizing the Metadata Pane

You also can specify what types of metadata you want to display.

■ In Version 7, you get two options: All and EXIF. The EXIF option displays only metadata stored by digital cameras, which typically includes aperture, shutter speed, and other camera settings. Choose All to also view general file information, such as pixel dimensions and creation date. Make your choice from the Metadata options pop-up menu, labeled in Figure 3.3.

■ In CS, choose Metadata Display Options from the Metadata palette menu, as shown in Figure 3.4. You then see a dialog box in which you can select the metadata categories you want to display. In addition to EXIF and the general file information (labeled File Properties in CS), you can view several additional types of metadata, including IPTC (International Press Telecommunications Council) metadata. IPTC data is used by press photographers to pass along information such as the credit line, suggested caption, and

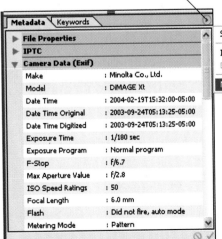

Figure 3.4: The Metadata pane displays a variety of file information, including digital-camera capture settings.

Pencil icon

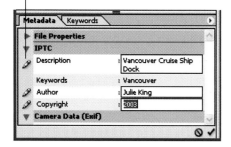

Figure 3.5: Click the pencil icon to edit IPTC metadata in CS.

so on. You can add and edit IPTC metadata by clicking the pencil icon labeled in Figure 3.5 and typing the new text.

Setting CS File Browser Preferences

CS The Preferences dialog box offers additional options for customizing the CS browser. To open the dialog box with the File Browser panel at the foreground, as shown in Figure 3.6, choose Edit | Preferences from the File Browser menu bar. I suggest that you stick with the default settings, with a few exceptions:

- **Custom Thumbnail Size** The File Browser offers three preset thumbnail sizes: Small, Medium, and Large. If Large isn't big enough, enter your desired thumbnail width, in pixels, into the Custom Thumbnail Size box. Photoshop generates that size thumbnail when you select Custom Size from the View menu in the File Browser.

- **Render Vector Files** If you create vector files, such as those produced by Adobe Illustrator, turn on the Render Vector Files check box so that you can preview that type of file in the browser as well as image files.

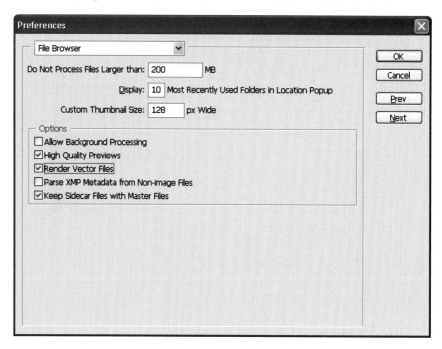

Figure 3.6: In CS, the Preferences dialog box contains several File Browser settings.

- **High Quality Previews and Allow Background Processing**
  By default, the High Quality Previews option is selected, which renders better previews in the browser. However, the option can slow down the thumbnail display. To speed things up, turn off this option. Also experiment with the Allow Background Processing option, which gives the browser permission to steal some computer processing power to pre-generate thumbnails and metadata information.

Organizing and Deleting Image Files

Both the Version 7 and CS File Browsers enable you to do basic file management from inside Photoshop, as follows:

- **Moving files between folders** To move a file from one folder to another, drag the file's thumbnail to the new folder in the Folders pane, as illustrated in Figure 3.7.

Figure 3.7: Drag a thumbnail to a folder to move the file to that folder.

- **Copying files** To put a copy of a file in another folder, hold down the CTRL key (Windows) or the OPTION key (Mac) as you drag and drop the thumbnail. A plus sign appears next to your cursor to indicate that you're copying the file.
- **Deleting files** Click the file's thumbnail and then press DELETE or click the Trash icon. In CS, the icon appears on the File Browser toolbar, as shown in Figure 3.7. The Version 7 icon hangs out in the lower-right corner of the browser.
- **Renaming files** In the Thumbnails pane, click the filename to make the name area active, type the new name, and press ENTER.

Searching for Photos in CS

CS Not sure where you stashed an image file? Don't waste time hunting through dozens of folders—instead, use the new search function provided in the CS File Browser.

1. Click the Search icon, labeled in **Figure 3.7.**

Or choose File | Search from the File Browser menu bar. Either way, you see the Search dialog box, shown in Figure 3.8.

2. Use the Source options to tell Photoshop what folders to search.

The program will search the folder selected in the Look In drop-down list. To change the folder, click the Browse button and select the folder from the resulting dialog box, which works like any Windows or Mac file-opening dialog box. To search subfolders in the selected folder, select the Include All Subfolders check box.

3. Select a general search category from the left Criteria drop-down list.

For example, to turn up all files created on a certain day, select Date Created, as shown in Figure 3.8.

4. Enter the exact search parameters.

Now use the other Criteria drop-down list and the adjacent text box to specify the exact parameters of

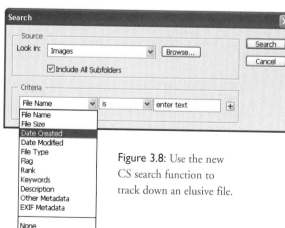

Figure 3.8: Use the new CS search function to track down an elusive file.

the search. Your options here depend on what you select as the general search category. If you select Date Created, choose from the three list options shown in Figure 3.9, for example, and then type the date in the text box.

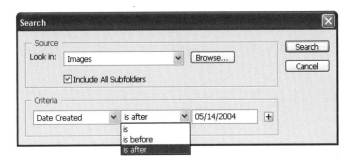

Figure 3.9: Click the plus sign to enter additional search parameters.

To use more than one category of information as the basis for a search, click the plus button to the right of the text box. The dialog box expands to offer a second row of Criteria controls. You can add as many as 12 additional search parameters. To remove a parameter, click the minus button to the right of its text box.

5. Click the Search button.

Photoshop conducts the search and displays thumbnails for all images that match your search criteria. To open a file, double-click its thumbnail.

To display a little box showing the file's folder location, as shown in Figure 3.10, pause your cursor over the thumbnail. The Show Tool Tips option on the General panel of the Photoshop Preferences dialog box must be turned on; see Chapter 1 for details about setting program preferences. This trick doesn't work if you set the browser to Details view.

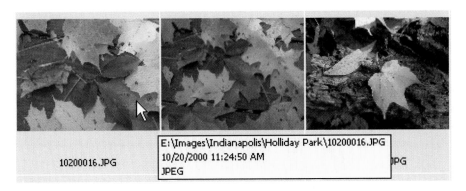

Figure 3.10: Pause your cursor over a thumbnail to discover the file's location.

Alternatively, choose View | Reveal Location in Explorer (Windows) or View | Reveal Location in Finder (Mac) from the File Browser menu bar. Photoshop then opens either Windows Explorer or the Mac Finder with the relevant folder selected.

Adding Keywords for Easier Searching

CS Like any good image-management tool, the CS File Browser enables you to assign *keywords* to image files. A keyword is a descriptive label that you add so that you later can search for files based on subject matter or some other criteria. For example, you might assign the keyword *flowers* to botanical images. To view thumbnails of all your flower photos, you can then run a File Browser search based on that keyword.

You can add multiple keywords to each file to make tracking down specific images even faster. Instead of browsing through all your floral photos to find close-ups of tulips, for example, you could search for files tagged with the keywords *flowers, close-up,* and *tulips.*

To assign a keyword to a file, follow these steps:

1. Click the file's thumbnail in the File Browser.

2. Click the Keywords tab to display it in front of the Metadata tab, as shown in Figure 3.11.

The tab contains several keyword category folders. Click the triangle next to a category folder to see keywords in that folder.

3. To assign a keyword, click the column to the left of that keyword.

A check mark appears next to the keyword, as shown in the figure, and Photoshop tags the file with the keyword. To remove a keyword tag, just uncheck its box.

You can create custom keywords and otherwise edit the keywords list as follows:

- **Add a new keyword** Click the keyword folder where you want to put the new keyword. Then click the New Keyword icon, labeled in Figure 3.11. A new row appears in the palette, with a text box for the keyword. Type the keyword and press ENTER.

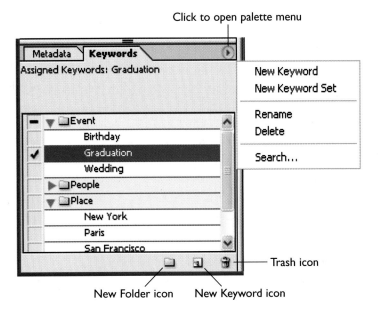

Figure 3.11: Tag files with keywords to enable searching by subject matter.

- **Add a keyword folder** Click the New Folder icon, also labeled in Figure 3.11. A new folder row appears; type the folder name and press ENTER.

- **Delete a keyword or folder** Click the item you want to remove and click the Trash icon, labeled in Figure 3.11. Note that this step *doesn't* remove keyword tags from any image files. To delete the tag from a file, scroll down the list of keywords to the Other Keywords folder, which shows deleted keywords that are still associated with files. Then uncheck the keyword box.

- **Rename a keyword or folder** Click the item you want to change and then open the Keywords palette menu by clicking the arrow labeled in the figure. Choose Rename from the menu and type the new name.

To search for files by keyword, follow the steps outlined in the preceding section, but choose Keywords from the category list in Step 3.

Remember

Some aspects of how Photoshop opens your photos depend on settings that you establish in the File Handling panel of the Preferences dialog box, covered in Chapter 1, and in the Color Settings dialog box, explained in Chapter 14.

Opening Image Files

To open a photo file, use any of these options:

- Double-click the image thumbnail in the File Browser.
- Choose File | Open or press CTRL-O (Windows) or ⌘-O (Mac) to display the Open dialog box. The dialog box design varies depending on your computer operating system; Figure 3.12 shows the Windows XP version. Track down your file as you do in any program and then click Open.

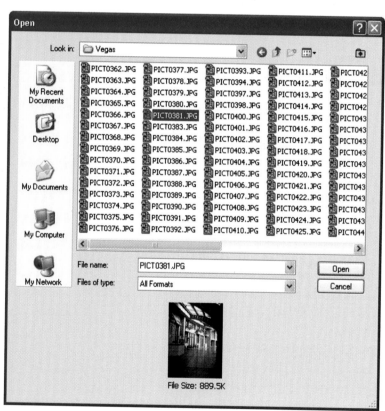

Figure 3.12: The Photoshop Open dialog box conforms to the normal Windows or Mac operating system design.

Time Saver

In Windows, double-click an empty area of the Photoshop workspace to display the Open dialog box quickly.

When you open some types of files, you see a second dialog box containing further options. The next section explains the choices you need to make when opening Camera Raw files, the most common photo format that involves this second dialog box.

Working with Camera Raw Files

If you own a digital camera, it may be able to capture images in the Camera Raw format. In this format, the camera does not apply any white balancing, noise removal, or other processes that occur when you shoot in the JPEG or TIFF format. Instead, you get "uncooked" data straight from the image sensor.

v.7 Most programs, including Photoshop 7, can't open Camera Raw files. Adobe used to sell a plug-in that enabled you to open Camera Raw files in Version 7, but pulled the product when CS was launched. If you don't own the plug-in, use the software that came with your camera to open the file and save a copy in the TIFF format, which Photoshop can open.

CS Photoshop CS offers a built-in Camera Raw converter, shown in Figure 3.13. However, each camera manufacturer uses its own flavor of Camera Raw, and the CS utility doesn't support all of them. Adobe updates the utility every now and then, so visit the Adobe Web site (www.adobe.com) to make sure that you have the latest version and find out whether your camera is supported.

PHOTO COURTESY JEFF MCCARTY.

Figure 3.13: You can open raw files from some digital cameras in Photoshop CS.

Assuming that your camera is on the list, the following steps explain how to bring Camera Raw files into Photoshop CS. The basics are the same for the Version 7 plug-in, but you don't have access to all the CS options, and the dialog box layout is different.

1. **Open the file via the File | Open dialog box or File Browser, as explained in the preceding section.**

You see the Camera Raw plug-in window, shown in Figure 3.13.

2. **Set the basic file characteristics using the controls under the image preview.**

You can specify four characteristics:

- **Space** sets the working color space, a topic explained in Chapter 14. Adobe RGB is always a good choice.
- **Size** controls pixel dimensions, explained in Chapter 2. Leave the setting as is to retain the original pixel count. Choose one of the other options to add or delete pixels; remember that adding pixels reduces image quality.
- **Depth** determines bit depth, or the amount of color information possible in the file. Normally, 8 bits is adequate. But if your image has serious exposure or color problems, you may want 16 bits. Chapter 2 details bit depth.
- **Resolution** establishes the initial output resolution (ppi) for printing. You can adjust the value after opening the file; the option is presented here just as a convenience. (See Chapter 2 for help on determining the appropriate value.) For Web images, this value is meaningless, so ignore it.

3. **Use the other dialog box controls to enhance the image (optional).**

The right side of the dialog box offers tools that enable you to tweak the image before you open it in Photoshop proper. Click the Advanced button near the top-right corner of the window to display four tabs of corrective controls, as shown in Figure 3.13. See the information following the steps for my take on the most helpful tools and which corrections I think are better handled after opening the file.

When you adjust a setting, the preview updates to show you the result. Use the Zoom and Hand tools in the upper-left corner of the image to magnify and scroll the preview. (The tools work like their counterparts in the Photoshop toolbox; see Chapter 1.)

4. **Click OK to close the converter and finish opening the picture.**

5. **Save a working copy of your file in the Photoshop (PSD) format.**

Chapter 4 provides specifics about this critical step. Don't try to save in the Photoshop RAW format, by the way—it's not the same thing as Camera Raw.

Now for some explanation about the corrective tools that I so conveniently skimmed over in Step 3. The following list explains the tools I find most useful:

- **Vignetting Amount and Vignetting Midpoint** Use these controls, on the Lens tab, to correct *vignetting*, a defect that makes the image appear darker in the corners. The left half of Figure 3.14 shows vignetting; the right half shows the problem removed.

Vignetting   Vignetting Removed

Figure 3.14: You may be able to correct vignetting using controls on the Lens tab.

- **Chromatic Aberration** If you notice *color fringing*—areas where objects appear to be ringed with a halo of color—experiment with these two controls, also on the Lens tab. You may not be able to correct all color fringing this way.

■ **Luminance Smoothing and Color Noise Reduction** Found on the Detail tab, these controls take different approaches to removing noise, a defect that gives images a speckled look. (Chapter 12 shows you other ways to defeat noise.) Zoom in on the preview and monitor the image details when using these two controls; both adjustments have the side effect of softening focus.

As for color, contrast, and sharpness, I prefer to perform any needed corrections after opening the file. Inside the Camera Raw dialog box, you can't take advantage of selections or layer masks, which means that you can't change just a portion of the photo. You also don't have access to adjustment layers and other helpful correction features discussed later in this book. Finally, you can't *soft proof* your image—preview the colors as they will appear when printed. (Chapter 14 explains soft proofing.)

Assuming that you want to make the same correction to the entire photo, however, you may be able to save time by using the Camera Raw options to do a "rough edit." You then can fine-tune after opening the file. If you go this route, I recommend that you first explore the chapters on exposure, color, and focus adjustments so that you better understand how to approach these corrections.

Scanning Photos into Photoshop

If you own a scanner, the software that came in the scanner box should include a scanning utility, which you use to select the scanner settings, and a *Twain driver.* A Twain driver is a bit of code that enables the scanner and computer to communicate. After installing the scan utility and Twain driver, you can scan images directly into Photoshop as follows:

1. Choose File | Import.

A submenu appears, listing all installed Twain devices on your system.

2. Choose your scanner name from the Import submenu.

Photoshop launches the scan utility. Every scanner manufacturer offers its own utility, so you'll need to read your scanner manual for specifics.

3. **Select the desired scan settings in your scanner software.**

For help setting the scan resolution and bit depth—the two main options you'll have to consider—see Chapter 2. Bypass any scanner tools for adjusting exposure, color, and sharpening and instead use the Photoshop filters for these functions.

4. **After the scan is done, close the scan utility and save the image in the PSD format.**

Watch Out!

Until you save, the file is only temporary. Chapter 4 provides details on saving files.

Importing Files Directly from a Digital Camera

Photoshop can access files from a digital camera that's connected to your computer. How you get to those files depends on your camera and computer operating system.

- With newer cameras and operating systems, your computer "sees" the camera as a removable drive, just as it does a floppy drive or CD. (You may need to install the USB driver that shipped with the camera for the computer to recognize the camera.) In this case, you can access files from the File Browser or the File | Open command as outlined earlier in this chapter.
- With older cameras and operating systems, you need to install the Twain driver that came with your camera. Then, to open files, select the camera name from the File | Import submenu. Photoshop launches your camera's image-transfer software, and you can open files as you normally do using that software. (Sorry, you'll have to read your camera manual for specifics.)

Remember

If you captured your images in the JPEG format, always save a copy in the PSD format before you do any editing. Then use that PSD version as your working copy. See Chapter 4 to find out how to create a working copy; refer to Chapter 15 for details about JPEG.

PART I | INTO THE DIGITAL DARKROOM

Creating a New Image Canvas

Every image in Photoshop rests on a virtual *canvas.* Normally, the canvas matches the image size exactly, so you don't see the canvas. The canvas becomes visible only if you delete pixels in the image, as discussed in Chapter 8, or enlarge the canvas, as discussed in the next section.

On occasion, you may want to create a new, blank image canvas. For example, if you're putting together a photo collage, you may want to start with a new canvas and then paste the collage elements into it. To create a new canvas, take these steps:

1. Choose File | New or press CTRL-N (Windows) or ⌘-N (Mac).

You see the New dialog box. Figure 3.15 shows the CS version of the dialog box, which contains a few new options.

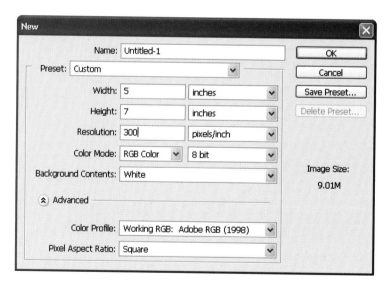

Figure 3.15: Choose File | New to display the New dialog box and create an empty image canvas.

2. Enter a file name in the Name box.

3. Set the canvas size.

You can choose a predefined size from the Preset drop-down list or enter custom dimensions in the Width and Height boxes. If you set a custom size, select a unit of measurement from the adjacent drop-down lists. To match the canvas size to a selection that you just copied or moved to the Clipboard via the Edit | Copy or

Edit | Cut command, leave the Width and Height values as is—Photoshop sets them automatically for you.

4. Set the Resolution value.

Watch Out!

If you set the Width and Height in any unit of measurement other than pixels, the Resolution value determines the pixel count of your new image. Photoshop multiplies the Resolution value by the Width and Height values to calculate the number of image pixels. For example, if you set the canvas size to 4 × 6 inches and the Resolution value to 300, you get 1200 × 1800 pixels. If you use Pixels as the unit of measurement, ignore the Resolution value. You get however many pixels you specify in the Width and Height boxes.

Either way, create enough pixels for your intended final output, as discussed in Chapter 2.

5. Choose a color model from the Color Mode menu.

Chapter 2 discusses color models thoroughly. RGB is the norm for color images.

6. Set the bit depth.

CS In CS, use the drop-down list next to the Color Mode option to establish the initial bit depth. See Chapter 2 for details on bit depth.

7. Select a canvas content option.

You can fill the new canvas with white, with the current background color, or with transparent pixels. In Version 7, click the Contents button to make your choice; in CS, select an option from the Background Contents drop-down list.

8. Set the Advanced options (CS only).

CS In CS, click the Advanced button to reveal the Color Profile and Pixel Aspect Ratio options as shown in Figure 3.15. Using the first options, you can specify a color profile for the document or turn off color management. See Chapter 14 for advice on color-management issues.

The Pixel Aspect Ratio drop-down list allows you to specify square or rectangular pixels. For photos, choose Square.

55

Remember

When you paste a selection into an empty canvas, the selection takes on the output resolution of the canvas. As a result, the apparent size of the pasted object may change. See Chapter 8 for help with this issue and others related to building photo collages.

9. **Click OK to create the new canvas and then save the file in the PSD format.**

Until you save, your new canvas—and anything you add to it—are only temporary. See Chapter 4 for help with saving files.

Adjusting the Canvas Size

You can adjust the canvas size at any time by taking the following steps:

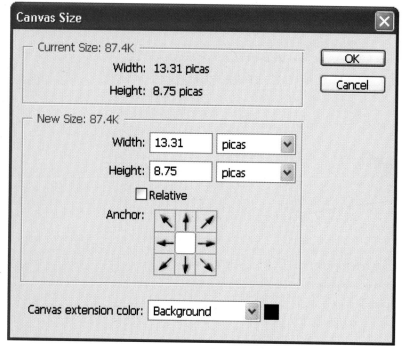

Figure 3.16: Use the Anchor boxes to specify the location of the image with respect to the canvas.

1. **If enlarging the canvas, set the background color to the desired canvas color.**

v.7 This step applies to Version 7 only. Photoshop uses the background color as the canvas color. See Chapter 5 to find out how to establish the background color.

2. **Choose Image | Canvas Size to display the Canvas Size dialog box, shown in Figure 3.16.**

3. **Set the desired canvas dimensions.**

You can go about this in two ways:

■ Deselect the Relative box and enter the canvas dimensions in the Width and Height boxes. Specify the unit of measurement using the adjacent drop-down lists.

■ Select the Relative box and use the Width and Height boxes to specify how much you want to add or subtract from the existing canvas. If you enter 2 in the Width box, for example, you add 2 inches to the canvas width; if you enter –2, you reduce the width by 2 inches.

Remember

To quickly add a solid border around a photo, extend the canvas on all four sides. Set the canvas color to your desired border color.

Watch Out!

Assuming that your image currently covers the entire canvas, reducing the canvas size crops your photo. See Chapter 4 for other information about cropping.

4. **Use the Anchor control to position the image on the newly sized canvas.**

The empty square represents your image. Click to set the position of the image with respect to the new canvas. If you click the center box, your image is centered on the canvas.

5. **If enlarging the canvas, set the canvas color (CS only).**

CS Select an option from the Canvas Extension Color drop-down list or click the adjacent color swatch to select a custom color. Again, Chapter 5 explains how to choose colors.

6. **Click OK to close the dialog box.**

Rotating the Canvas (and Your Image)

You can rotate the image canvas—and the image on it—by choosing Image | Rotate Canvas and choosing an option from the submenu that appears. If you want to rotate the image with respect to the canvas, use the Edit | Free Transform command, detailed in Chapter 13.

In Photoshop CS, you can rotate an image without opening the file by following the instructions outlined in the section "File Browser Basics." But heed my warning in that discussion about doing so with JPEG files.

First Steps: Protect and Crop

4

A digital image has a potentially unlimited life span—if you take a few steps to protect it. This chapter covers this critical aspect of your Photoshop life, explaining how to safeguard original image files, undo editing mistakes, and save completed images. You'll also find out how to crop away unwanted portions of a photo.

Pairing these topics may seem odd—first I talk about preserving your images, and then I discuss destroying parts of them? But after protecting your original file, the second step in every photo project should be a loose cropping. Cropping reduces the size of an image file, which enables Photoshop to process your other changes more quickly.

Protecting Your Originals

Watch Out!

Never edit an original image file. Instead, save a copy of the file immediately after you open it and apply any alterations to this working copy. Remember to resave your working copy before you close your image, too; if you don't, all your changes are lost. Also get in the habit of saving periodically during each editing session, because your edits are vulnerable if your system crashes while the image is open.

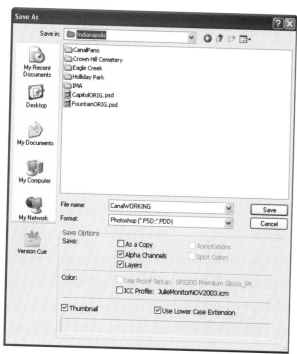

Figure 4.1: Choose File | Save As to save a working copy of your original image.

Photoshop offers four file-saving commands:

- **File | Save As** produces the Save As dialog box, which varies depending on your operating system. Figure 4.1 shows the Windows XP version. Regardless of your system, you will find the standard controls for selecting the folder where you want to store the image, naming the file, and specifying the file format. In addition, you'll get a few Photoshop-specific options. The next two sections offer advice about file formats and discuss the Photoshop-related options. Use Save As to create your working copy and to preserve multiple versions of an image—for example, to save copies at various print sizes or in different file formats.

- **File | Save** overwrites the open file with the current version of the image without displaying any dialog box. Photoshop saves the file applying the same settings you used when saving the file for the first time. Use this command to safeguard edits as you work and before closing the file.

- **Save for Web** launches a tool that simplifies the job of saving a Web-ready copy of an image. Chapter 15 explains this feature.

- **Save a Version** relates to the CS Version Cue system. If you use Photoshop in a workgroup environment, ask your workgroup administrator how to implement this and other Version Cue features.

SPEED KEYS: Save Command Shortcuts		
Command	Windows	Mac
Save	CTRL-S	⌘-S
Save As	SHIFT-CTRL-S	SHIFT-⌘-S
Save for Web	ALT-SHIFT-CTRL-S	OPTION-SHIFT-⌘-S

File Format Options

The Format drop-down list in the Save As dialog box offers more than a dozen choices. But for everyday photography projects, you need just three:

- **Photoshop (.PSD)** This is Photoshop's own format, or *native format,* which is designed to preserve special Photoshop features such as layers and alpha channels. PSD also allows the fastest processing of your edits. Always save your working copies in this format. In fact, there's no reason to save in any other format unless you want to use an image on the Web or in a program that can't open PSD files.

- **TIFF (.TIF)** TIFF, pronounced *tiff,* as in spat, is a print format. You may need to create a TIFF version of your image to import it into a page-layout program or have it printed at a commercial imaging lab. Chapter 15 explains the options that appear when you save in this format.

- **JPEG (.JPG)** Pronounced *jay-peg,* JPEG is a screen-display format used for Web, e-mail, and multimedia images. After finalizing a photo, create a JPEG copy using the Save for Web command, explored in Chapter 15.

Photoshop-Only Save Options

The lower portion of the Save As dialog box contains the following options, which are specific to Photoshop (refer to Figure 4.1). A few items become available only when you save in the PSD or TIFF format.

- **As a Copy** If you turn this option on, Photoshop doesn't save the open image but instead creates a copy of the image at its present state. However, you must give the copy a new name, or you will overwrite the open image. Also, be sure to save your open image before you close it, using File | Save, or any changes made during the current editing session won't be retained in that file.

- **Alpha Channels (PSD or TIFF only)** Select this box to retain alpha channels, explained in Chapter 7.

Remember

To save a
16-bit image,
select PSD
or TIFF as the
file format.

- **Layers (PSD or TIFF only)** Select the Layers check box to preserve individual layers, discussed in Chapter 8. If you deselect the box, all layers are merged.

- **Annotations (PSD or TIFF only)** Using the Notes tool, you can add the digital equivalent of yellow sticky notes to your image. I have never in my life used this feature, but if you think it's keen, select this check box to preserve your notes.

- **Spot Colors (PSD or TIFF only)** If you're producing an image for output on a commercial press, you can add spot-color ink specifications to the file. This book doesn't get into that arena, but if you do, select the box to include the specifications.

- **Use Proof Setup** This option, related to Photoshop's color-management features, applies only to a few formats that aren't part of the photographer's core set. Ignore it.

- **ICC Profile (Windows) and Embed Color Profile (Mac)** Another color-management option, this one allows you to include— *embed*—a color profile. Embedding profiles causes problems in some scenarios; see Chapter 14 for details.

- **Image Previews (Mac)** These options enable you to save tiny previews with a file. You get four choices: Macintosh Thumbnail creates a preview that appears in the Photoshop Open dialog box, as shown in Figure 4.2. Windows Thumbnail creates a preview that appears on Windows systems; Icon turns the desktop file icon into a tiny thumbnail; Full Size creates a low-resolution image that can be used in programs that can't open high-resolution images. Each preview adds to the file size, so turn these options off unless you absolutely need them.

Time Saver

To avoid dealing with this issue each time you save, open the File Handling panel of the Preferences dialog box, introduced in Chapter 1 and shown again in Figure 4.3. Select Always Save or Never Save from the Image Previews pop-up menu, depending on your feelings about previews. If you choose Always Save, select the boxes for the previews you want to create. Now Photoshop implements your preview choices automatically. To specify the preview options each time you save, select Ask When Saving. (The options appear in the Save As dialog box only if you go the Ask When Saving route.)

Figure 4.2: To include previews in the Open dialog box, save files with the Macintosh Thumbnail option selected.

- **Thumbnail (Windows)** This option saves a thumbnail preview with the image file. In Windows, the Photoshop Open dialog box displays thumbnails regardless of whether you save the preview, however. In fact, most newer Windows programs offer this capability. Again, because the preview increases the size of the image file, turn this feature off. Better yet, open the File Handling panel of the Preferences dialog box and select Never Save from the Image Previews pop-up menu.

- **Append File Extension/Use Lower Case (Mac) and Use Lower Case Extension (Windows)**
If you're a Mac user who needs to share images with a Windows user, your file names must include the three-letter Windows file extensions (.psd, .tif, .jpg). You can tell Photoshop to add the extension automatically: Open the File Handling panel of the Preferences dialog box and select Always from the Append File Extension pop-up menu, as shown in Figure 4.3. If you instead select Ask When Saving, the Save As

Figure 4.3: Don't enable all four previews; each one increases file size.

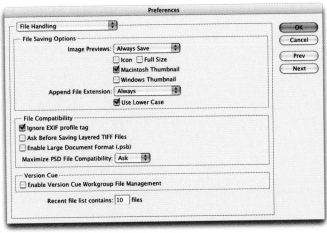

dialog box offers an Append check box so that you can make the call on a case-by-case basis. As for the Use Lower Case (Mac) or Use Lower Case Extension (Windows) option, it simply tells Photoshop whether to add the extension in lowercase or capital letters. It doesn't make a hoot of difference unless you're preparing the photo for a specific use that requires lowercase file names.

Tracking and Undoing Changes

With Photoshop, you don't have to worry about "breaking" your image. First, assuming that you always work on a copy of your original file, you can go back to square one if you really botch an editing project. Second, Photoshop gives you a number of safety nets that enable you to undo bad editing decisions:

- **Edit | Undo and Edit | Redo** Undo takes you back one step in time, reversing your last edit. Undo then morphs into the Redo command, which enables you to undo your undo.

- **Edit | Step Backward and Edit | Step Forward** To reverse a series of steps, use the Step Backward and Step Forward commands, respectively, rather than Undo and Redo. Each time you choose a command, you undo or redo another step. By default, you can undo and restore 20 edits. This value is controlled by the History States option in the Preferences dialog box, explained in Chapter 1.

- **File | Revert** This command undoes all edits made during the current editing session. And guess what—you can undo the Revert command, which is helpful in case you totally lose your mind or your patience and then find either again.

- **History Palette** Not a command but a palette full of restorative power, the History palette offers a quicker way to undo and redo a long sequence of edits than Step Backward and Step Forward. The next section tells all.

You'll use the four Edit menu commands frequently, so commit the keyboard shortcuts in the "Speed Keys: Undo/Redo Keyboard Shortcuts" table to memory. Undo and Redo share the same shortcut; press the shortcut once to undo and again to redo. (These shortcuts assume that you stick with the default shortcut settings discussed in Chapter 1.)

SPEED KEYS: Undo/Redo Keyboard Shortcuts		
Command	Windows	Mac
Undo/Redo	CTRL-Z	⌘-Z
Step Backward	ALT-CTRL-Z	OPTION-⌘-Z
Step Forward	SHIFT-CTRL-Z	SHIFT-⌘-Z

Using the History Palette

Undo and its brethren work fine for reversing a few recent changes to a photo. But for real undo and redo power, choose Window | History to take advantage of the History palette, shown in Figure 4.4.

The History palette is a complex feature, and I could spend a whole chapter discussing all its options. Because most everyday photography projects don't require extensive editing—and thus don't involve a lot of undoing and redoing—I'll introduce you to just the basics here.

Each time you apply an alteration to an image, Photoshop creates a *history state,* which logs the change in the History palette. In Figure 4.4, the palette contains six states. By accessing different states, you can move between current and previous versions of your image, as follows:

- Click a state to return to the image as it existed at that point.
- All states following the one you click appear dimmed. If you apply a new edit, the dimmed edits disappear from the palette.
- To restore a dimmed state and the edit it represents, click the state. All states above the one you click also get restored.
- If you set the History palette to *nonlinear mode,* you can delete and

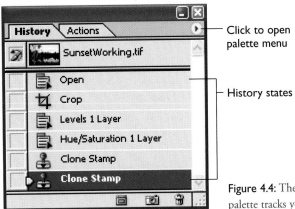

Click to open palette menu

History states

Figure 4.4: The History palette tracks your edits.

restore a state without affecting states above or below. To switch to this setup, choose History Options from the History palette menu to display the dialog box shown in Figure 4.5 and select Allow Non-Linear History. Working in this mode can be confusing, though, because the result of an edit may depend on what you did before or after applying that change. So undoing a state may affect your image in ways you don't expect. I recommend that you turn the option on only when you encounter situations that require it.

■ In either regular or nonlinear mode, you can undo a state change by choosing the Undo command.

Figure 4.5: Turn on Allow Non-Linear History to undo/redo one state without affecting other states.

The number of states the History palette tracks depends on the History States option on the General panel of the Preferences dialog box. The default limit is 20. When you apply the twenty-first change to your image, the first state drops off the History palette and the most recent change goes on the list.

Raising the History States value sounds appealing, but every edit that Photoshop tracks taxes your computer resources more. If you're worried about not being able to undo more than 20 edits, you can take advantage of *snapshots,* explained next. Regardless of your decision, remember that history states aren't saved with the image file—so if you close the image, you lose the chance to access those states.

Taking History Snapshots

A snapshot "takes a picture" of your image at its current appearance. You can tell Photoshop to restore your image to the snapshot version, which enables you to revert to a particular state even if the History palette no longer displays that state.

By default, Photoshop automatically creates a snapshot when you open your image. This snapshot appears at the top of the History palette, as shown in Figure 4.6.

To create a new snapshot, click the New Snapshot button, labeled in the figure. Click a snapshot to return to that version of your photo. To delete snapshots that you no longer need, drag them to the Trash icon at the bottom of the History palette.

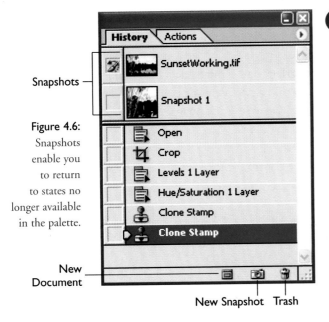

Snapshots —

Figure 4.6:
Snapshots
enable you
to return
to states no
longer available
in the palette.

New
Document

New Snapshot   Trash

Watch Out!

Like history states,
snapshots are not
saved with the image
file. To preserve a
snapshot, you must
save it as a new
image. You can do
this by dragging the
snapshot to the New
Document icon,
labeled in Figure 4.6.
Then save the result-
ing new image.

Remember

If Photoshop
starts behaving
sluggishly or
exhibiting other
low memory
symptoms, try
using the Edit |
Purge | All com-
mand. This com-
mand frees some
memory by dump-
ing the current
Undo tracking
data, History
States tracking
data, and Clipboard
data (which is
created when you
use the Edit | Copy
and Edit | Cut
commands). You
can't undo the
command, though,
so use caution.

PART 2 | PHOTOSHOP BASICS

Cropping Your Pictures

The smaller the image file size, the faster Photoshop can process your alterations.
Because every pixel adds to file size, always crop your photo loosely after you
create your working copy. After editing your photo, you can crop again more
closely if needed.

Watch Out!

One exception applies: If you need to fix a tilting horizon line or convergence, don't
apply the crop before making the correction. Those corrections often cause part of
your image to be lost, so you should start with as much original image area as possible.
See Chapter 13 for details about these corrections.

With that caveat in mind, the rest of this chapter explains five ways to crop an
image in Photoshop.

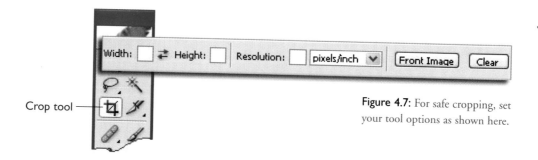

Crop tool

Figure 4.7: For safe cropping, set your tool options as shown here.

Using the Crop Tool

For loose cropping, the Crop tool provides the quickest solution. Crop this way:

1. Press c or click the Crop tool icon in the toolbox, labeled in Figure 4.7.

2. Set the tool options as shown in Figure 4.7.

These options enable you to specify a specific crop size and output resolution (ppi). However, this approach isn't a good way to go. If you enter a Resolution value, the image is resampled, which may degrade image quality. And if you don't enter a Resolution value, you may not wind up with enough pixels to produce a decent print or the right screen display size. See the next section for a better solution.

Crop boundary

3. Drag to create a crop boundary, as shown in Figure 4.8.

A dotted outline indicates the crop boundary. Anything inside the dotted outline will be retained when you apply the crop.

When you release the mouse button, the options bar changes to offer the following controls, shown in Figure 4.9.

- **Cropped Area** This option is available for multiple-layer images. If you choose Hide, Photoshop doesn't dump cropped pixels, but simply hides them. Because your pixels are still hanging around, file size isn't reduced, which makes cropping a little pointless, at least for initial loose cropping. So set the option to Delete.
- **Shield** If you select this check box, Photoshop applies a colored tint to areas outside the crop boundary, as shown in Figure 4.10. Adjust the tint opacity and color using the controls next to the Shield control.

Figure 4.8: Drag to create the initial crop boundary.

- **Perspective** This option enables you to correct convergence distortion and crop the image at the same time. Turn this option off and instead correct convergence using the Free Transform command, discussed in Chapter 13. Transform enables you to preview your correction before committing to it, a benefit you don't get with the Crop tool.

Figure 4.9: These options are available after you create your crop boundary.

4. Adjust the crop boundary as needed.

- To resize the boundary, drag the square handles that appear around the perimeter (see Figure 4.10).
- To move the boundary, drag inside it. Or press the arrow keys to nudge the boundary one pixel in the direction of the arrow. Press SHIFT plus an arrow key to nudge the boundary 10 pixels.

5. Press ENTER or click the Accept check mark at the end of the options bar.

If you move your cursor outside the crop boundary in Step 3, the cursor turns into a double-headed arrow, which is Photoshop's signal for "rotation possible." By dragging, you can rotate the crop boundary. This feature enables you to rotate an image and crop it in one action. However, I suggest that you instead use the Free Transform command to rotate the image so that you can see a live preview of the rotation. Again, see Chapter 13 for help.

Handle

Figure 4.10: Drag a handle to resize the crop boundary.

Rectangular Marquee tool

Figure 4.11: Specify the size of the crop boundary on the options bar.

Cropping to a Specific Size or Aspect Ratio

In addition to the Crop tool, Photoshop offers a Crop command. Use this command to crop to specific dimensions.

1. Choose the Rectangular Marquee tool, shown in Figure 4.11, and set the Feather value to 0.

2. Choose Fixed Size from the Style pop-up menu on the options bar.

3. Type the desired image dimensions in the Width and Height boxes.

Be sure to type the unit of measurement you want to use after the numbers you enter, as shown in Figure 4.11. You can use picas, inches, and other standard units of measurement. For Web images, you should use pixels, for reasons discussed in Chapter 2.

Watch Out!

Use pixels for low-resolution images you plan to print, too. This way, you know that after you crop, you still have enough pixels to produce a good print. Multiply the desired resolution by the desired print size to come up with the pixel values. For example, if you want to output a 4 × 6–inch print at 200 pixels per inch, set the Width and Height values to 800 and 1200 pixels, respectively. Of course, you can't crop those dimensions unless your original image is at least that large.

4. Click on your image to display a selection outline.

5. Move your cursor inside the outline and then drag the outline over the part of the image you want to keep.

6. Choose Image | Crop.

Photoshop crops the image to the boundaries of the selection outline.

In addition to cropping to a specific size, you can use this technique to crop to a particular aspect ratio. Just choose Fixed Aspect Ratio instead of Fixed Size from the Style pop-up menu in Step 2. This time, drag in the image window to create your selection outline. Photoshop limits the Rectangular Marquee tool to drawing an outline that matches the proportions you entered in the Width and Height boxes on the options bar.

With either of these methods, you need to visit the Image Size dialog box to establish the output resolution before printing. For Web images, you may need to adjust the pixel dimensions after cropping if you go the Fixed Ratio route.

See Chapter 2 for more information about pixels and output resolution. Chapter 6 provides details about the Rectangular Marquee tool, and Chapter 15 shows you how to establish output resolution and adjust the pixel count.

Trimming with Precision

As covered in Chapter 3, every image in Photoshop rests on an invisible canvas, which you can resize via the Image | Canvas Size command. When you reduce the canvas size, Photoshop clips off pixels that fall outside the new canvas area, which means that you can use Canvas Size as a cropping tool.

Time Saver

This option provides the fastest way to clip a specific number of picas, inches, pixels, or whatever from one or more edges of an image. Just match the dimensions of the canvas to the size you want your cropped image to be.

Chapter 3 details the process of adjusting the canvas size, so I won't waste space going into everything again here.

Trimming by Color

Introduced in Photoshop 7, the Image | Trim command makes short work of clipping a colored border from an image. But it works only if all pixels along the edge you want to trim are exactly the same color.

You specify what border you want to trim via the two options in the Trim dialog box shown in Figure 4.12:

- **Based On** This option tells Photoshop which corner pixel to use

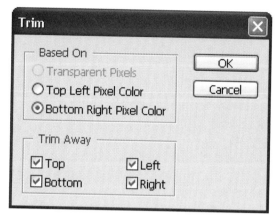

Figure 4.12: Use the Image | Trim command to clip away a solid border from an image edge.

when searching for a border to clip. You can base the trimming on either the top-left pixel or the bottom-right pixel. If the image contains transparent pixels, you can base the crop on those pixels as well.

■ **Trim Away** Select the check boxes for the image edges you want to trim. Again, the trimming occurs only if all pixels on the selected edge are the same color, regardless of whether the box is checked.

Cropping to an Irregular Shape

All digital images are rectangular. But you can create the *illusion* that your image has some other shape by using a "faux cropping" technique. After selecting the area of the photo you want to retain, you simply fill the rest of the image with a solid color. If you match that color to the color of your photo paper or Web page background, the photo appears to have an irregular shape. I used this technique to "crop" the sunset image in Figure 4.13. (I added a border so that you can see the actual dimensions of the image.)

In essence, this technique creates an invisible digital matte. Try it with the sample image Sunset.jpg. These steps show you how to produce a white, circular matte like the one I used in Figure 4.13.

1. Select the Elliptical Marquee tool, labeled in Figure 4.14.

2. Set the tool options as shown in Figure 4.14.

3. Hold down the SHIFT key as you drag from one corner of the area you want to retain to the other.

Figure 4.13: All digital images are rectangular (top), but a little trickery creates the illusion of an image that has some other shape (bottom).

A blinking *selection outline* appears, as shown in Figure 4.15. The outline indicates the area of your photo that will be affected by your next edit. If you need to reposition the outline, place your cursor inside the outline and drag it into place.

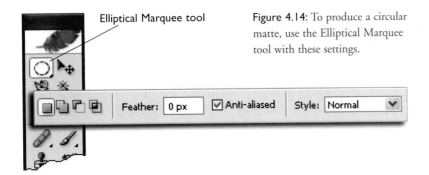

Elliptical Marquee tool

Figure 4.14: To produce a circular matte, use the Elliptical Marquee tool with these settings.

Feather: 0 px   ☑ Anti-aliased   Style: Normal

4. Choose Select | Inverse.

This command reverses the outline, so that it now encompasses the area you want to hide with the matte.

5. Press D to set the background paint color to white.

6. Press DELETE.

The unwanted background turns white, creating a circular matte. Crop away any excess white using the Trim command, explained in the preceding section.

You're not limited to creating a white circular matte—you can make the matte any shape or color you want. See Chapters 6 and 7 for details about working with the Elliptical Marquee tool as well as other tools that produce selection outlines. Chapter 5 shows you how to mix a custom paint color.

Figure 4.15: First, select the area you want to retain; then choose Select | Inverse to select the rest of the picture.

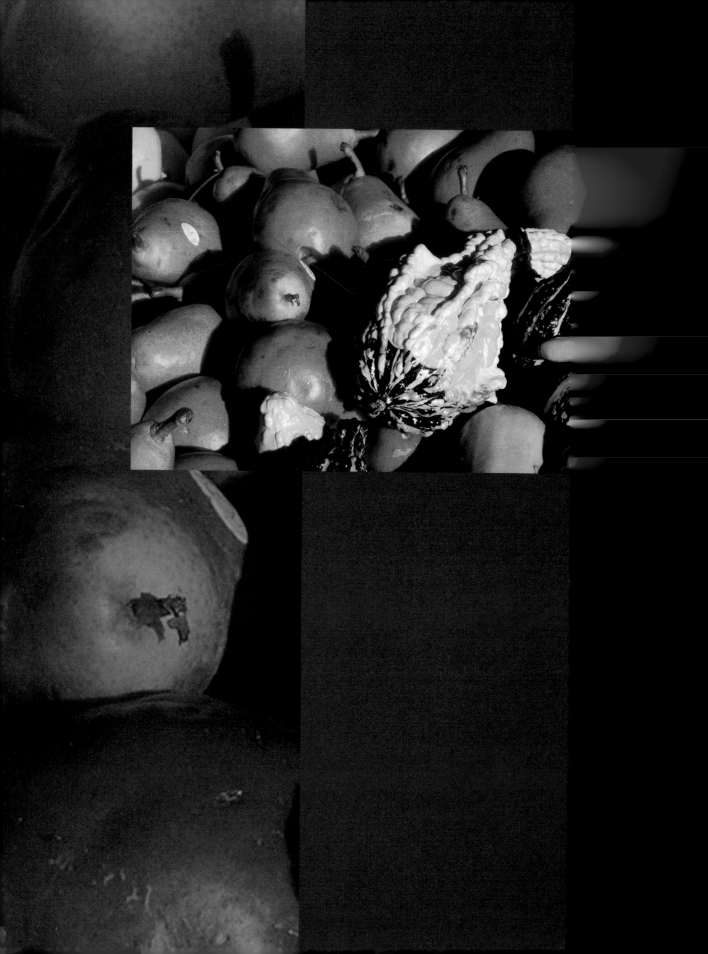

Field Guide to Brush Options and Color Controls

5

When you work with the Photoshop retouching and painting tools, you can customize the tool brush to suit the job at hand. In fact, the Brushes palette, which stores all the brush settings, contains such a dizzying array of options that it's probably the quickest route to a freak-out for the Photoshop novice.

Only a handful of the brush settings play a role in everyday photographic work, however. In fact, this chapter covers all the important options and still has room left over to explain how to establish your paint colors. In other words, freak out no more—this bit of Photoshop business is easier than it looks!

In This Chapter:

- ☐ How brush options affect your tools

- ☐ Shortcuts for changing brush opacity, size, and hardness

- ☐ Special settings for tablet users

- ☐ Tips for using the Color Picker and Color palette

- ☐ Ways to save time with the Eyedropper and Swatches palette

Accessing the Brush Options

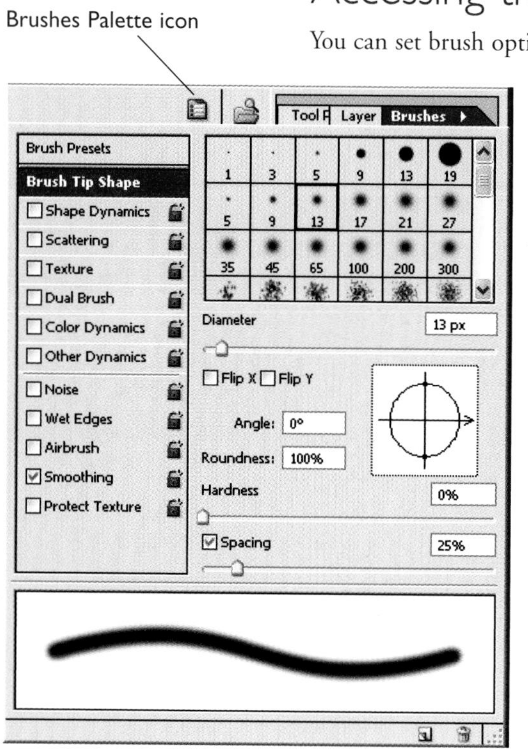

Brushes Palette icon

You can set brush options in two places:

Figure 5.1: The Brushes palette contains the entire array of brush adjustments.

- **Brushes palette** The Brushes palette, shown in Figure 5.1, contains all the available settings. By default, the palette appears docked in the palette well. To open the palette, click its tab in the palette well or press F5. When any tool that uses brushes is selected, you also can click the Brushes Palette icon, labeled in Figure 5.1. (If your palette doesn't look like the one in the figure, open the palette menu and select the Expanded View and Small Thumbnail options.)

  The left side of the palette contains a list of option categories; click a category to display related settings on the right side of the palette. In Figure 5.1, for example, you see the options in the Brush Tip Shape category. This category is the only one that's always in force. You must select the check boxes next to the other categories to enable their related options.

- **Options bar** Click the down-pointing arrowhead labeled in Figure 5.2 to display a mini-palette that provides quick access to controls for adjusting brush size, shape, and, in CS, hardness. You can vary the brush preview appearance via the palette menu; again, I've selected the Small Thumbnail menu option for this figure.

Because the default settings for the advanced brush controls are appropriate for basic photo retouching, there's no need for CS users to mess with the main Brushes palette unless you're working with a pressure-sensitive tablet (such as a Wacom Graphire). If so, you may want to head to the palette to adjust brush dynamics features, explained later in this chapter. In Version 7, unfortunately, you must access the main palette to set brush hardness.

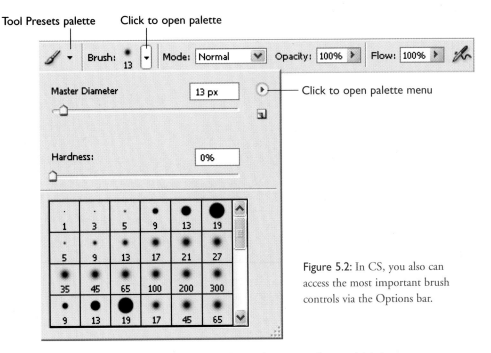

Tool Presets palette

Click to open palette

Brush: 13   Mode: Normal   Opacity: 100%   Flow: 100%

Master Diameter   13 px   — Click to open palette menu

Hardness: 0%

1	3	5	9	13	19
5	9	13	17	21	27
35	45	65	100	200	300
9	13	19	17	45	65

Figure 5.2: In CS, you also can access the most important brush controls via the Options bar.

With either version, you can ignore the Tool Presets palette, which hangs out on the options bar, to the left of the mini Brushes palette, as shown in Figure 5.2, as well as in the main Brushes palette and the palette well. This feature enables you to save custom brushes so that you can reuse them without setting the brush characteristics again. However, the only options you need to adjust for most projects are brush size and hardness, which you can change easily and quickly. So saving brushes doesn't offer much, if any, added time saving or convenience.

Narrowing Your Brush Options

As I mentioned in the introduction to this chapter, most brush options aren't related to photography work—they're provided mainly for Photoshop artists who produce digital paintings and other original imagery.

The next several sections introduce you to the options that do deserve your attention. Don't panic if you don't fully understand them all on first read; they'll become clearer when you work through techniques presented in later chapters. For now, just familiarize yourself with the basics.

Note that not all the brush-based tools offer all these options, and a few tools offer controls unique to their operation. I discuss these tool-specific settings in sections of the book that explain techniques involving said tools.

The Big Three: Size, Shape, and Hardness

The top three brush settings to consider are size, shape, and hardness. I won't insult your intelligence by explaining size, except to say that it's measured in pixels.

100% **50%** **0%**

By default, brushes are round, which is convenient because round brushes are appropriate for almost every photo retouching task.

Brush hardness determines whether your tool lays down sharp-edged strokes or *feathered*—fuzzy—strokes. Hardness is measured in percentages, with 100 percent producing the hardest edge and 0 percent the softest. Figure 5.3 gives you a look at a stroke painted at 0, 50, and 100 percent hardness. The appropriate hardness setting depends on the task at hand; you'll find my recommendations as you explore the various techniques throughout the book.

Figure 5.3: Use a low Hardness value to produce fuzzy strokes and a high setting for sharp-edged strokes.

Figure 5.4: Click an icon to use a prefab brush; open the palette menu to load more prefab brushes onto the palette.

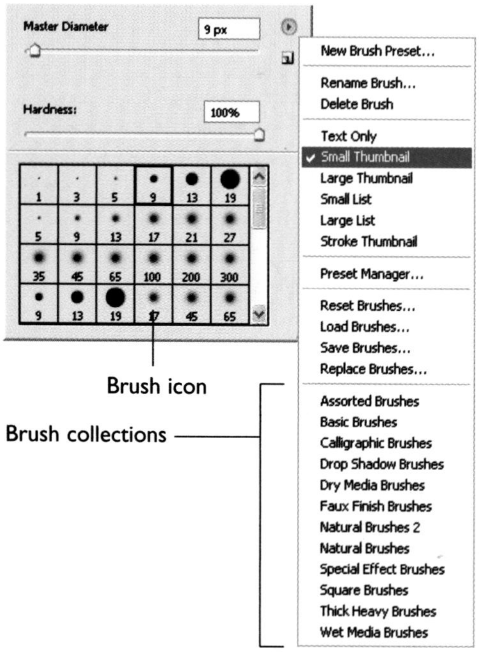

The icons in the Brushes palettes (see Figures 5.1 and 5.2) represent prefab brushes, each of which has a different size, shape, and hardness. Pause your cursor over an icon to see a description of the brush, and click an icon to use that brush. You can access additional predefined brushes by opening the palette menu, shown in Figure 5.4, and selecting a brush collection at the bottom of the menu.

After selecting a brush, you can adjust its size, shape, or hardness as follows:

- **Adjust brush size** Use the Master Diameter control in the mini-palette. Or, in the main Brushes palette, select the Brush Tip Shape category and use the Diameter control.

- **Adjust brush shape** Open the main Brushes palette, select the Brush Tip Shape category, as shown in Figure 5.1, and adjust the Angle, Roundness, and, in CS, the Flip X and Flip Y controls. However, as I said earlier, using anything but the default round brush is rarely necessary for retouching. On occasion, you may want a square brush; to get one, open the Brushes palette menu and load the Square Brushes collection. (Setting the Roundness value to 0 doesn't give you a square brush, as you might expect, but instead produces a brush that looks like a deflated beach ball.)

Brush icon

Brush collections

- **Adjust brush hardness**
  In CS, use the Hardness
  control in either palette.
  In Version 7, the control
  lives only in the main

brushes palette, in the Brush Tip Shape category of options.

Blending Modes

By changing the tool *blending mode,* you can affect how Photoshop calculates the
new hue, brightness, and saturation of pixels that you alter with a painting tool
or any editing tool except the Eraser, Dodge, Burn, and Sponge tools. You set the
blending mode via the Mode menu on the options bar. (The Mode control for the
Eraser and Sponge tools adjusts tool-specific behavior and not blending mode.)

The math behind the blending modes is pretty complicated, and even if you know
the formulas involved, predicting the outcome of a particular blending mode isn't
easy. Fortunately, for most retouching work, you use the Normal mode, which is
the default setting.

Blending modes are also available for mixing layers in multilayer images, a topic
discussed in Chapter 8.

Opacity

When you work with any
painting tool and some
editing tools, the options
bar offers an Opacity control. At 100 percent opacity,
the altered pixels completely
obscure the originals. At
anything less than 100
percent opacity, the original
pixels remain partially
visible. In Figure 5.5, I
painted white lines across
the image using different
Opacity values.

Figure 5.5: At 100 percent opacity, a paint
stroke obliterates the underlying pixels.

PART 2 | PHOTOSHOP BASICS

You can adjust the Opacity setting quickly by pressing the number keys. For 100 percent opacity, press 0; for 10 percent, press 1; for 20 percent, press 2; and so on. To adjust opacity in smaller increments, type the specific value—for example, for 25 percent opacity, press 25.

However you adjust opacity, the setting remains in force until you change it again (as do all the other brush options). So if a tool isn't providing the coverage you anticipate, revisit the Opacity control.

Airbrush and Flow

A few painting tools offer an Airbrush option, which you toggle on and off by clicking the icon labeled in Figure 5.6. When you enable the option, your tool mimics a traditional airbrush. As long as you hold down the mouse button, the tool pumps out paint. This feature also applies to some editing tools.

Watch Out!

I suggest that you disable the Airbrush option and leave its companion control, Flow, at 100 percent. Otherwise, predicting the impact of the tools is difficult, which is just what you don't need for precision retouching. In addition, when the Airbrush option is disabled, lowering the Flow value affects tool opacity, which makes things even more confusing. The one exception applies to the Sponge tool; see Chapter 10 for further information.

Figure 5.6: Turn off the Airbrush option and keep the Flow value set to 100 percent for more predictable tool results.

Airbrush icon

Brush Dynamics

Without question, the most valuable addition to any Photoshop studio is a pressure-sensitive tablet such as the Wacom Graphire, shown in Figure 5.7 (www.wacom.com). With these devices, which start at about $100, you trade in your mouse for a pen-like stylus, which makes precision editing much easier, more intuitive, and less stressful on the wrist. In addition, through a feature called *brush dynamics,* you can vary brush size, shape, opacity, and some other characteristics by simply adjusting stylus pressure.

For photo retouching, the brush dynamic option that I use most often is Opacity. To access this option, open the main Brushes palette and select the Other Dynamics category. Underneath the Opacity Jitter option, select Pen Pressure from the Control pop-up menu, as shown in Figure 5.8. Now tool opacity depends on how hard you press with the stylus. At full pressure, the tool applies your edit or paint stroke at the Opacity value you set on the options bar. (You must turn brush dynamics on and off for each paint or edit tool individually; changing the setting for one tool doesn't affect other tools.)

Figure 5.7: A pressure-sensitive tablet such as the Wacom Graphire makes precision editing easier.

PHOTO COURTESY WACOM TECHNOLOGY CO.

However, if you want consistent opacity for a retouching project, don't enable brush dynamics because it isn't likely that you'll be able to keep the same pressure on the pen for every stroke. Ditto for times when you want full opacity—keeping the maximum pressure on the pen can get tedious.

Photoshop provides a way for mouse users to vary opacity on the fly, too, but the feature is too limited to be very useful. In the same menu where you enable the Pen Pressure option, you find an option called Fade. With this option, the tool starts out at the opacity established by the Opacity control and fades to zero opacity over the course of your drag. You can specify how quickly you want the fading to occur by adjusting the value in the box that appears next to the Control pop-up menu when the Fade option is enabled. Finding the right fade value is difficult, though, so you wind up doing a lot of trial and error to produce the results you want. In addition, all strokes wind up at 0 percent opacity, a limit you don't en-counter with the Pen Pressure option. If you find yourself wanting to use opacity dynamics regularly, do yourself a favor and invest in a pressure-sensitive tablet.

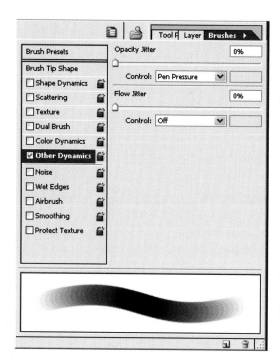

Figure 5.8: The Pen Pressure option enables you to adjust opacity by varying stylus pressure.

Watch Out!

One more bit of brush dynamics business for tablet users: Adobe enables the Shape Dynamics option by default. The first time you use each tool, disable the Shape Dynamics check box, as shown in Figure 5.8, so that your brush size remains consistent no matter how much stylus pressure you apply.

Tool Tricks

You can force a painting tool to produce a horizontal or vertical line by pressing SHIFT as you drag. You also can paint a straight line at any angle by clicking to set one end of the line and then clicking where you want the line to end. These tricks also work for the editing tools.

Choosing the Foreground and Background Colors

When working with any tool that applies paint, you need to specify the paint color *before* you click or drag. The following toolbox controls, labeled in Figure 5.9, indicate the current colors and enable you to select a new color.

Eyedropper

Swap Colors

Foreground Color

Background Color

Default Colors

Figure 5.9: Click the Foreground or Background swatch to open the Color Picker.

The toolbox controls work as follows:

- **Foreground Color** This swatch indicates the *foreground color*. The Brush and Pencil tools apply this color. Click the swatch to open the Color Picker and choose a new color, as explained in the next section.

- **Background Color** This swatch controls the *background color*. The Eraser tool applies the background color when you work on a single-layer image or on the Background layer of a multilayer image. (See Chapter 8 for information about layers.) Again, just click the swatch to open the Color Picker.

- **Default Colors** Click this icon or press D to return to the default foreground and background colors, which are black and white, respectively.
- **Swap Colors** Click this icon or press X to make the foreground color the background color and vice versa.

You can also set the foreground and background colors via the Eyedropper and Color and Swatches palettes, discussed later in this chapter.

SPEED KEYS: Color Shortcuts

Action	Windows	Mac
Restore default colors (foreground, black; background, white)	D	D
Swap foreground/background colors	X	X
Select Eyedropper tool	I	I
Access Eyedropper while paint tool is active	ALT	OPTION
Match foreground color to image color	Click color with Eyedropper	Click color with Eyedropper
Match background color to image color	ALT-click color with Eyedropper	OPTION-click color with Eyedropper
Open Color palette	F6	F6

Matching an Image Color with the Eyedropper

You can use the Eyedropper, labeled in Figure 5.9, to quickly match the foreground or background color to a color in your photo:

- Click in the image to set the foreground color to the color you click.
- ALT-click (Windows) or OPTION-click (Mac) to set the background color.

When you select the Eyedropper, the options bar offers a single control, called Sample Size. Choose Point Sample to match the color to the pixel you click. If you choose 3 by 3 Average or 5 by 5 Average, the tool analyzes a 3-by-3-pixel area or 5-by-5-pixel area underneath your cursor and then averages those pixel colors to come up with the new color.

Tool Tricks

When any painting tool is active, you can temporarily switch to the Eyedropper by holding down the ALT key (Windows) or OPTION key (Mac) and then click a color in your image to set the foreground color. Release the key to return to the formerly active tool.

Selecting Colors via the Color Picker

Clicking either the foreground or background color swatch in the toolbox produces the Adobe Color Picker, shown in Figure 5.10. (If you instead see the Windows or Mac OS color picker, see Chapter 1 to find out how to switch to the more capable Adobe version.)

The Color Picker looks intimidating at first, but the controls are actually simple after you know what's what. In the lower-right portion of the dialog box, you find boxes where you can enter specific color values, using the HSB, RGB, Lab, or CMYK color models discussed in Chapter 2. You also can enter an HTML color code, used to specify colors on Web pages in the HTML language. But don't panic—you don't have to do any number-crunching to select a color.

Instead, use the slider bar and color field, labeled in Figure 5.10, to visually choose a color. The slider bar and color field change depending on which of the color-model buttons you select. For the most intuitive way of doing things, click the H button, as shown in the figure. The Color Picker then works as follows:

■ To set the hue, drag the triangles on either side of the slider bar or just click in the bar.

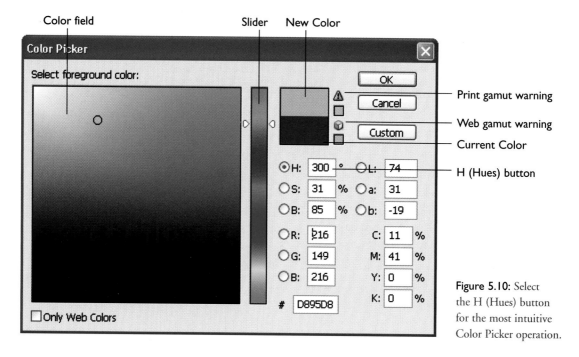

Figure 5.10: Select the H (Hues) button for the most intuitive Color Picker operation.

- To adjust saturation and brightness, drag or click in the color field. The little black circle indicates your current position in the color field.

- As you drag or click in the slider or color field, the values in the color-model boxes update automatically.

- The Current Color swatch shows you the current foreground or background color, depending on which swatch you clicked to open the dialog box. The New Color swatch shows you the new color you've chosen.

- If you select a color that can't be reproduced in print—an *out-of-gamut* color—Photoshop displays a little warning triangle next to the New Color swatch, as shown in the figure. To select the closest printable color, click the tiny color swatch underneath the warning triangle.

- A second alert, this time next to the Current Color swatch, appears if you select a color that's outside the so-called *Web-safe color* spectrum. This spectrum includes a limited palette of colors that can be displayed by all Web browsers and all operating systems. Again, to choose the closest Web-safe color, click the little swatch underneath the alert. You also can select the Only Web Colors check box beneath the color field to restrict the field and slider to the Web-safe palette.

Keep in mind that your photo likely contains many colors that are outside the printable gamut and even more that are beyond the Web-safe gamut. When you're retouching a photo, select the color that produces the best results on your screen and don't worry about the out-of-gamut warning. Otherwise, you may find it impossible to make your corrections invisible. When you ship your image to the printer or Web, all the image colors will be mapped to the appropriate color gamut together. However, if you're adding a border or some other solid-color element, such as text, it makes sense to stick within the color gamut of your final output.

Using the Color Palette

If your project calls for lots of painting, you may want to choose colors via the Color palette, shown in Figure 5.11, instead of the Color Picker. You can leave the palette on-screen so that you don't have to keep opening and closing the Color Picker. Choose Window | Color or press F6 to display and hide the palette. To specify which color you want to set, click the foreground color or background color swatch, both labeled in the figure.

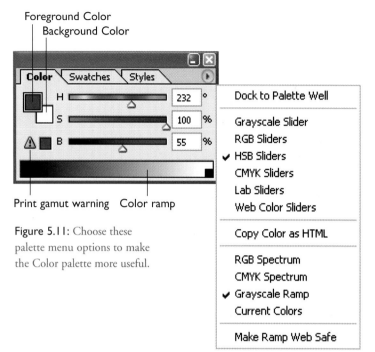

Foreground Color
Background Color

Print gamut warning   Color ramp

Figure 5.11: Choose these palette menu options to make the Color palette more useful.

The palette contains sliders corresponding to the primary components of a particular color model. By default, you get a red, green, and blue slider so that you can specify colors according to the RGB color model, explained in Chapter 2. At the bottom of the palette, you see a bar that contains a spectrum of colors—a color *ramp,* in Photoshop lingo. You can click in this bar to select a color instead of using the sliders. By default, the bar is set to display colors in the CMYK color model.

In my opinion, this setup makes life more difficult than it need be. To make the palette easier to use, open the palette menu and select the HSB Sliders and Grayscale Ramp options, as shown in the figure. Now the sliders correspond to the HSB color model. You get sliders for choosing the hue, brightness, and saturation of the color, which is more intuitive for anyone not schooled in RGB color mixing. And you can easily select a shade of gray by clicking in the ramp bar.

As with the Color Picker, an out-of-gamut warning appears if you select a color that's beyond the printable spectrum. See my comments at the end of the preceding section for my advice on this issue. The Color palette doesn't offer a Web-safe gamut warning, but if you select Make Ramp Web Safe from the palette menu, the color bar displays only colors in that gamut.

Storing Colors on the Swatches Palette

Never one to hold back in offering you multiple approaches to the same task, Photoshop also enables you to set the foreground and background colors via the Swatches palette, shown in Figure 5.12. Choose Window | Swatches to open the palette, which contains swatches for a basic set of colors.

- Click a swatch to set the foreground color.
- CTRL-click (Windows) or ⌘-click (Mac) to set the background color.

For color picking, the Swatches palette is most useful to graphic artists who need to specify colors using a particular color library, such as a PANTONE library. You select the library you want to use from the palette menu. As you can imagine, finding just the right color to match a particular photographic element this way can be time consuming.

PART 2 | PHOTOSHOP BASICS

Time Saver

The Swatches palette does have one benefit for photographers, though: you can store swatches for colors that you select via the Color Picker, Eyedropper, or Color palette so that you can easily reuse the same color.

For example, if you nail down just the right skin color when retouching a portrait, add that color to the Swatches palette so that you don't have to remix the color every time you work on the photo.

Follow these steps to add a swatch:

1. Make the color that you want to save the foreground color.

If you want to create a swatch for the current background color, click the Swap Colors icon in the toolbox or press X to make the background color the foreground color and vice versa.

2. Click the New Swatch icon, labeled in Figure 5.12.

Alternatively, if you want to give the swatch a name—such as "Joe's skin"—click an empty area underneath the existing swatches. You then see a dialog box where you can name the swatch. Passing your cursor over the swatch displays the swatch name.

3. To delete a swatch, drag it to the Trash icon, labeled in the figure.

Watch Out!

Your custom swatches are stored as part of the Photoshop Preferences file. If that file becomes corrupt, you lose your custom swatches. To ensure the preservation of the swatches, choose Save Swatches from the Swatches palette menu. With this command, you create a custom Swatch library that you can load via the palette menu the next time you start Photoshop. When saving, accept the default storage location for the file.

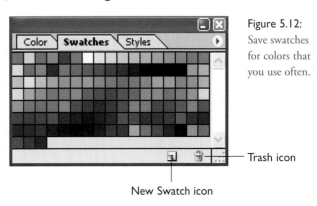

Figure 5.12: Save swatches for colors that you use often.

Trash icon

New Swatch icon

Selective Editing: Masking in Photoshop

6

When printing photos in a traditional darkroom, photographers sometimes selectively expose the image by covering part of the paper with a light-blocking material, or *mask*. You may be familiar with one type of masking material, Rubylith, which looks like a sheet of red acetate. Regardless of the material, the mask prevents the underlying area from being altered by the exposure, just like the masking tape that you may use to protect your baseboards when you paint a room.

Photoshop not only offers the digital equivalent of Rubylith but also a slew of other tools that enable you to limit changes to a specific area of your photo. This chapter introduces the basics of setting editing boundaries, and Chapter 7 explores advanced techniques.

Figure 6.1: I selected the background before applying a blur filter, creating the illusion of shortened depth of field.

Understanding Photoshop Selections: Masks in Reverse

In the darkroom, you limit changes to an image by applying a mask over the area that you don't want to alter. In Photoshop, you take the opposite approach, specifying the area you *do* want to affect. This process is called *selecting,* and the area you designate as ready for editing is called a *selection.* In Figure 6.1, I altered the apparent depth of field by selecting just the background before applying a blur filter. The unselected flower pixels remain unchanged. (Chapter 13 provides step-by-step instructions for creating this effect.)

Selecting isn't a requirement when you work with an editing tool, such as the Brush or Clone tool. But if you do select an area of the image, tools can affect only those pixels, providing you with a safety net. Suppose that you want to paint a tint over the flower in Figure 6.1, for example. If you select the flower, you don't have to worry about accidentally getting paint on the leaves.

Selection Lingo: Masks, Marquees, and Marching Ants

When I was a Photoshop novice, the selection process was one of the most perplexing aspects of the program. Looking back, I realize that much of my confusion stemmed from the fact that the terms used to describe selection techniques varied depending on who was doing the describing. In hopes of starting you off on better footing, here's an overview of selection lingo:

- **Masking versus selecting** Some people use these terms interchangeably. But technically speaking, *masking* means *preventing* changes to an image area, and *selecting* means marking the pixels that you *do* want to edit. That's how I use the terms in this book.

- **Selection outlines, marquees, and marching ants** To specify what pixels you want to edit, you use the techniques covered in this chapter and Chapter 7 to create a *selection outline,* also known as a *selection marquee* or just *marquee.* Photoshop indicates the boundaries of a selection outline with a blinking, dashed line, which you can see in Figure 6.2. The term *marquee* stems from the blinking effect—the outline is supposed to resemble a theatre marquee.

  If that's not creative enough for you, many Photoshop gurus instead use the term *marching ants.* Having just battled real marching ants in my home, I find that particular selection slang unpleasant, not to mention a little cutesy. If Adobe ever puts six little legs on each blinking line, I may reconsider, though. As for *marquee,* I don't use that one to avoid confusion with the Marquee tools, which I discuss later in this chapter.

Remember

A selection outline sometimes prevents you from getting a clear view of what's happening to your photo. You can hide the outline by pressing CTRL-H (Windows) or ⌘-H (Mac); press again to redisplay the outline. Unfortunately, this shortcut also toggles the display of guides, the grid, and some other on-screen aides that you may still want to see. To remedy this problem, choose View | Show | Show Extras Options. In the resulting dialog box, check the elements that you want the shortcut to affect.

PART **2** | PHOTOSHOP BASICS

Note that in Figure 6.2, as well as in other figures that show a selection outline, I made the outline thicker and, in some cases, added a tint so that you can see it more clearly. I applied these changes in Photoshop; you can't adjust the actual on-screen appearance of selection outlines. Not to worry—the outlines are perfectly visible on-screen in their natural clothing; they just don't reproduce well in print.

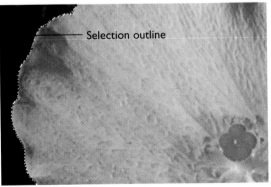

Selection outline

Figure 6.2: Selection outlines appear as dashed, blinking lines.

Fading Versus Precise Selection Outlines

Figure 6.3: Too much background steals emphasis from the subjects.

Before you create a selection outline, you need to consider whether you want to create a sharp, distinct boundary between the edited and unchanged areas in your photo or have the alteration fade out gradually along that border.

Figures 6.3 and 6.4 illustrate the difference between a hard-edged selection outline and a fading one, which is said to be *feathered.* The first figure shows my uncropped original, which contains too much background. To create the images in Figure 6.4, I used the "faux cropping" technique discussed at the end of Chapter 4, which hides a portion of the image with a white, digital matte. For the left image, I created the matte using an unfeathered selection outline, resulting in a cleanly defined boundary.

For the right example, I used a feathered outline, setting the feathering effect to spread over 20 pixels. Now pixels along the edge of the selection outline fade gradually into nothingness, resulting in a soft vignette effect.

Figure 6.4: Here you see the results of deleting the excess background using an unfeathered outline (left) and a feathered outline (right).

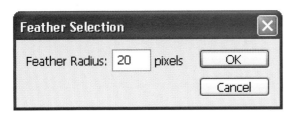

Figure 6.5: A higher Feather Radius value produces a more feathered outline.

Whether you should use a hard-edged or feathered selection outline depends on what you're trying to accomplish. If a hard-edged outline creates an unwanted visual break after you apply an edit, undo your changes and try again with a slightly feathered outline. You need to experiment to see how much feathering creates the look you want. You may even need an outline that's hard-edged along part of the border and feathered in another. (Use the Quick Mask technique outlined in the next chapter to accomplish that trick.)

Photoshop gives you two ways to specify which outline treatment you want:

- Some selection tools can create either type of outline. For these tools, you make the call via the Feather control on the options bar.
- You also can apply feathering after creating a selection outline by choosing Select | Feather, which displays the Feather Selection dialog box, shown in Figure 6.5.

In both cases, a higher value produces a more feathered outline.

Anti-aliased Selection Outlines

When you work with some selection tools, the options bar offers an Anti-aliased check box. *Anti-aliasing* is a process that smoothes out the jagged edges that can occur along curved or diagonal lines in a digital image.

To understand the impact of this option, see Figure 6.6. Both examples show a close-up of a portion of the unfeathered image in Figure 6.4. For the top example in Figure 6.6, I created the selection outline used to produce the white matte with the Anti-aliased option off. Notice the jagged edges?

Anti-aliased off

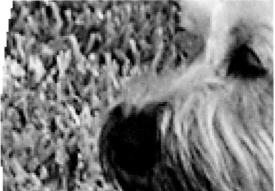

Anti-aliased on

Figure 6.6: Anti-aliasing smooths the edges of a selection outline.

Remember

Many techniques in this book involve *layers,* a feature that you can explore in Chapter 8. When you work on a multilayered image, a selection outline normally affects only the active layer. However, techniques covered in Chapter 8 allow you to perform some changes to multiple layers at a time.

Compare that result with the lower example. For that version, I created an anti-aliased selection, producing a smoother edge.

As with feathering, the decision to anti-alias depends on your photo-editing goal. For projects such as the matte illustration, anti-aliasing is clearly a good thing. But when you need a precise outline, you may want to turn the feature off because anti-aliasing can cause your outline to stray from the boundaries of the area that you want to alter.

Watch Out!

Be sure to set the Anti-aliased control *before* you create your selection outline. You can't apply this effect after the fact.

Choosing the Right Selection Technique for the Job

Photoshop gives you three basic features for creating selection outlines:

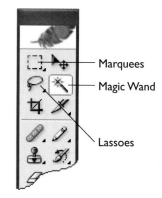

Figure 6.7: The selection tools are grouped at the top of the toolbox.

- **Selection tools** Three toolbox slots, labeled in Figure 6.7, contain eight selection tools. You get four Marquee tools, three Lassoes, and the Magic Wand, with the Marquees and Lassoes grouped in two flyout menus:
  - **Marquee tools** create rectangular or elliptical outlines.
  - **Lasso tools** produce irregularly shaped outlines.
  - **The Magic Wand** selects pixels based on color.
- **Select menu commands** The Select menu offers five commands that create a selection outline:
  - **All** selects the entire image, or, in a multilayered image, all pixels on the current layer.
  - **Deselect** gets rid of an existing outline.
  - **Reselect** resurrects the previous outline.

- **Inverse** reverses the outline, so that what was previously selected becomes not selected, and vice versa.
- **Color Range** selects pixels based on color or brightness.

The Select menu also offers commands that enable you to adjust an existing outline and save an outline for future use.

- **Quick Mask mode** You can throw Photoshop into *Quick Mask mode,* which enables you to create a Rubylith-like mask by painting on your image and then convert the mask to a selection outline.

You need to be familiar with all these selection features because no single option provides the best solution for all projects. However, in general, I recommend that you assign selection tasks as follows:

- For simple rectangular or oval selections, use the Marquee tools.
- To create rough, initial selection outlines, use one of the Lassoes.
- To select areas by color, use the Magic Wand or Select | Color Range.
- To select highlights or shadows, use Select | Color Range.
- To select an intricate subject or refine a rough outline, switch to Quick Mask mode.

This chapter explains the Marquees, Lassoes, and Select | Inverse command as well as tricks for adjusting an existing outline. For information about the Magic Wand, Color Range, Quick Mask mode, and saving selection outlines, see Chapter 7.

As for the All, Deselect, and Reselect commands, there's nothing more to tell except to guide you to the Selection Tools and Commands Speed Keys table. Commit at least the All and Deselect shortcuts to memory—you'll use those commands often.

> **Remember**
>
> After you create a selection outline, don't click or drag in the image window with any selection tool. When the Selection Mode control on the options bar is set to New Selection, your click or drag eradicates your selection outline and starts a new one. If you accidentally click or drag, just press CTRL-Z (Windows) or ⌘-Z (Mac) to undo your mistake and get your original outline back. See "Adjusting a Selection Outline" later in this chapter for more about the Selection Mode controls.

SPEED KEYS: Selection Tools and Commands

Tool/Command	Windows*	Mac*
Rectangular Marquee	M	M
Elliptical Marquee	M	M
Lasso	L	L
Polygonal Lasso	L	L
Magnetic Lasso	L	L
Magic Wand	W	W
Select | All	CTRL-A	⌘-A
Select | Deselect	CTRL-D	⌘-D
Select | Reselect	SHIFT-CRTL-D	SHIFT-⌘-D
Select | Inverse	SHIFT-CTRL-I	SHIFT-⌘-I
Select | Feather	ALT-CTRL-D	OPTION-⌘-D**

*Press SHIFT plus the key to toggle through tools that share a shortcut. **In OS X, disable conflicting system shortcut; see Chapter 1.

Selecting Rectangular or Elliptical Areas

Figure 6.8 offers a look at the four Marquee tools, which share a flyout menu. Given their prominent position in the toolbox, you'd think that these tools are vitally important. But for photo editing, you almost never need them. Why? Because these tools create only perfectly rectangular or elliptical selection outlines, and photographs rarely feature subjects that are perfectly rectangular or elliptical.

New Selection icon
Selection Mode icons

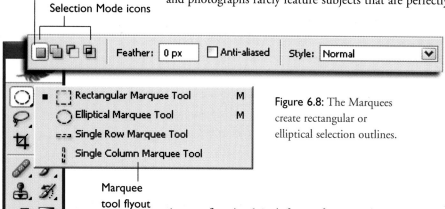

Figure 6.8: The Marquees create rectangular or elliptical selection outlines.

Marquee tool flyout

Because of their restricted geometric nature, the Marquee tools shine for two functions only (in my rarely humble opinion, anyway). You can use the Rectangular Marquee tool to crop a picture to a specific size—to fit a 4 x 6–inch frame, for example. You also can use either the Rectangular or Elliptical Marquee tool to create framing effects like the ones shown earlier, in Figure 6.4. See the Chapter 4 section related to cropping for details about both techniques.

As for the Single Row and Single Column Marquee tools, I'll trade you mine for a latte, maybe even a plain old coffee-of-the-day. About the only function they have is to add a rule across an image or to trim a row of pixels off the edge of the image, and you can accomplish both goals more easily with the Brush tool and Canvas commands, respectively. (See Chapter 5 to find out more about working with the Brush tool; check out Chapter 3 for information on the Canvas command.)

When you do have occasion to select the Rectangular or Elliptical Marquee tool, the options bar offers the controls shown in Figure 6.8. Starting from the left, the controls work as follows:

- **Selection Mode icons** These icons determine whether the tool creates a new selection outline or adjusts an existing outline. Click the New Selection icon, labeled in Figure 6.8, to begin a new outline; see "Adjusting a Selection Outline" later in this chapter to find out how the neighboring three icons work.

- **Feather and Anti-aliased** These options work as described earlier in this chapter.
- **Style** These options affect the possible proportions and size of the selection outline:
  - **Normal** In this mode, you can make your outline as tall and wide as you like.
  - **Fixed Aspect Ratio** This mode limits the tool to creating an outline that adheres to proportions that you establish in the Width and Height boxes. If you want an outline that's twice as tall as it is wide, for example, enter 1 in the Width box and 2 in the Height box.
  - **Fixed Size** Choose this mode to produce a selection outline with specific dimensions. Enter values in the Width and Height boxes, remembering to type the unit of measurement after the number (inches, pixels, picas, and so on.)

In Normal or Fixed Aspect Ratio mode, create your selection outline by dragging from one corner of the area you want to select to the other, as illustrated in Figure 6.9. (I added the arrow; you don't see it on-screen.) In Fixed Size mode, just click in the image.

The Single Row and Single Column Marquee tools offer only the Selection Mode icons and the Feather control. A single click with either tool creates the outline.

Tool Tricks
When the Normal style is selected, hold down the SHIFT key while dragging with the Rectangular or Elliptical Marquee to force the tool to draw a square or circular selection outline, respectively.

See "Adjusting a Selection Outline" at the end of this chapter to find out how to reposition or otherwise refine your initial outline if needed.

Figure 6.9: Drag to create a selection outline with the Rectangular or Elliptical Marquee tool.

Selecting with the Lasso Tools

In homage to all the cowpokes in the digital darkroom, Photoshop provides a selection tool called the Lasso. The Lasso ropes pixels into a selection corral—get it? Anyway, you get three Lasso variations, all accessible from the Lasso flyout menu (refer to Figure 6.7).

- **Lasso** The plain old Lasso enables you to draw a selection outline as if you were drawing with a pen.
- **Polygonal Lasso** This tool assists you with drawing straight-sided polygonal outlines.
- **Magnetic Lasso** This one automatically lays down a selection outline along a border between contrasting areas. (Don't worry—that description probably won't make sense until you see the tool in action.)

Figure 6.10: Try out the Lassoes using the Needlework.jpg sample image.

Earlier, I offered to sell you my Single Column and Single Row Marquee tools for a cup of java, and I'd like to now expand that proposition by offering all three Lassos for a bagel with a schmear. Doing precision selecting with them is difficult and time consuming, if not impossible. Even if you're incredibly skilled with a mouse or stylus, I think that you'll agree that the Quick Mask feature, explained in the next chapter, makes working with the Lassoes seem like roping cattle with dental floss.

That said, I do sometimes use the Lassoes to draw rough selection outlines before switching to Quick Mask mode to finish the job. So that you can take advantage of your Lassoes in the same way, the next three sections walk you through the pixel-ropin' possibilities, using the sample photo Needlework.jpg, featured in Figure 6.10, as an example of how to use each tool.

Creating Freeform Outlines with the Lasso

Using the Lasso couldn't be simpler: Just drag around the object that you want to select. To select the red buttons in the needlework photo, for example, start your drag anywhere along the outer boundary of the group and snake your way around the neighboring measuring gauge and thread. A solid line trails your mouse to show you where the outline will appear, as shown in Figure 6.11. Release

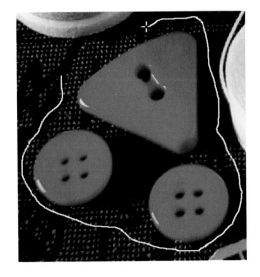

Figure 6.11: Drag around the objects you want to select.

the mouse button when you get back to where you started.

Watch Out!

In an attempt to be helpful, Photoshop automatically closes your selection outline with a straight segment if you release the mouse button before you get back to your starting point. That may or may not be a good thing, depending on the shape of the area you want to select.

As for Lasso options, you can get the standard Selection Mode icons as well as the Feather and Anti-aliased controls, all described earlier in this chapter. Remember that you must select anti-aliasing *before* you create your selection outline. You can apply feathering either before you start the outline, via the Feather control on the options bar, or after, via Select | Feather.

Selecting Polygonal Shapes

The measuring gauge in the Needlework.jpg image provides a good example of the type of subject that responds well to the Polygonal Lasso, which is designed to assist you with selecting straight-sided polygonal regions.

The Polygonal Lasso offers the same Selection Mode icons and Feather and Anti-aliased options described earlier in this chapter; I won't bore you by explaining them again here. After setting the tool options, follow these steps to create your outline. (Again, I've emphasized the outline edges by enlarging and tinting them yellow to make them easy to see in the figures.)

1. Click at the spot where you want the selection outline to begin.

If you're working along with the example image, click at the position marked "first click" in Figure 6.12.

2. Click at the spot where you want to end the first segment in the outline.

In the example, click the spot marked "second click." Photoshop creates a straight outline segment between the first and second pixels you clicked.

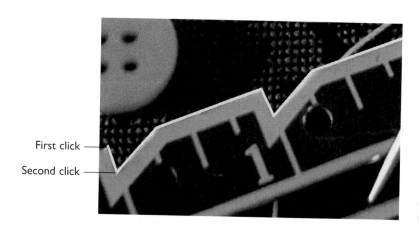

First click —

Second click —

Figure 6.12: Click to set each corner in the selection outline.

3. **Keep clicking to create additional segments until you surround the area you want to select with the outline.**

If you mess up, press DELETE to get rid of the last corner you created; click to redraw the segment. When you reach the start of the outline, a little circle appears next to the cursor, as illustrated in Figure 6.13.

4. **Click to finish the outline.**

You also can double-click to automatically create a final segment between the last pixel you clicked and the starting point.

Tool Tricks
Hold down the ALT key (Windows) or OPTION key (Mac) to temporarily shift the Polygonal Lasso into standard Lasso mode, and vice versa. This trick enables you to use either tool to create an outline that contains both curving and straight lines.

Selection — close cursor

Figure 6.13: When you get back to the selection starting point, a circle appears next to the cursor.

Selecting Between Boundaries with the Magnetic Lasso

The Magnetic Lasso is designed to automate the process of selecting an object that's surrounded by contrasting pixels—a white flower set against a dark green background, for example. As you move your cursor around the edges of the object, the Magnetic Lasso lays down a selection outline along the boundary between contrasting regions, as if pulled by a magnetic force. (Photoshop gurus refer to areas where contrasting pixels meet as *edges,* by the way.)

This tool sounds more complex than it really is, but you can't know that until you try it for yourself. So open Needlework.jpg (refer to Figure 6.10) and pretend that your creative soul is just dying to select that light blue spool of thread on the left. Then pick up the Magnetic Lasso, ignoring the tool options for now, and follow these steps:

1. **Center your cursor over the boundary between the object you want to select and the background.**

Your cursor looks like a cross-hair within a circle, as shown in Figure 6.14. (See the Chapter 1 section related to tool cursor options if your cursor instead looks like the tool icon.)

2. **Click to start your selection outline.**

3. **Move your mouse cursor along the perimeter of the object.**

Keep the cursor centered over the edge between the object and the background. As you move the mouse, Photoshop follows your cursor with a selection outline. Every so often, the tool shoots out little squares called *fastening points* to tack

Fastening point   Magnetic Lasso cursor

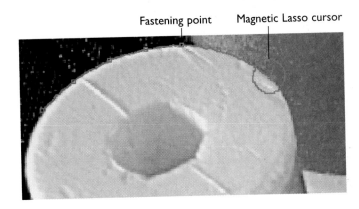

Figure 6.14:
Move the mouse
along the edge
of the object you
want to select.

down the outline. If a segment of the outline doesn't fall where you want it, try these tricks:

- Move your cursor over the last fastening point and press DELETE. The fastening point disappears, and you can re-create that portion of the outline. You can delete as many fastening points as needed.
- Click to add your own selection points. Don't go hog wild; too many points results in a jagged outline.
- Hold down the ALT key (Windows) or OPTION key (Mac) to temporarily switch to the regular Lasso and then drag to create the segment without Photoshop's help. If you click instead of drag, the tool behaves like the Polygonal Lasso. Release ALT or OPTION to return to the Magnetic Lasso.

4. **When you reach the starting point of the outline, click to complete it.**

To let you know that you've reached the starting point, Photoshop displays the tool's icon-style cursor with a little circle to the side, similar to the Polygonal Lasso close cursor shown in Figure 6.13. Be careful to single-click and not double-click, or Photoshop automatically creates a segment to join the last fastening point with the starting point.

Like the Lasso and Polygonal Lasso, the Magnetic Lasso offers the Selection Mode icons and the Feather and Anti-aliased controls, both explored earlier in this chapter. You also can tweak this tool's behavior by using the following options bar controls, shown in Figure 6.15.

- **Width** This control sets the length of the Magnetic Lasso's leash. If you use a high value, the tool can stray farther from the cursor

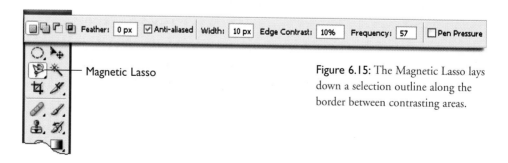

Magnetic Lasso

Figure 6.15: The Magnetic Lasso lays down a selection outline along the border between contrasting areas.

position to look for an edge. The diameter of the tool cursor reflects the width setting.

Time Saver

Press the [(left bracket) key to lower the Width value; press] (right bracket) to raise it.

- **Edge Contrast** This value controls the tool's sensitivity to contrast. If the contrast between object and background is minimal, use a low value.
- **Frequency** This control tells the tool to add fastening points at closer or wider intervals. The higher the value, the more points you get.
- **Pen Pressure** This option is designed for users working with a pressure-sensitive tablet. When you select this option, you can adjust the Width value on the fly by applying more or less pressure with the stylus. I think the Magnetic Lasso is unpredictable enough without throwing in this option, but be your own judge. Note that the value in the Width box doesn't change as you vary pen pressure, but the cursor size does, so that's something.

Time Saver

The Magnetic Lasso does a decent job when a high degree of contrast exists between subject and background. But I can't recommend that you spend hours trying to perfect your Magnetic Lasso technique because you can drive yourself nuts pretty quickly trying to achieve perfection with this tool. (Some say that's what caused my bizarre mental state, in fact.) So take advantage of the Magnetic Lasso to draw your initial selection outlines if the necessary image contrast exists, but then rely on Quick Mask mode, covered in the next chapter, for refining the outline.

Adjusting a Selection Outline

However you create a selection outline, don't worry if you don't achieve perfection on the first stab. Photoshop gives you a variety of ways to adjust an existing outline. The next several sections tell all. To work along with the examples, download the image Lanterns.jpg, shown in Figure 6.16, and use the Lasso to draw a rough outline around any portion of the image that interests you.

Figure 6.16: To practice refining selection outlines, open the Lanterns.jpg image and create a rough outline anywhere with the Lasso.

Moving a Selection Outline

To reposition an outline, first make sure that one of the selection tools (Marquees, Lassoes, or Magic Wand) is active. Then use either of these techniques:

- **Drag the outline with a selection tool** Put your cursor inside the selection outline. Your cursor changes to look like the one in Figure 6.17. Now drag the outline to move it. You can even drag a selection outline from one image window to another.
- **Press the arrow keys** Each press of an arrow key moves the outline one pixel in the direction of the arrow. Press SHIFT plus an arrow key to nudge the outline 10 pixels.

Watch Out!

Don't get confused and try to move a selection outline with the Move tool. That tool moves the pixels enclosed in the outline, not just the outline.

Selecting Additional Pixels

You can use a number of techniques to expand a selection outline:

- **Add Selection Mode** When one of the selection tools is active, click the Add Selection Mode icon on the options bar, labeled in Figure 6.18. Then use the tool to select the new pixels you want to add to the selection, as shown in Figure 6.19. You can create as many additional selection outlines as you need.

Outline move cursor ⎯

Figure 6.17: To move an outline, move the cursor inside the outline and drag.

Time Saver

You also can simply press and hold the SHIFT key to throw a selection tool into additive mode. This trick works regardless of which Selection Mode icon is active. Hold down the ALT key (Windows) or OPTION key (Mac) to temporarily throw a selection tool into deselect mode.

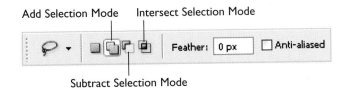

Add Selection Mode   Intersect Selection Mode

Subtract Selection Mode

Figure 6.18: The Selection Mode icons determine whether a selection tool creates a new outline or adjusts an existing outline.

- **Select | Modify | Expand** To expand an outline by a set number of pixels around the entire perimeter, choose this command. Enter the number of pixels in the resulting dialog box and click OK.
- **Select | Transform Selection** If you don't know how many pixels you want to expand an outline, try this command, which is a variation of the Free Transform command covered in Chapter 13. Your selection outline becomes surrounded by little boxes, known as *handles;* drag the handles outward to enlarge the outline and press ENTER.
- **Select | Grow and Select | Similar** Both commands add pixels to an outline based on color. Grow snatches up adjacent pixels that are similar in color to those at the edges of the selection outline. Similar selects similarly colored pixels no matter where they're located.

  Both Grow and Similar select pixels based on the current Tolerance setting of the Magic Wand tool, which I discuss in the next chapter. A low Tolerance value tells Photoshop to add only pixels that are extremely close in color to the selected ones.

Deselecting Pixels

Round up too many pixels with your initial selection outline? To deselect just some pixels, use these tactics:

- **Subtract Selection Mode** Pick up one of the selection tools and then click the Subtract Selection Mode icon on the options bar, labeled in Figure 6.18. Now your selection tool works in reverse, deselecting pixels instead of selecting them.
- **Select | Modify | Contract** Use this command to shrink the outline by a specific number of pixels around the entire perimeter. Enter the number of pixels you want to trim and click OK.
- **Select | Transform Selection** After

Figure 6.19: In Add mode, you can create multiple selection outlines.

PART 2 | PHOTOSHOP BASICS

choosing this command, drag inward on the transformation handles (the little boxes that appear around the outline) and press ENTER.

To get rid of a selection outline entirely, walk this way:

- **Select | Deselect** Press CTRL-D (Windows) or ⌘-D (Mac) to choose the command quickly.
- **Click with a selection tool** This one works only when the tool is in New Selection mode.

Creating Intersecting Outlines

Truth be told, I almost didn't include the Intersect option here, which you access by clicking the Intersect Selection Mode icon (see Figure 6.18). In Intersect mode, you can create intersecting selections. Try this: Click the New Selection icon, grab the Rectangular Marquee tool, and draw a small outline. Now click the Intersect icon and create a second outline that overlaps just one corner of your existing outline. Photoshop then selects just the area of overlap.

What's my problem with Intersect mode? Nothing; it works fine. I just find it less mentally challenging to create a brand-new outline that selects that overlapping area. But your brain may work differently than mine, so feel free to intersect away!

Inversing a Selection Outline

The Select Inverse command reverses an existing selection outline, so that pixels that previously were selected become deselected, and vice versa. (Photoshop experts refer to this process as *inversing the outline.*) Inverse makes your life easier in two important ways. First, you may sometimes want to apply one correction to a foreground subject and another process to the background. You need only one selection outline to do both jobs. Select the subject, apply the first correction, and then use Inverse to select the background.

Second, you can take a "backwards" approach to selecting if the area you *don't* want to alter is easier to select than the region you do want to change. Suppose that you wanted to apply a correction to just the buildings in Figure 6.20. Creating an outline around all the peaks and valleys of those buildings would be a tedious affair. But selecting the sky behind the buildings is a piece of cake with

Figure 6.20: To quickly select the buildings, use the Magic Wand to select the sky and then inverse the selection outline.

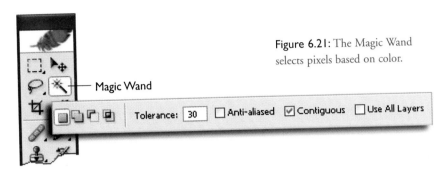

Figure 6.21: The Magic Wand selects pixels based on color.

Magic Wand

Tolerance: 30 ☐ Anti-aliased ☑ Contiguous ☐ Use All Layers

the help of the Magic Wand, which selects pixels based on color. With one or two clicks in the sky, you can easily select the entire background and then choose the Inverse command to select the buildings instead.

The next chapter details the Magic Wand, but if you want to try out this backwards-selection thing now, open the image Indianapolis.jpg and follow these steps:

1. **Select the Magic Wand and set the options bar controls as shown in Figure 6.21.**

2. **Click anywhere in the sky.**

3. **Hold down the SHIFT key and keep clicking sky pixels until you've selected the entire sky.**

4. **Choose Select | Inverse to select the buildings.**

5. **Just for kicks, choose Image | Adjustments | Invert.**

Invert is different from Inverse; Invert is a special-effects feature. It creates a negative image of your selection, as shown in Figure 6.22.

Rotating and Distorting Outlines

Chapter 13 explores the topic of rotating and distorting images via the Free Transform command. You can apply the same transformations to a selection outline, by choosing Select | Transform Selection. Because you use the same techniques for either process, I won't repeat all the maneuvers here.

Figure 6.22: Don't confuse Select | Inverse with Image | Adjustments | Invert, which creates this negative-image effect.

Power Selection Techniques

7

You may find it surprising that creating selection outlines is the only topic given two chapters in this book. Is selecting really that important? In a word, yep. In two words, you betcha. The quality of your selection outlines determines whether the alterations that you make to your photos are undetectable to the viewer or announce to all the world, "Photoshop was here!"

To build on the basic selection skills covered in Chapter 6, this chapter introduces power techniques that enable you to precisely select even the most difficult subject. You'll also find out how to save an outline for future use.

In This Chapter:

☐ Techniques for selecting pixels based on color or brightness

☐ Guide to the Magic Wand and Color Range command

☐ Quick Mask mode: Using paint tools to create selection outlines

☐ Tricks for selecting hair and other difficult subjects

☐ How to preserve and reuse selection outlines

Figure 7.1: To change a solid colored background, first select it with the Magic Wand or Color Range command.

Selecting Similarly Colored Areas

Two of the most valuable selection tools in the Photoshop arsenal are the Magic Wand tool and Select | Color Range command. Both select pixels based on color, which is often the fastest route to a selection outline, especially for selecting subjects shot against a contrasting background.

For an example, see the top image in Figure 7.1. Suppose that you want to paint the background black, as shown in the lower image. Selecting the background with the Lassoes or Marquee tools would be a nightmare because of the tiny nooks and crannies between the jewels. But with the Magic Wand or Color Range, you just tell Photoshop to select all the burgundy pixels. Now suppose that instead of altering the background, you want to apply a sharpening filter to just the brooch. The Magic Wand and Color Range serve you well in this task, too. First, use either option to select the background. Then choose Select | Inverse to reverse the outline, deselecting the background and selecting the brooch.

Tapping Pixels with the Magic Wand

When you click a pixel with the Magic Wand, labeled in Figure 7.2, Photoshop selects similarly colored pixels. Couldn't be simpler.

You get five options for fine-tuning the Wand's performance:

■ **Selection Mode icons** Click the New Selection icon, labeled in Figure 7.2, to get rid of any existing selection outline and create a new one. The other three icons shift your tool into modes that enable you to refine an outline. See Chapter 6 for details.

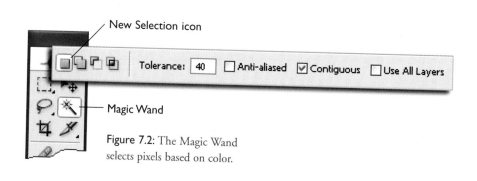

New Selection icon

Magic Wand

Figure 7.2: The Magic Wand selects pixels based on color.

Tolerance 20, Contiguous on

Figure 7.3: I clicked at the spot marked by the X to produce the examples in Figures 7.4 through 7.7.

Figure 7.4: With the Contiguous option turned on, no pixels inside the brooch were selected.

- **Tolerance** This setting determines how closely a pixel must match the color of the pixel you click in order to be selected. At a Tolerance value of 0, only exact matches are selected. Raise the value to include more color variations in the selection.

- **Anti-aliased** Select Anti-aliased to smooth jagged edges along curved or diagonal segments of the outline. Chapter 6 has further information on this option as well.

- **Contiguous** If you enable this option, Photoshop selects only pixels that are contiguous—directly connected, in plain English—to the pixel that you click. If you turn off the option, the tool can select matching pixels throughout the image.

- **Use All Layers** This option applies only to multilayered images, which you can learn about in the next chapter. If you turn on the option, Photoshop creates the outline based on the colors of pixels in all layers. This *doesn't* mean that pixels on all layers are actually selected; a selection outline always affects just the active layer. To base the outline only on colors in the current layer, uncheck the Use All Layers box.

Figures 7.3 through 7.7 illustrate how the Tolerance and Contiguous settings work together to affect the outcome of a Magic Wand selection. After setting the Tolerance value to 20 and selecting the Contiguous check box, I clicked at the position marked by the white X in Figure 7.3. The blue areas in Figure 7.4 show the extent of the resulting outline. (I filled the selection with blue to make the illustration clearer; in real life, you see only the dotted selection outline.)

Tolerance 20, Contiguous off

Tolerance 50, Contiguous on

Background pixels inside the perimeter of the brooch aren't selected because pixels of another color fall between them and the pixel I clicked—those interior pixels are noncontiguous, in Photoshop lingo. Some pixels outside the brooch also miss the cut because they don't meet the Tolerance limit.

Figure 7.5: Disabling the Contiguous option selected some interior pixels.

Figure 7.6: Here, I raised the Tolerance value and turned on the Contiguous option.

For Figure 7.5, I turned off the Contiguous option but left the Tolerance value at 20. This time, the Magic Wand selected a handful of the interior background pixels. Most of those pixels are not selected, however, because they are significantly darker than the pixel I clicked.

For Figures 7.6 and 7.7, I raised the Tolerance value to 50. With the Contiguous option enabled, the Magic Wand selected nearly all the background pixels outside the brooch, as shown in Figure 7.6. When I turned the option off, the tool grabbed nearly all the background pixels regardless of their position in the image. However, if you peer at the image closely, you can see that some pixels in the brooch also became selected. At the higher Tolerance value, the Magic Wand includes a broader range of shades to be included in the selection, and the brooch has some pixels that fall within that range.

In most cases, a single click of the Magic Wand isn't sufficient to produce a perfect selection outline, no matter what Tolerance/Contiguous combo you use. Not to worry—if the tool didn't grab all the areas you want to select, hold down the SHIFT key and click those areas to add them to the selection outline. If the tool overstepped its bounds, hold down the ALT key (Windows) or OPTION key (Mac) and click the pixels that you want to deselect. You can also use the Selection Mode icons, discussed in Chapter 6, to formally set the Magic Wand to Add or Subtract mode, in which case you don't have to press the modifier keys.

> **Remember**
>
> When you work with any selection tool, establish tool settings before you apply the tool. The settings have no impact on a selection outline after the fact. Also, don't forget that if a tool doesn't offer a Feather option, you still can produce a feathered outline. Just choose Select | Feather after you create your outline. (See Chapter 6 to find out what I mean by a feathered outline.)

Tolerance 50, Contiguous off

Figure 7.7: These settings selected most of the background, but also picked up some brooch pixels.

Using the Color Range Command

Tucked away on the Select menu, the Color Range command offers two important selection features: You can select pixels based on brightness, as explained in the next section, or based on color, as with the Magic Wand.

The following steps show you the basics for using Color Range as a boxed version of the Magic Wand; see the sections following the steps for variations. Try out the steps with the sample image Brooch.jpg.

1. Choose Select | Color Range to open the Color Range dialog box.

In the left half of the dialog box, a black-and-white selection preview area appears, as shown in Figure 7.8. White areas indicate selected pixels and black areas indicate deselected pixels. Gray pixels are partially selected. (If you see a preview of your actual image instead of the black-and-white preview, click the Selection button

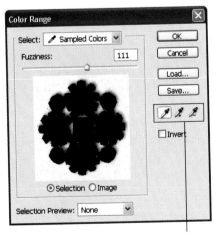

Eyedropper icons

Figure 7.8: White areas in the preview indicate selected pixels.

underneath the preview.) The initial selection is based on the current foreground paint color.

2. **Choose Sampled Colors from the Select drop-down list at the top of the dialog box.**

3. **Select None from the Selection Preview list at the bottom of the dialog box.**

4. **Click the leftmost Eyedropper icon in the dialog box, if that icon is not already selected, as shown in the figure.**

5. **In the image window, click the color that you want to select.**

The preview updates to show you what regions the tool selected. You can adjust the selection as follows:

- Drag the Fuzziness slider to the right to include a larger range of colors; drag left to select fewer colors.
- Click the Add or Subtract Eyedropper icon and then click in the image window to add a new color to the outline or remove an existing color, respectively.
- To start fresh, click the leftmost Eyedropper and click in the image window a second time.
- To reverse the outline—as if you had used Select | Inverse—click the Invert box.

You also can click inside the black-and-white preview with the Eyedroppers instead of clicking in the image window.

6. **Click OK to close the dialog box and generate the selection outline.**

If you prefer, you can use the regular Eyedropper tool—the one in the toolbox—to change the foreground color to the color you want to select before choosing the Select | Color Range command. (You still get access to the Eyedroppers within the dialog box.)

Used as just described, the Color Range command offers much the same functionality as the Magic Wand. The main difference is that Color Range enables you to preview and adjust the selection outline before you create it. With the Magic

Wand, you have to choose your tool settings and then click to see what those settings produce. On the other hand, the Color Range dialog box preview doesn't give you a very detailed view of the selection boundaries. You can't see the outline on top of your image, as you can with the Magic Wand.

Stepping back to the plus side, Color Range offers a few additional twists that you don't get with the Magic Wand. The next two sections introduce you to the color-selecting features; following that, you can read about how to use Color Range to select highlights, midtones, or shadows.

Select a Range of Colors or Unprintable Colors

Instead of specifying the colors you want to select with the Color Range Eyedroppers, you can instead choose one of six colors from the Select drop-down list, shown unfurled in Figure 7.9. This option isn't as useful as you may expect, though, because a pixel doesn't get fully selected if it contains even a trace of some color other than the one you choose from the list. Non-pure hues are only partially selected, which means that they won't receive the full impact of whatever edit you apply next. In addition, you no longer have access to the Fuzziness control to adjust the scope of the selection.

The Out of Gamut option, at the bottom of the list, is more helpful. This option selects colors that are outside the printable range of colors, or *gamut.* (For more about color gamuts, see Chapter 2.) After selecting the out-of-gamut colors, you can replace them with printable shades or, as I usually do, just accept the fact that those colors will look slightly different when printed.

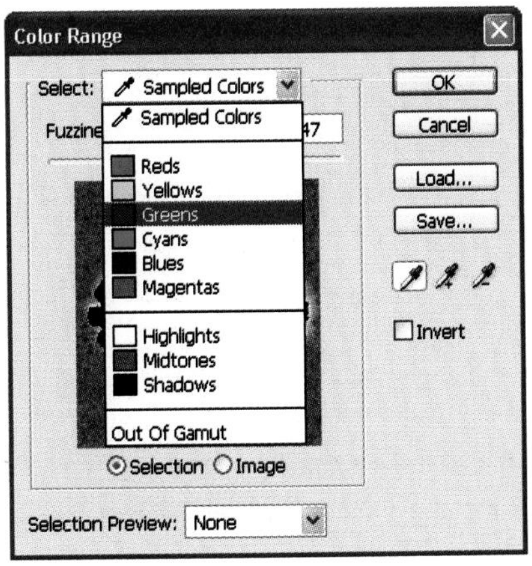

Figure 7.9: Selecting a color range from the list tells Photoshop to select only pixels of a certain hue.

Select Within a Selection

Perhaps the best reason to abandon the Magic Wand in favor of Color Range is that you can draw a selection outline before opening the Color Range dialog box to force Photoshop to select qualified pixels within the boundaries of the outline.

For example, say that you want to select just the blue portion of the sewing gauge in the Needlework.jpg image shown on the left in Figure 7.10. First, draw a rough outline around the perimeter of the gauge, using the Polygonal Lasso perhaps. Then open the Color Range dialog box and click a blue pixel in the gauge. Photoshop selects just blue pixels within the original selection borders. (Although the dialog box preview appears to indicate that areas outside your original selection outline will be selected, after you click OK to create the outline, those pixels are not, in fact, part of the selection.)

Selecting just the blue gauge pixels with the Magic Wand would be a much more difficult proposition. If you turned off the Contiguous option, the Magic Wand would select the similarly colored blue background. But with the Contiguous option enabled, the selection would stop each time Photoshop reached one of the silver measurement lines, so you'd have to click about a zillion times to grab all the blue.

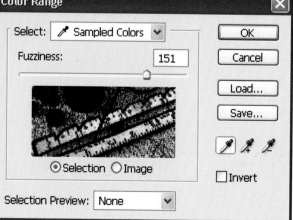

Figure 7.10: Draw a selection outline before choosing the Color Range command to select matching pixels within the outline borders.

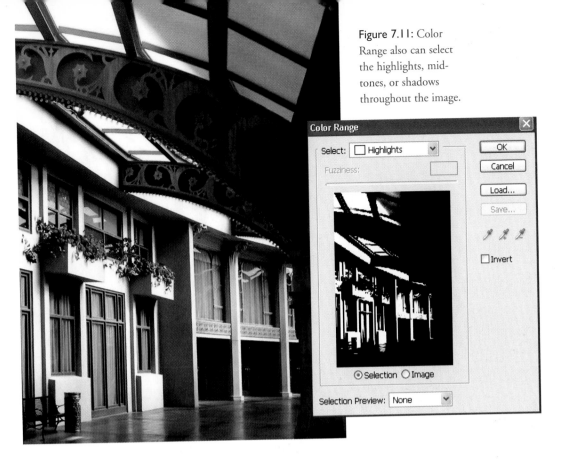

Selecting Highlights and Shadows

If the area you want to select is significantly brighter or darker than the rest of the image, a function of the Select | Color Range command can make short work of the job. Color Range, you say? Yep, even though you would never guess so from the command name, Color Range enables you to select pixels based on brightness.

To try it out, open the MorningLight.jpg image, shown in Figure 7.11, and follow these steps:

1. Choose Select | Color Range.

2. Choose Highlights from the Select drop-down list at the top of the dialog box.

Or, if you want to instead select all dark pixels or all pixels of medium brightness, choose Shadows or Midtones, respectively.

3. Click OK to generate the selection outline.

Unfortunately, you don't get a Fuzziness slider or Eyedroppers as you do when selecting by color, so you can't fine-tune the outline from inside the dialog box. (All the other functions work as described in the preceding sections.) However, as you can see from Figure 7.11, this technique is a speedy way to establish a rough selection outline.

Selecting Like the Pros: Quick Mask Mode

The Magic Wand and Color Range command can work like a charm, but they're of no help for selecting subjects such as the one in Figure 7.12. The colors in the iguana are too varied and too similar to the background to enable either of the color-based tools to generate a decent selection outline.

Figure 7.12: In Quick Mask mode, you paint a Rubylith-like mask on areas you want to protect from changes.

To solve this selection dilemma, make friends with Photoshop's Quick Mask option. As its name implies, this feature enables you to quickly create a *mask,* which prevents changes to the area of the image that it covers. The Quick Mask feature is designed to mimic the sheets of Rubylith that are sometimes used to mask photos in a traditional darkroom.

You create a mask by painting a translucent overlay on your image, using the Brush, Pencil, or any other tool that applies paint. In the right image in Figure 7.12, I created a mask to cover everything but my scaly friend—well, not so much a friend as a favorite subject at the zoo.

After you complete the mask, you switch back to regular editing mode. The mask overlay disappears, and a selection outline appears around the unmasked area. You can switch back to Quick Mask mode at any time to refine your mask and then regenerate the selection outline.

Although the Quick Mask feature is at first a little harder to understand than the standard selection tools, it makes creating perfect selections so much easier and faster that mastering it is well worth your time. In fact, I'm betting my favorite SpongeBob SquarePants action figure that after you try Quick Mask selecting, you'll rarely pick up any of the other selection tools—and I'm a *huge* SBSP fan. (Wearing SpongeBob slippers as I write, in fact!)

Quick Mask Basics

The best way to understand Quick Mask selecting is to try it for yourself. To that end, the following steps show you how to use Quick Mask mode to create an unfeathered (hard-edged) selection outline. To work along with the steps, open the file Iguana.jpg.

Keep in mind that these steps show you just one approach to creating selection outlines via Quick Mask mode. After you try out this technique, read the subsequent sections for variations on the theme.

1. **Shift to Quick Mask mode by clicking the Quick Mask tool-box icon (see Figure 7.13) or pressing Q.**

The foreground and background colors should automatically switch to black and white, respectively. If they don't, press D to make it so.

2. **Select the Brush tool and set the tool options as shown in Figure 7.14.**

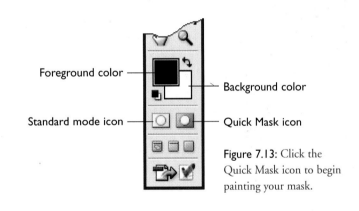

Foreground color

Background color

Standard mode icon

Quick Mask icon

Figure 7.13: Click the Quick Mask icon to begin painting your mask.

Also set the brush Hardness value to 100 percent, which will produce an unfeathered selection outline, and turn off Brush Dynamics, accessible via the main

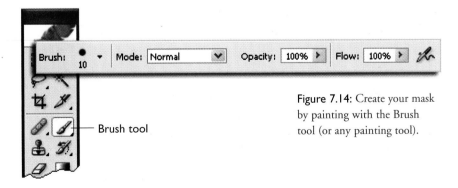

Brush tool

Figure 7.14: Create your mask by painting with the Brush tool (or any painting tool).

Figure 7.15: Masked areas are represented by a translucent red overlay.

Brushes palette. For help with setting these and other brush options, refer to Chapter 5.

3. Zoom in on the iguana's snout and paint along the border between iguana and background, as shown in Figure 7.15.

In Quick Mask mode, you paint with black to apply the mask and paint with white to remove it. However, you don't see black or white paint in the image window; instead, the mask appears translucent red. In unmasked areas, the image appears unchanged.

4. Continue painting along the border until you have outlined the entire subject, as shown in Figure 7.16.

Adjust the brush size as necessary as you work. If you make a mistake, paint with white over the portion of the mask you want to remove.

5. Expand the mask over the rest of the background.

Switch to a large brush and swab over the background.

6. Exit Quick Mask mode by clicking the Standard mode icon in the toolbox, labeled in Figure 7.13.

The unmasked area appears inside a regular selection outline, as shown in Figure 7.17.

Figure 7.16: Start by painting the mask along the border between subject and background; then extend the mask over the rest of the background.

Figure 7.17: After you exit Quick Mask mode, the unmasked area appears inside a selection outline.

Watch Out!

At this stage, your selection outline is a fragile babe! Don't click in the image window with any of the selection tools, or you'll lose that outline. To protect yourself, immediately save the selection outline as discussed in the upcoming section "Preserving Selection Outlines."

If you need to refine the mask, just switch back to Quick Mask mode. Any areas not currently selected again appear under the red overlay.

Remember

If the Quick Mask overlay is difficult to distinguish because your photo contains similarly colored red areas, you can change both the color and translucency of the overlay. Double-click the Quick Mask mode icon in the toolbox (see Figure 7.13) to open the Quick Mask Options dialog box. Click the Color swatch to open the Color Picker and establish a new overlay color. You also can choose the Selected Areas option in the dialog box to create a "reverse mask." That is, the area that you cover with the overlay will become selected, not protected, when you exit Quick Mask mode.

Quick Mask Master Class

The really cool thing about Quick Mask selecting is that you can use any of the normal Photoshop painting and selection tools to produce the mask. This presents you with a world of ways to reduce the amount of time required to create the mask and also a much greater degree of selection flexibility than you get with any other selection method.

The next few sections pass along some of my favorite Quick Mask tricks.

Masking Large Areas with the Fill Command

To mask a large area, save time with the Fill command, as follows:

1. After entering **Quick Mask mode, use any selection tool to select the area you want to mask.**

2. Set the foreground paint color to black.

3. Press ALT + DELETE **(Windows) or** OPTION + DELETE **(Mac) to mask all pixels within the selection outline.**

If you're not keen on keyboard shortcuts, use Edit | Fill instead. Choose Foreground Color from the Use drop-down list, select Normal as the blend mode, and set the Opacity value to 100 percent.

Creating a Feathered Mask

To create a mask that will produce a feathered selection outline, use a soft-edged brush when painting the outer border of the mask. The lower you set the Hardness value for the brush, the greater the feathering. (Stick with a hard brush for the interior of the mask; a soft brush can sometimes leave stray pixels unselected.)

Keep in mind that you can create a mask that is hard-edged along some regions of the border and feathered along others. Just adjust the brush Hardness setting before you paint each segment of the mask.

I often use this technique when retouching portraits. For example, I wanted to brighten the face in the lower image shown in Figure 7.18, but leave the hair alone. In cases like this, I use a hard-edged outline along areas of the face that aren't bordered by hair and switch to a soft brush to paint around the hairline. The exposure change then gradually fades into the hair, leaving no visible boundary between the retouched and original pixels, as shown in Figure 7.19.

You also can lower the opacity of your paint tool as you paint along the boundary of the mask. This creates additional fading because pixels covered by a partially transparent mask become only partially selected.

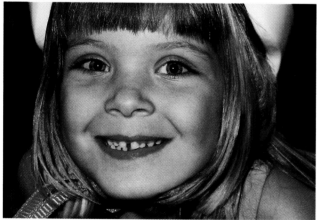

Figure 7.18: When masking a face, use a soft brush around the hairline and a hard brush around the rest of the face.

Figure 7.19: The exposure correction fades out gradually in areas where the mask was soft.

For example, if you set your paint tool to 50 percent opacity, Photoshop applies your subsequent edit at only 50 percent strength.

Create a Gradient Mask

A *gradient mask* is a special masking technique that enables you to fade an exposure change or some other effect from full strength to zero strength. The technique is similar to working with a feathered outline, except that a regular feathered outline fades at the edges of the selection outline. With a gradient mask, the fading occurs over the entire width or height of your outline.

To try this technique, open the image Ixtapa.jpg, shown in Figure 7.20, and follow the bouncing ball:

1. **Press Q to enter Quick Mask mode.**

2. **Make sure that the foreground and background paint colors are black and white, respectively.**

3. **Select the Gradient tool, labeled in Figure 7.21.**

4. **Choose the first gradient from the Gradient picker.**

To open the picker, click the arrow labeled in Figure 7.21. By default, the first gradient fades from the current foreground color to the background color.

Figure 7.20: Starting with this image, I used a gradient mask to produce the fading special effect shown in Figure 7.22.

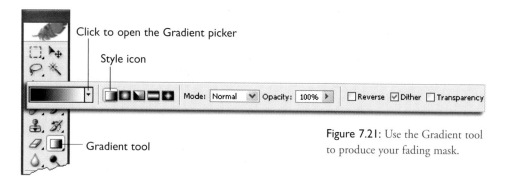

Click to open the Gradient picker

Style icon

Gradient tool

Figure 7.21: Use the Gradient tool to produce your fading mask.

5. Select the first Style icon, as shown in Figure 7.21.

6. Set the remaining tool options as shown in Figure 7.21.

7. Drag from the left edge of the image to the right edge.

Your mask should look like the one in Figure 7.22.

8. Press Q to exit Quick Mask mode and produce the selection outline.

Don't be fooled by the selection outline. Although it indicates that your outline has a clean-cut edge, it really is feathered. To prove it to yourself, choose Filter | Pixelate | Crystallize, which applies a special-effects filter. Set the cell size to 15, click OK, and your photo should look something like the one in Figure 7.22. The effect is nonexistent at the left edge of the frame and fades gradually to full strength at the right edge.

"Pulling" Hair (and Fur!)

Without a doubt, masking strands of hair or pieces of fur is one of the most difficult and tedious selection tasks. I can't offer any magical solutions, unfortunately, but I can offer one trick that may save you some time. Open the image Bear.jpg to try this technique, which I call "pulling hair."

1. Press Q to enter Quick Mask mode.

2. Using the Brush tool with a hard, round brush, mask the interior of the bear, as shown in Figure 7.23.

Get close to the edge of the bear, but don't paint any of the fringes of hair.

Figure 7.22: After creating the mask, I applied the Crystallize filter; the filter effects fade into view from left to right.

3. Select the Smudge tool, labeled in Figure 7.24.

Use a small, medium soft brush and set the other tool options as shown in the figure. Turn off all Brush Dynamics options. (See Chapter 5 if you need help.)

Figure 7.23: To select a furry beast, start by masking its interior.

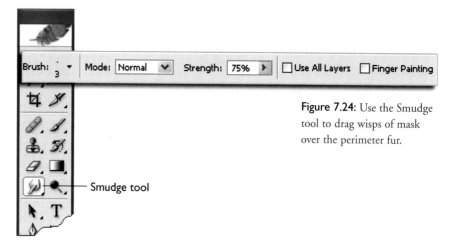

Smudge tool

Figure 7.24: Use the Smudge tool to drag wisps of mask over the perimeter fur.

4. Zoom in on the boundary between bear and background.

In Figure 7.25, I focused on the area between the two front legs.

5. Drag outward from the edge of the mask along the fringes of fur, as illustrated in Figure 7.25.

The Smudge tool smears paint from the start of your drag, fading the paint toward the end of your drag. This enables you to create tapered wisps of mask that create a more natural-looking selection outline.

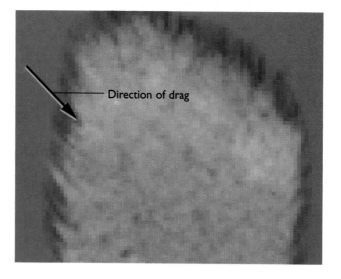

Direction of drag

Figure 7.25: Drag outward from the edge of the mask along the fringes of the fur.

You won't grab every strand of fur or hair using this technique, and you may need to do some touch-up work later, but you should at least get close to an accurate selection outline.

Preserving Selection Outlines

"Never do something twice if you can get away with doing it just once"—that's my motto. Some people call that lazy; I call it efficient. If you're of like mind, you'll appreciate the Save Selection and Load Selection commands. These commands enable you to save a selection outline so that if you later want to alter the same area of your photo, you don't have to create a new outline from scratch.

Photoshop preserves selection outlines as *alpha channels,* also known as *mask channels.* Either way, these channels are just like the regular channels that make up your photo except that they hold selection outline data instead of pixel brightness data. (See Chapter 2 if you're new to channels.)

To store your outline in a channel, choose Select | Save Selection to display the Save Selection dialog box, shown in Figure 7.26. The dialog box options work as follows:

- **Document** You can store the channel as part of the current image, ship it to another open image, or create a new image just to hold the channel. Make your selection from the Document drop-down list.
- **Channel** Select New to create a new channel to hold the outline information. You also can replace or modify an existing mask channel by selecting it from the drop-down list.
- **Name** Type a name that will remind you what you selected with your outline, such as "bear" or "background." Otherwise, Photoshop assigns the name Alpha 1 to your first saved outline, and Alpha 2, Alpha 3, and so on, to subsequent outlines.
- **Operation** If you select New from the Channel drop-down list, you don't have to worry about this one. But if you selected an existing mask channel, you have the option of replacing it or modifying it. (The New button changes to Replace Channel.) The Add, Subtract, and Intersect options work just

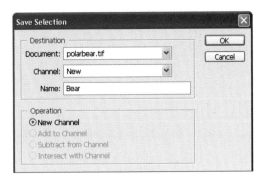

Figure 7.26: Choose Select | Save Selection to preserve a selection outline for future use.

like the Selection Mode icons described in Chapter 6. Frankly, I find it less confusing to just create a brand-new mask every time and delete ones I want to replace or modify.

Time Saver

If you simply want to preserve your selection outline as a new channel in the current image, you can bypass the Save Selection dialog box. Just click the Save Selection icon at the bottom of the Channels palette, labeled in Figure 7.27.

However you save your selection outline, you can resurrect it in two ways:

■ Choose Select | Load Selection to display the Load Selection dialog box, shown in Figure 7.28. The dialog box is very similar to the Save Selection dialog box. Select the image file that contains the mask channel you want to use from the Document list; select the channel itself from the (surprise!) Channel list. The Invert option accomplishes the same thing as Select | Inverse, reversing the outline that the mask channel produces.

If you open the Load Selection dialog box while a selection outline is currently active, you can create a new outline or add to, subtract from, or intersect the existing outline. Again, Chapter 6 spells out these outline-editing tricks.

Figure 7.27: To preserve a selection outline as a new channel, click the Save Selection icon in the Channels palette.

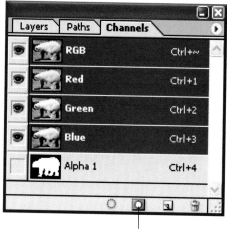

Save Selection icon

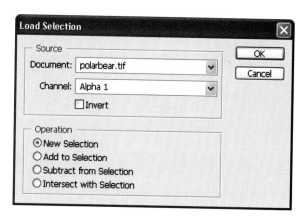

Figure 7.28: You can access saved selection outlines via the Select I Load Selection command.

- Open the Channels palette and CTRL-click (Windows) or ⌘-click (Mac) the channel name in the palette. Of course, this one works only to reload a selection outline stored as a channel in your current image.

Watch Out!

Before closing your image, save it in either the Photoshop (PSD) or TIFF format and select the Alpha Channels check box in the Save As dialog box. Other formats can't preserve mask channels. See Chapter 4 for additional file-saving information.

Also, when you create a selection outline using Quick Mask mode, Photoshop automatically creates a mask channel named "Quick Mask," which you can see if you open the Channels palette. This channel is only temporary, though, and disappears when you exit Quick Mask mode. You must save the outline as just described if you want to preserve it.

Layers: The Photo Editor's Best Weapon

8

If you're like most people, you probably weren't drawn to this chapter when you first thumbed through the book looking for a fun place to dive in. First, you may not even know what I mean by layers—there's no equivalent in the traditional photographic world. Second, this isn't a topic that lends itself to dramatic illustrations. Heck, even I think this chapter is less visually compelling than, say, the chapters on color effects or exposure corrections.

Trust me, though, that what this chapter lacks in eye candy is far overwhelmed by the Photoshop power you'll gain by discovering layers. Like wheels on suitcases, layers are one of those inventions that make you wonder how you ever lived without them after you discover their benefits.

Introducing Layers

Are you old enough to remember overhead projectors? For the young 'uns in the crowd, an overhead projector is the ancestor of today's digital projector. You draw bar charts, company slogans, or whatever on sheets of transparent acetate—transparencies, for short—and the machine projects the transparency contents onto a screen. To present a series of ideas, you can stack one transparency on top of another, with each sheet adding a new element to the projected image.

Photoshop layers are based on the same idea. Every image begins life with one layer, called the Background layer, which is opaque throughout. On top of the Background layer, you can create additional layers that can be opaque, translucent, or transparent. Wherever a layer is transparent, the underlying layer shows through. Translucent pixels allow underlying pixels to be partially visible.

As an example, the large image in Figure 8.1 is a collage that contains three layers. I used a close-up of a tree stump as my Background layer. On top of that, I added a second layer, into which I copied a flower taken from another photo. Then I created a third layer to hold the butterfly, taken from yet another picture. Underneath the collage, you see representations of the individual layers; the checkerboard pattern indicates transparent areas.

Figure 8.1: Where a layer is transparent, the underlying layer shows through.

Background layer   Middle layer   Top layer

Figure 8.2: Swapping the order of the flower and butterfly layers changes the composition.

Each layer exists on its own virtual plane, which gives you several advantages:

- Changes to one layer don't affect other layers. So you could, for example, apply a sharpening filter to the butterfly in the collage without sharpening the flower and wood—and without having to first draw a selection outline around the butterfly. (If you do want to alter several layers at once, you can; see the upcoming sections "Moving Layer Elements" and "Applying Corrections with Adjustment Layers.")
- You can vary the composition of an image by shuffling the vertical arrangement of the layers—the *stacking order,* in imaging lingo. I swapped the butterfly and flower layers to produce Figure 8.2.
- You can reposition and rotate layer elements without harming the underlying image. In the left image in Figure 8.3, I moved and rotated the butterfly, for example. Making the same alteration in a single-layer

Figure 8.3: You can reposition objects in a multilayer image (left); moving pixels in a single-layer image creates a colored hole (right).

image creates a hole in your photo, as shown in the right image. Photoshop fills the hole with the background paint color—white, in the figure.

■ You can delete an element by simply deleting its layer. In a single-layer image, deleting pixels creates a background-colored hole.

Upcoming sections show you how to take advantage of these and other layer benefits. But first, explore the next two sections, which cover additional layer fundamentals.

Layer Central: The Layers Palette

The Layer menu contains scores of layer-related commands. But the Layers palette, shown in Figure 8.4, provides quicker access to nearly all those commands.

Open the palette by choosing Window | Layers or pressing F7. In the palette, you see thumbnails representing each image layer, as shown in Figure 8.4. The layers appear according to their stacking order.

Visit the palette to perform these basic layer operations:

■ **Make a layer active** Click a layer name to make that layer the *active layer,* which is the only one affected by your next edit. The active layer appears highlighted in the palette, and a little brush icon appears to the left of the thumbnail. (A few commands, such as Crop, Image Size, and Mode, affect all layers; these operations can't be applied on a single-layer basis.)

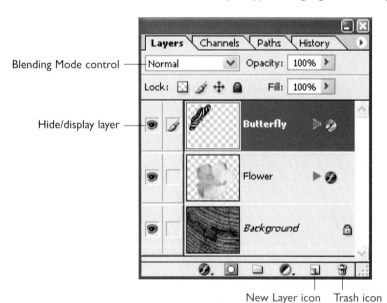

Blending Mode control

Hide/display layer

New Layer icon   Trash icon

Figure 8.4: The Layers palette offers quick access to layer-management controls.

- **Create a new layer** Click the New Layer icon, labeled in Figure 8.4. The new layer appears above the layer that was active when you clicked. Photoshop then makes the new layer the active layer.
- **Delete a layer** Drag the layer name to the Trash icon, also labeled in the figure. All pixels on the layer go kaput.
- **Hide/display layers** To hide a layer, click the eyeball icon to the left of the layer name (refer to Figure 8.4). Click the column again to redisplay the layer.

Time Saver

You can quickly hide all layers but the one you want to view by ALT-clicking (Windows) or OPTION-clicking (Mac) the eyeball for that layer. ALT- or OPTION-click the eyeball again to redisplay all hidden layers.

- **Name a layer** Photoshop automatically names the bottom layer *Background* and assigns numbers to new layers—*Layer 1, Layer 2,* and so on. You can rename any layer but the Background layer by double-clicking the name and typing the new name. Naming layers helps you remember the purpose of each layer.

  Double-clicking the Background layer name produces the New Layer dialog box, which contains a layer-name option. But this action does more than rename your layer. It also converts the Background layer into a regular layer. For more on this subject, see "Freeing the Background Layer," near the end of this chapter.

- **Prevent changes to a layer** Use the four Lock icons to protect layer pixels from accidents. From left to right, the icons work as follows:
  - **Lock Transparency** protects transparent pixels.
  - **Lock Image Pixels** protects the entire layer from the painting and editing tools. You can still move the layer, however.
  - **Lock Position** prevents any pixels from being moved unless you first create a selection outline.
  - **Lock All** prevents any changes to the layer.

  When you want full editing access to a layer, disable all four options. (Clicking the icons toggles the locks on and off.)

Remember

Hidden layers do not print. However, when you save the image in a format that supports layers (PSD or TIFF), hidden layers remain part of the file so that you can continue to access them. When you save in other formats, hidden layers get dumped.

PART 2 | PHOTOSHOP BASICS

The Blending Mode, Opacity, and Fill Controls

By using the following Layers palette controls, you can fine-tune the way that pixels on one layer blend with underlying pixels.

■ **Blending Modes** The Blending Mode control, labeled in Figure 8.4, determines how pixels on one layer mix with pixels on the layers below. In Normal mode, the top pixels obscure underlying pixels, assuming that those top pixels are opaque. In other blending modes, Photoshop uses some properties from the upper layer and some from the underlying layer, which can produce some interesting results. In Figure 8.5, I set the butterfly layer to the Difference mode and the flower layer to the Hard Light mode. Blend modes aren't just for special effects, however; they also can be useful for retouching, as you'll discover in later chapters.

Figure 8.5: Changing the blending mode alters how layer pixels mix with underlying pixels.

The Photoshop Help system spells out the formulas used for each mode, but frankly, predicting the outcome of a blend mode isn't easy even when you have that information. So when you're not sure which mode to choose, just click your way through all of them and see which one you like best.

- **Opacity** This control enables you to reduce the opacity of an entire layer. As you reduce the opacity, the underlying pixels become more visible, as illustrated in Figure 8.6. I reduced the opacity of the flower to 50 percent, producing an area that's half flower, half wood. As an alternative, you can adjust the opacity of just some pixels on a layer by using techniques explored in the upcoming section "Erasing Unwanted Layer Pixels."

Figure 8.6: Reducing the opacity of the flower layer to 50 percent allows the underlying wood pixels to become partially visible.

- **Fill** This control relates to special effects that you can add via a feature called *layer styles*. (The drop-shadow effect discussed later in this chapter is one layer-style possibility.) When you leave the Opacity control at 100 percent but reduce the Fill value, Photoshop makes the regular layer pixels translucent but doesn't alter the opacity of the layer effect. I don't think you'll have much call for this option; I explain it mostly because it's easily confused with the Opacity control.

Building a Multilayer Photo Collage

Creating a simple photo collage is a great way to get acquainted with basic layer techniques. The next few sections explain this process; to work along with the steps, download the sample images TreeRing.jpg, Hibiscus.jpg, and Butterfly.jpg, all shown in Figure 8.7.

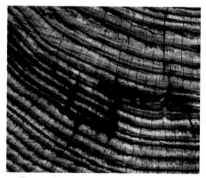  

Figure 8.7: To create the sample collage, download the TreeRing.jpg, Hibiscus.jpg, and Butterfly.jpg images.

Step 1: Combining Photos

Your first step in creating a collage is to copy and paste the collage elements into the background image. Follow these steps:

1. Open the Layers palette by pressing F7.

2. Open the image that you want to use as the collage background.

For the example collage, open TreeRing.jpg.

3. Open an image that contains an element you want to add to the collage.

This time, open Hibiscus.jpg.

4. Check the output resolution (ppi) of both images.

Watch Out!

When you paste one image into another, the pasted image takes on the output resolution (ppi) of its new home. As a result, the relative size of the pasted image may change. To avoid this, match the resolution of each collage element to the background image before you copy and paste. The sample images already match, so you're good to go. If you're working with your own images, visit Chapter 15 to learn how to use the Image | Image Size command to adjust output resolution.

5. **Draw a loose selection outline around the first collage element, as shown in Figure 8.8.**

For the flower image, use the Lasso tool, explained in Chapter 6. You don't have to be precise—you'll get rid of unwanted pixels around the flower later.

6. **Copy the selected area to the background image.**

You can do this in two ways:

- **Copy and Paste commands** Press CTRL-C (Windows) or ⌘-C (Mac) to quickly apply the Edit | Copy command. Next, click the background-image window and press CTRL-V (Windows) or ⌘-V (Mac), which is the shortcut for the Edit | Paste command.
- **Drag and drop** Alternatively, press V to select the Move tool. Place your cursor inside the selection outline, as shown in Figure 8.8, and then drag the selection into the background-image window. (The selection initially disappears from its original home, but when you release the mouse button, the selected pixels are restored.) See the upcoming section "Positioning Layer Elements" for details about the Move tool.

Your combined image should look something like the one in Figure 8.9. If you check the Layers palette, you see that the copied flower appears on a new layer above the Background (tree) layer.

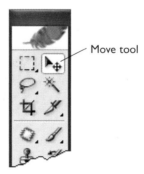

Move tool

Figure 8.8: Loosely select the flower and then drag it into the TreeRing.jpg image.

Figure 8.9: The tree ring shows through transparent areas in the flower layer.

To continue building the collage, close the flower image and open the Butterfly.jpg image. Following the same process, copy the butterfly into the background image, creating the third layer in your collage.

Step 2: Erasing Unwanted Layer Pixels

Your next step is to eliminate the unwanted pixels that exist around the perimeter of the butterfly and flower. You can do this in two ways:

- **Select and delete** After creating a selection outline, press the DELETE key. All selected pixels become transparent. This option works best for getting rid of large or easy-to-select areas.
- **Rub out with the Eraser** Touching pixels with the Eraser tool also makes them invisible. Go this route to wipe out small areas or pixels that would be difficult to select with precision. The following steps give you the low-down on the Eraser; try it out using your sample collage.

Watch Out!

Remember, you can't make Background-layer pixels transparent; these techniques apply just to other layers. On the Background layer, Photoshop paints pixels with the current background color when you delete or erase.

1. **In the Layers palette, click the layer containing the pixels you want to erase.**

For the sample collage, click the Flower layer.

2. **Make sure that the Lock icons in the Layers palette are inactive.**

3. **Select the Eraser tool, labeled in Figure 8.10.**

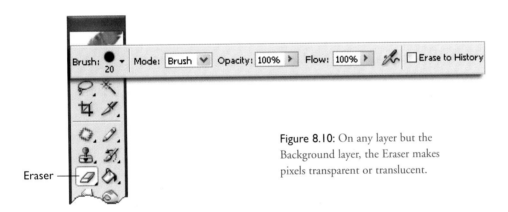

Eraser

Figure 8.10: On any layer but the Background layer, the Eraser makes pixels transparent or translucent.

4. **Choose a tool mode (Pencil, Brush, or Block) from the Mode control.**

In Brush or Pencil mode, the Eraser works just like the Brush or Pencil tool, respectively, except that it "paints" transparency onto pixels instead of applying the foreground color. You get all the standard brush-control options. In Block mode, you get a hard, square brush that can't be adjusted.

For the example project, choose Brush.

5. **Set the other tool options.**

In Brush and Pencil mode, the options bar also offers the following controls. In Block mode, you get only the last control, Erase to History.

- **Brush** For this project, start with a 20-pixel round brush, setting the Hardness value to 100 percent so that your Eraser strokes produce a nice, clean edge. Turn off Brush Dynamics. Other projects may call for different brush characteristics; Chapter 5 provides more information on what each setting does.

- ■ **Opacity** At any setting less than 100, pixels aren't completely erased but instead become translucent. Each swipe of the Eraser makes the pixels more translucent. For the sample project, use 100 percent.

- ■ **Flow and Airbrush** I recommend leaving the Flow value at 100 percent and turning off the Airbrush option for all eternity; Chapter 5 explains why.

- ■ **Erase to History** When you enable this option, the Eraser copies pixels from a selected history state instead of applying transparency. See Chapter 4 to find out what I mean by "history state." And for normal Eraser performance, turn the option off.

6. **Hide all other layers (optional).**

Just ALT-click (Windows) or OPTION-click (Mac) the eyeball icon for the active layer. If you're working on the sample project, you now see just the flower image, as shown in Figure 8.11. Remember, the checkerboard pattern indicates transparent areas.

7. **Drag over or click on the pixels you want to erase.**

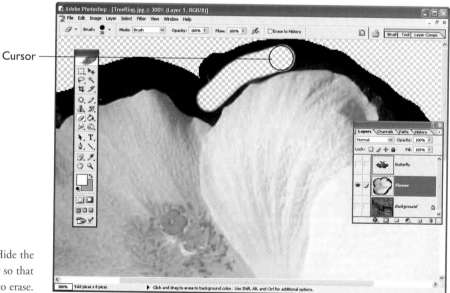

Figure 8.11: Hide the background layer so that you can see where to erase.

Assuming that you hid other layers in Step 6, the pixels you erase are replaced by the checkerboard pattern, as shown in Figure 8.11. You may need to adjust the brush size as you work.

That's all there is to it. Just keep dragging or clicking with the Eraser until you get rid of all the extraneous pixels on your layer. Then ALT-click (Windows) or OPTION-click (Mac) the layer's eyeball icon to redisplay other layers, if you hid them.

To continue building the sample collage, repeat the preceding steps, this time working on the Butterfly layer.

Time Saver

Of course, you can always eliminate the need to do any erasing by precisely selecting your collage elements before copying and pasting them. But even when you're careful, you can easily miss a few of the element pixels when you draw your selection outline. For that reason, I prefer to include a small boundary of unwanted pixels in the original selection—I find erasing excess pixels easier than returning to the original image and grabbing pixels that I missed on the first try.

Step 3: Positioning Layer Elements

When you copy and paste elements into your collage, they may not fall at the positions you want for the final design. The next three sections show you how to reposition and rotate elements and also how to change the layer stacking order.

Moving Layer Elements

The Move tool, labeled in Figure 8.12, is key to moving objects on layers. To select the Move tool, click its toolbox icon or press V.

Tool Tricks

When you're working with any tool other than the Slice, Path, Hand, or Shape tools, you can temporarily access the Move tool by holding down the CTRL key (Windows) or ⌘ key (Mac). Release CTRL or ⌘ to return to the previously active tool.

When the Move tool is selected, the options bar offers these controls:

■ **Auto Select Layer** If you enable this option, Photoshop automatically activates the layer that contains the pixel you click with the

143

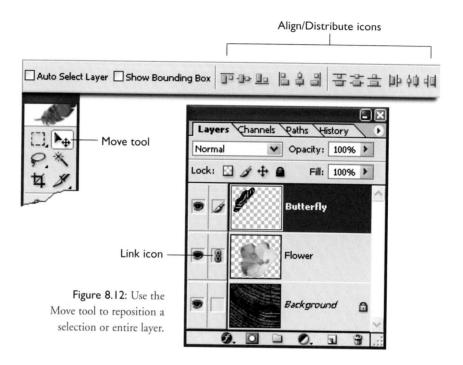

Align/Distribute icons

Move tool

Link icon

Figure 8.12: Use the Move tool to reposition a selection or entire layer.

Move tool, saving you a trip to the Layers palette. This feature works great unless your layers hold very small or translucent elements, in which case clicking just the right pixel to grab the layer you want can be a challenge. I normally leave the option turned off for that reason.

■ **Show Bounding Box** This option, when selected, displays a dotted outline around the contents of the selected layer. The outline enables you to see clearly the boundaries of the layer contents, but it's also dangerous for new users. If you drag an edge of the outline, you shift into layer-transformation mode, as if you had selected the Edit | Free Transform command. See the upcoming section about rotating layers for an introduction to this command.

■ **Align and Distribute icons** Labeled in Figure 8-12, these icons provide one-click access to the Layer | Align Linked and Layer | Distribute Linked commands. You can use these commands to align layer elements with respect to each other and spread elements evenly across a specified distance. These tasks don't fall in the camp of everyday projects, so I respectfully decline to discuss them further.

To sum up, I recommend that you set your Move tool options as shown in Figure 8.12. Then use the tool as follows to position your collage elements:

1. In the Layers palette, click the layer that contains the object you want to move.

2. To move only some pixels on the layer, select them using the techniques outlined in Chapters 6 and 7.

3. Drag or nudge to move.

Just drag with the Move tool, releasing the mouse button at the spot where you want to position the moved pixels. You also can press an arrow key to nudge the selection or layer one pixel in the direction of the arrow. Press SHIFT plus an arrow key to nudge stuff ten pixels in the direction of the arrow.

Manipulating Multiple Layers

You can reposition two or more layers at the same time by *linking* them. In the Layers palette, click the name of one of the layers that you want to move. For the other layers, click the column between the layer name and the eyeball to display a link icon, as shown in Figure 8.12. Photoshop moves all the linked layers as a unit. To unlink the layers, just click that link icon to make it disappear. Note that if you want to include the Background layer in the link group, you must first convert it to a regular layer, as explained in the upcoming section, "Freeing the Background Layer."

> **Tool Tricks**
>
> SHIFT-drag with the Move tool to restrict it to moving the selection or layer in 45-degree increments. ALT-drag (Windows) or OPTION-drag (Mac) to copy a selection or layer instead of moving it.

Rotating a Layer

When adding the flower to the sample collage, I kept the flower at its original orientation. But if you refer to Figure 8.1, you'll see that the butterfly in the collage appears at a different angle than in the original photo, shown in Figure 8.7.

Bounding box   Handle   Rotate cursor

Figure 8.13: Drag near a corner handle to rotate the layer contents.

Follow these steps to rotate the contents of any layer but the Background layer:

1. Select the layer by clicking its name in the Layers palette.

To rotate multiple layers, link them as described in the preceding section.

2. Choose Edit | Free Transform or press CTRL-T (Windows) or ⌘-T (Mac).

The options bar changes to offer a slew of controls, and a rectangular outline, known as a *bounding box,* appears around the nontransparent layer pixels, as shown in Figure 8.13. Tiny squares called *handles* appear around the perimeter of the box.

3. Position your cursor outside the box, near one of the corner handles.

The cursor turns into a curved, two-headed arrow, as shown in Figure 8.13.

4. Drag to rotate the contents of the layer.

You also can enter a specific rotation angle in the box labeled in Figure 8.14. Enter a value up to 180 to spin the layer clockwise. Enter a minus sign before the value to rotate counterclockwise.

5. Press ENTER or click the check mark at the right end of the options bar to apply the rotation.

You must press ENTER twice if you typed a specific rotation value.

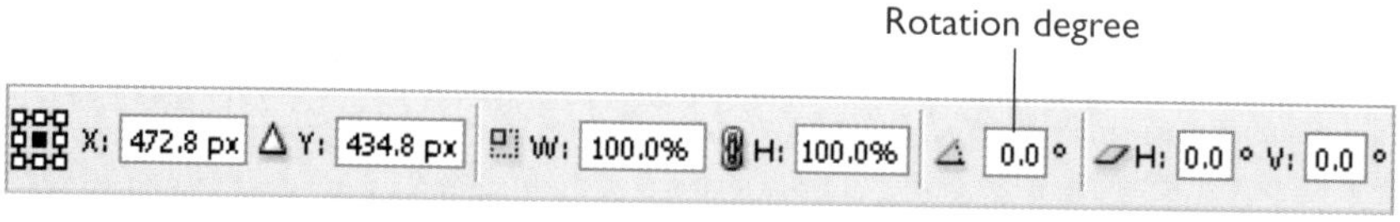

Rotation degree

Figure 8.14: Enter a specific degree of rotation here.

X: 472.8 px   Y: 434.8 px   W: 100.0%   H: 100.0%   0.0°   H: 0.0°   V: 0.0°

Try not to apply more than one rotation to a layer. Every time you rotate, Photoshop has to shuffle the pixels to rebuild the rotated element, a process that can lead to a loss of picture quality.

For information about the other changes you can make with Free Transform, see Chapter 13.

Changing the Layer Stacking Order

By changing the layer stacking order, you can alter its composition, illustrated by Figures 8.1 and 8.2. (Don't take this step if you're working along with the example collage.)

To change the stacking order of a layer, just drag the layer name up or down the list of layers in the Layers palette. As you drag, your cursor changes to a little clenched fist to let you know you've got a layer by the tail, as shown in Figure 8.15.

If you want to reposition the Background layer, see "Freeing the Background Layer," later in this chapter.

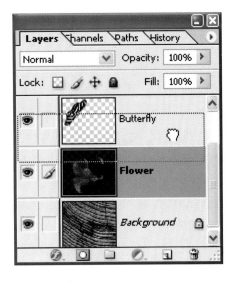

Figure 8.15: Drag a layer up or down to change its position in the layer stack.

Step 4: Adding Shadows with Layer Styles

If you're working along with the sample project, your collage should look something like the one on the left side of Figure 8.16 at this point. Notice anything different between your collage and the one on the right? Look closely, and you can see that the right image looks more realistic because the butterfly and flower cast shadows on the wood, adding separation between the three elements.

Both objects cast shadows in their original images. So why not just copy the shadows from one image to the other? Because you wind up bringing some of the original background with that shadow. For example, refer to the original butterfly image in Figure 8.7. If you copied the shadow underneath the left

Figure 8.16: Adding shadows produces a more lifelike image.

wing, it would look weird in the collage because the butterfly would appear to be casting a green shadow.

Photoshop offers a remedy for this situation. Copy and paste just the object, sans shadow, into your collage, and then add a shadow by using a *layer style*. Here's how:

1. **In the Layers palette, click the layer to which you want to add the shadow.**

2. **Click the Layer Style icon, labeled in Figure 8.17, to display a pop-up menu of effects.**

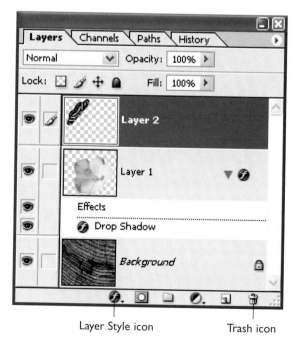

Figure 8.17: Click the Layer Style icon to access the drop shadow effect.

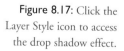

Layer Style icon   Trash icon

Drag to adjust shadow angle

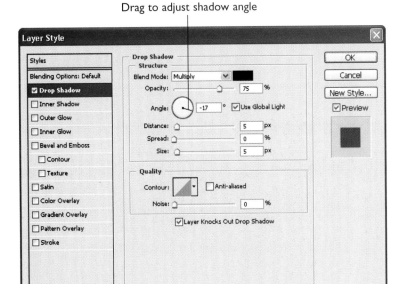

Figure 8.18: Drag the angle control to adjust the shadow position with respect to the layer element.

3. Select Drop Shadow to open the Layer Style dialog box.

Figure 8.18 shows this freakishly complex dialog box. Because you selected Drop Shadow from the pop-up menu, Photoshop displays options related to that effect in the right portion of the dialog box. In the Styles column on the left side of the dialog box, clear all boxes except for Drop Shadow.

4. Tweak the shadow controls until you get an effect you like.

First, set the Quality options as shown in the figure (these are the default settings, so you probably don't need to change them). Now focus on the Structure options in the upper part of the dialog box. Again, stick with the default Blend Mode and shadow color—Multiply and black, respectively. In fact, the default settings for the other Structure options work pretty well in most cases, too, but you can play with them to adjust the distance from the object and shadow size, opacity, and spread (fuzziness). Drag the bar in the Angle circle to change the angle of the shadow. Select the Preview box in the upper-right corner of the dialog box so that you can see the effect of your changes in the image window.

5. Click OK to close the dialog box.

The Layers palette now contains a Drop Shadow item, as shown in Figure 8.17. To adjust the shadow, double-click the Drop Shadow item, which reopens the Layer Style dialog box.

To remove a layer shadow, drag the Drop Shadow item to the Trash icon in the Layers palette or choose Layer | Layer Style | Clear Layer Style.

SPEED KEYS: Layer Shortcuts		
Action	Windows	Mac
Display/hide Layers palette	F7	F7
Copy selection to a new layer	CTRL-J	⌘-J
Move selection to a new layer	SHIFT-CTRL-J	SHIFT-⌘-J
Merge layer with underlying layer	CTRL-E	⌘-E
Merge visible layers	SHIFT-CTRL-E	SHIFT-⌘-E

Figure 8.19: Duplicate a layer by dragging it to the New Layer icon.

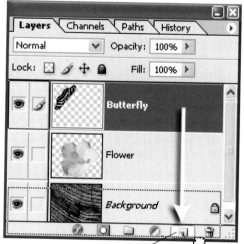

New Layer icon

Using Layers in the Retouching Room

Layers are invaluable for creating multiple-image compositions such as the example featured so far in this chapter. But layers also offer enormous benefits when you're retouching photos. By making your changes on a separate layer, you can protect your photo from irreparable harm—if you mess up, you just delete the edited layer. You also can fine-tune how edited and original pixels mix by using the layer Blending Mode and Opacity controls.

In addition, you can take advantage of *layer masks,* which enable you to hide part of a layer without permanently deleting it, and *adjustment layers,* which allow you to apply color and exposure corrections without permanently altering original pixel values.

The next three sections show you how to take advantage of layers in your retouching work.

Creating Editing Layers

Some retouching work calls for a new, empty layer, but other projects involve copying existing pixels to a new layer. I specify which route to take when providing instructions elsewhere in the book; for now, familiarize yourself with these techniques for creating your editing layers:

- **Create a new, empty layer** Click the New Layer icon in the Layers palette, labeled in Figure 8.19.
- **Copy a selection to a new layer** Press CTRL-J (Windows) or ⌘-J (Mac). Or choose Layer | New | Layer via Copy.
- **Duplicate an entire layer** Drag the layer name to the New Layer icon, as illustrated in Figure 8.19.
- **Move a selection to a new layer** Press SHIFT-CTRL-J (Windows) or SHIFT-⌘-J (Mac) or choose Layer | New | Layer via Cut.

In all cases, the new layer appears above the one that was previously active.

Hiding Parts of a Layer with a Layer Mask

A *layer mask* is a special feature that you can use to hide part of a layer. If you later want to see those pixels again, you just remove the layer mask.

Remember

You can select all non-transparent pixels on a layer quickly by CTRL-clicking (Windows) or ⌘-clicking (Mac) the layer name in the Layers palette. To quickly select all transparent pixels, first select nontransparent areas and then choose Select | Inverse.

Figure 8.20: The original Florence.jpg image (left) is too
light; its multiplied twin is too dark in some areas (right).

The advantages of layer masks probably won't become totally clear until you work
through later chapters, which present many techniques involving this feature. But to get
your feet wet, open the Florence.jpg image, shown in the left half of Figure 8.20. The
following example shows you how to use a layer mask to strengthen the washed-out colors in certain areas of the image. (For other tips on exposure correction, see Chapter 9.)

1. **Duplicate the Background layer by
dragging it to the New Layer icon.**

2. **Set the layer blending mode of
the new layer to Multiply, as
shown in Figure 8.21.**

Combining two layers using the Multiply
blending mode results in deeper, richer colors,
as shown in the right image in Figure 8.20.
However, some areas became too dark.

3. **Click the Layer Mask icon, labeled
in Figure 8.21.**

When you click the icon, a *mask thumbnail*
appears to the right of the image thumbnail,

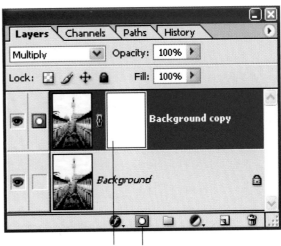

Mask thumbnail   Layer Mask icon

Figure
8.21: Use a
layer mask
to hide part
of a layer.

Image thumbnail   Mask thumbnail

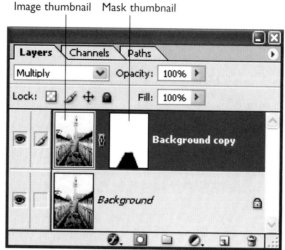

Figure 8.22: After multiplying the image, mask the duplicate layer where the results are too dark.

as shown in the figure. White areas in the thumbnail represent unmasked—visible—pixels. Black areas represent masked—hidden—pixels. If no pixels were selected when you created the mask, as in this example, the entire thumbnail is white. If you do select pixels before adding the mask, only selected areas appear white.

4. Select a paint tool.

The Brush tool works best for this example. Set the tool Mode to Normal, and set tool Opacity to 100 percent. Disable the Airbrush option, set the Flow value to 100 percent, and turn off Brush Dynamics. Choose a fairly small brush—say, 20 pixels—and set the brush Hardness to 50 percent. (Chapter 5 explains all these options.)

5. Set the foreground color to black.

Depending on what you were doing before you added the layer mask, Photoshop may have done this automatically.

6. Paint over too-dark areas to mask (hide) them.

The layer pixels you paint become hidden, and the mask updates in the Layers palette. You *don't* see black paint in the image window; rather, you see the effect of hiding the affected pixels. Figure 8.22 shows how the image and mask look after I painted with black over the street.

7. If necessary, redisplay masked areas by painting with white.

Pixels you touch with white reappear—become unmasked. Just keep alternating between painting with black and white to fine-tune the mask. (Press X to switch from black to white paint quickly.)

8. When you finish the mask, click the image thumbnail to return to normal editing mode.

You may be wondering why you couldn't simply select the areas that were too light, copy them to a new layer, and then multiply just those pixels. That's an entirely valid option. But in this case, you would need to create a complex selection outline, and you'd have to be psychic to predict which pixels would get too dark after multiplying. The masking technique offers an easier solution.

Now that you have the gist of layer masking, here are a few additional tips:

- You can edit the mask at any time by clicking the mask thumbnail and painting with black and white.
- By lowering the opacity of your paint tools, you produce a translucent mask, which allows pixels to remain partially visible. Translucent areas appear gray in the mask thumbnail. By adjusting opacity, you can fade an effect gradually into view. In the sample image, for example, you might want to slightly lighten the darkest portions of the buildings by painting with black at 50 percent opacity.
- You can also paint with a soft brush around the perimeter of the mask to soften the transition between hidden and visible pixels.
- To delete a layer mask, drag its thumbnail to the Trash icon. You get the option of either applying the mask permanently or discarding it.

Time Saver

To quickly mask or unmask a large area, select the area and then fill the selection with the current foreground color by pressing ALT-DELETE (Windows) or OPTION-DELETE (Mac). To fill the selection with the background color, press DELETE.

Applying Corrections with Adjustment Layers

Adjustment layers are a special breed of layer that offer a convenient way to apply the most frequently used exposure and color filters as an independent layer.

Filters that you apply via an adjustment layer affect not just the active layer, but all layers below, which saves you the trouble of correcting each layer individually. And because an adjustment layer is at heart a layer, it offers all the other layer features, including the option to adjust layer opacity, blending mode, and so on. Adjustment layers even come with a built-in layer mask.

The following steps show you the basic workings of adjustment layers. (Later chapters explain the specific filters that you can apply.) To work along with the steps, open the butterfly collage you created earlier in this chapter.

1. In the Layers palette, click the top layer that you want to receive the filter.

Remember, an adjustment layer affects all layers beneath it. For the sample project, click the flower layer so that your filter will affect the flower and the wood but not the butterfly.

2. Select the area that you want to alter (optional).

Normally, a selection outline affects just the active layer, but in this case, the selected area will change on *all* layers underneath the adjustment layer.

Time Saver

You don't have to create a selection outline if you want to edit all pixels on the affected layers, as is the case for the sample image.

3. Click the Adjustment Layer icon, labeled in Figure 8.23, to display a pop-up menu of filter choices.

4. Click the name of the filter you want to apply.

For this example, choose Hue/Saturation. Photoshop adds an adjustment layer item to the Layers palette, as shown in the figure, and opens a dialog box containing options for the filter you selected.

Dialog box thumbnail   Mask thumbnail

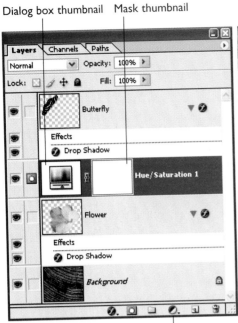

Figure 8.24: I used an adjustment layer to max out the saturation of the flower and wood layers.

Figure 8.23: Apply exposure and color filters via an adjustment layer.

Adjustment Layer icon

5. **In the dialog box, establish the filter settings you want to use.**

For the example collage, do something drastic, like cranking the Saturation value all the way up, so that you can clearly see the effects of the adjustment layer.

6. **Click OK to close the dialog box.**

In your sample collage, the flower and wood are infused with a blast of color, as shown in Figure 8.24. If you drew a selection outline before creating the adjustment layer, only selected pixels in the underlying layers are affected. In the layer mask thumbnail (refer to Figure 8.23), black areas represent unselected pixels and white areas indicate selected pixels, just as in any layer mask. In the example, the entire layer was selected, so the entire mask is white.

You can tweak the adjustment layer—and, thereby, the filter effect it applies— as follows:

- **Change the filter settings** To redisplay the filter dialog box, double-click the thumbnail labeled *dialog box thumbnail* in Figure 8.23.
- **Adjust the layer mask** Use the techniques outlined in the preceding section to hide and reveal the effect of the filter in certain areas.
- **Change the adjustment layer's opacity and blend mode** To lessen the effect of the filter without changing the filter settings,

reduce the layer opacity, as explained earlier in this chapter. You also can vary the blend mode to create different effects.

■ **Apply the adjustment to different layers** By changing the stacking order of the adjustment layer, you change what layers are affected by the filter. If you were to move the adjustment layer in the example image to the top of the layer stack, for example, all three layers would receive the saturation boost.

■ **Prevent an adjustment layer from affecting an underlying layer** You can do this by creating a *layer set* or *clipping mask*. Both features are advanced functions beyond the scope of this book, but I want you to know that the possibility exists. See the program Help system for details.

■ **Delete the adjustment layer** Drag the layer to the Trash icon in the Layers palette.

Time Saver

You can copy an adjustment layer from one image to another, which gives you a quick way to apply the same correction to multiple photos. Just drag the adjustment layer from the Layers palette into the image window of the other photo you want to correct.

Freeing the Background Layer

To transform the Background layer into a normal layer, double-click the layer name in the Layers palette or click the layer name and then choose Layer | New | Layer from Background. When the New Layer dialog box opens, give the layer a new name or stick with the default name, *Layer 0,* and click OK.

Although you can now create transparent areas on the Background layer, the empty areas are filled with a solid color if you save the image in any format but TIFF or PSD. You also must enable the Layers check box in the Save As dialog box.

Merging Layers

Every layer taxes your computer's resources. So when possible, combine finished layers, using these techniques:

■ **Combine a layer with the one immediately below** Click the top layer in the pair and choose Layer | Merge Down or press CTRL-E (Windows) or ⌘-E (Mac).

- **Combine multiple, nonconsecutive layers** First, hide all the layers that you don't want to merge (by clicking their eyeball icons in the Layers palette). Then choose Layer | Merge Visible or press SHIFT-CTRL-E (Windows) or SHIFT-⌘-E (Mac). Redisplay the hidden layers.
- **Combine all layers** To merge all layers, known as *flattening the image,* choose Layer | Flatten Image. If any layers are hidden, Photoshop displays a warning box asking for your permission to discard the hidden layers. To instead preserve the layer content, click Cancel, redisplay the layers, and choose the Flatten command again.

Watch Out!

After you flatten the image, you can no longer manipulate image elements, adjust transparency, or do any of those other things that make layers so useful. Your image exists solely on the Background layer. So before flattening, always make a backup copy in a format that preserves layers. See the next section for more information.

Preserving Layers

When you save your image file, you must select either the Photoshop (PSD) or TIFF file format if you want your image layers to retain their independence.

Watch Out!

Select any other format, and Photoshop flattens the image upon saving. Also be sure to select the Layers check box in the Save As dialog box, which you can explore in Chapter 4.

For works-in-progress, choose PSD over TIFF. This format enables Photoshop to process your edits more quickly. The layered TIFF option is provided for users who need to share TIFF files with others or import the files into a publishing program. Not all programs can work with layered TIFFs, however.

Remember

Here's a neat trick that you can do with the Merge Visible command. Create a new layer and then hold down the ALT (Windows) or OPTION (Mac) key as you choose the command. Photoshop creates a merged version of the image on the new layer but doesn't merge the other layers. You can use this technique to copy a merged version of the image to another photo.

Too Light?
Too Dark?
No Problem!

9

Photography books and magazines are loaded with information designed to help you expose your pictures properly. But even if you manage to digest all that advice, the occasional exposure problem is inevitable. Sometimes the film isn't as sensitive as the manufacturer claims. Sometimes the camera's autoexposure sensor or your light meter falters. And sometimes, the universe just wants to mess with you and blows a cloud over the sun just as you press the shutter button.

Whether your exposure problems stem from inexperience, mechanical failures, or bad karma—I recommend excuse number two, by the way—this chapter shows you how to fix pictures that are too light, too dark, or a bit of both.

In This Chapter:

☐ Fast exposure shifts with Screen and Multiply

☐ Introduction to histograms and tone curves

☐ Expert exposure and contrast corrections with Levels and Curves

☐ How to whiten teeth and emphasize eyes with the Dodge and Burn tools

☐ Tips for using the CS Shadow/Hightlight filter

Figure 9.1: Strong backlighting led to a too-dark subject.

Making Quick Changes with Screen and Multiply

One of the fastest routes to a darker or lighter image involves layer blending modes and layer masks, both discussed in detail in Chapter 8. After duplicating the Background layer, you set the blending mode of the copied layer to Multiply to darken the image or Screen to lighten the image. You can then add a layer mask to remove or soften the effect in areas that became too dark or too light.

The layer-masking section of Chapter 8 illustrates the Multiply version of this technique; if you want to try out the Screen variation, use the sample image Statue.jpg, shown in Figure 9.1.

1. Duplicate the Background layer by dragging it to the New Layer icon, labeled in Figure 9.2.

This assumes that you're working with a single-layer image; if not, duplicate the layer that contains the problem pixels.

2. Set the blending mode of the new layer to Multiply or Screen.

- Choose Multiply to darken the image.
- Choose Screen to lighten the image.

3. Add a layer mask by clicking the Layer Mask icon, labeled in Figure 9.2.

4. Paint with black over areas that became too dark or too light.

As you paint, the mask thumbnail updates, and the image itself gets lighter or darker. For the sample image, paint over everything but the statue to produce a mask that looks like the one in Figure 9.2. (See Chapter 5 for help using the paint tools.)

5. Adjust the effect as needed.

Are the remaining screened or multiplied areas too light or dark? Reduce the duplicate layer's opacity, using the Opacity slider in the Layers palette. To instead

Figure 9.2: After duplicating the Background layer, set the blending mode to Screen to lighten the image.

Blending Mode control   Mask thumbnail

Layer Mask icon   New Layer icon

produce a more pronounced change, duplicate the screened or multiplied layer. For example, in Figure 9.3, duplicating the first screened layer brought the brightness of the statue to the level you see in the accompanying image.

6. **When you're happy with the results, merge the screened or multiplied layers with the original.**

Or, if you want to retain the individual layers, click the image thumbnail (next to the mask thumbnail) to exit mask-editing mode.

As an alternative to using a layer mask, you can select the areas you want to change and then copy the selection to a new layer in Step 1. Press CTRL-J (Windows) or ⌘-J (Mac) to copy a selection to a new layer.

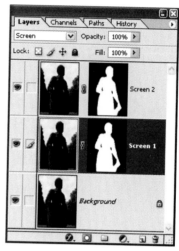

Figure 9.3: Duplicating the screened layer produces a stronger brightening effect.

Remember

Stay away from the Brightness/Contrast filter and the automatic exposure/contrast filters, including Auto Levels and Auto Contrast. These quick-fix exposure filters are easy to use but often destroy shadow and highlight detail.

Whichever option you choose, it's important to note that this technique doesn't affect black or white pixels. So if you're trying to fix blown highlights—areas that are so overexposed that they're completely white—Multiply won't help. Nor will Screen rescue shadow details that have gone to absolute black. In fact, you're not likely to get the results you want from any of the exposure tools; try using the touch-up techniques covered in Chapter 12 instead.

Tweaking Exposure with the Levels Filter

When you use the Screen/Multiply technique, Photoshop brightens or darkens all selected pixels (except white or black ones) by the same amount. With the Levels filter, you can adjust shadows, midtones, and highlights independently.

The next section explains *histograms,* a key component of the Levels filter. After that, you'll find general steps for applying the filter.

Analyzing Exposure and Contrast

To get acquainted with the Levels filter, open the sample image IndyCanal.jpg, shown in Figure 9.4. In this photo, the shadow values are good, but the midtones and highlights are too dark.

If colors appear faded after an exposure correction, use the Hue/Saturation filter, explained in Chapter 10, to strengthen them.

Figure **9.4**: The original IndyCanal.jpg photo is lacking in the highlight department.

Black ←————→ White

CS Below the photo, you see the Photoshop CS Histogram palette, which you display by choosing Window | Histogram. A *histogram* is a graph that plots image brightness values, with the darkest pixels on the left and the brightest pixels on the right. Possible brightness values range from 0 (black) to 255 (white). The vertical axis of the histogram shows you how many pixels fall at a particular brightness value. For example, the histogram in Figure 9.4 shows that the canal image has few pixels beyond the midpoint of the brightness spectrum.

Some Photoshop gurus really get into reading histograms and base all their exposure moves on what they read in that little black graph. Personally, I think the histogram gives you a good idea of what changes need to be made but should never take a front seat to what your eyes tell you when you look at the picture itself. (Be careful, however, that your monitor is properly calibrated so that you get a reasonably accurate view of things. See Chapter 14 for help.)

At any rate, the Levels dialog box contains its own histogram, so you don't have to fret if you're still using Version 7, and you can close the palette for now if you're a CS user. Then see the next section for specifics on applying the filter.

Applying the Levels Filter

You can access Levels from the Image | Adjustments menu, but doing so applies the correction directly to your image. Instead, always apply Levels via an adjustment

Dialog box thumbnail   Mask thumbnail

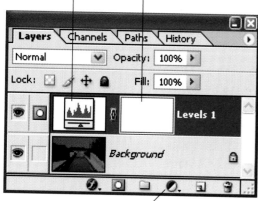

Adjustment Layer icon

Figure 9.5: Apply expo-
sure and color corrections
via an adjustment layer.

Histogram

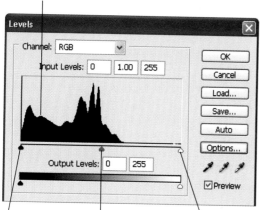

Black point slider Midtones slider White point slider

Figure 9.6: Drag the sliders to tweak shadows,
midtones, or highlights.

layer, a feature explained in Chapter 8. That way, if you
decide down the road that you aren't happy with the correction, you can modify the filter settings or simply trash the
adjustment layer and start over. You also can tweak the
correction by lowering the adjustment layer's opacity or
changing the blending mode.

Follow these steps to apply the filter, working along with
the sample image IndyCanal.jpg if you're in the mood.

**1. In the Layers palette, click the topmost layer
that you want to correct.**

Remember, an adjustment layer affects all layers underneath it. For single-layer
photos like the sample image, you can skip this step.

2. Select the area that you want to adjust (optional).

If you want the adjustment to affect all pixels on underlying layers, you don't need
a selection outline. For the example, don't select anything.

**3. Click the Adjustment Layer icon at the bottom
of the Layers dialog box, labeled in Figure 9.5.**

**4. Choose Levels from the pop-up menu to display
the Levels dialog box, shown in Figure 9.6.**

Select the Preview check box so that you can preview your
corrections in the image window.

5. Select RGB from the Channel menu.

**6. Drag the sliders underneath the histogram to
adjust exposure and contrast.**

You get three sliders, labeled in Figure 9.6. Use the sliders as follows:

■ **Deepen shadows** Drag the black point slider to the right to make
the darkest pixels darker. Photoshop finds all the pixels whose original
brightness value corresponds to the new slider position and makes
them black. Then it reassigns other pixels along the rest of the brightness spectrum.

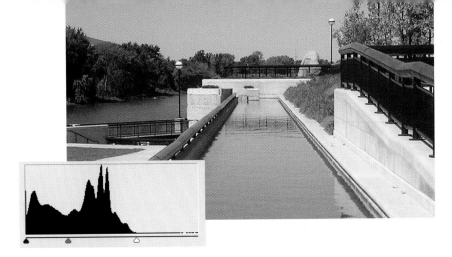

Figure 9.7: To brighten highlights, drag the high-light slider to the left.

- **Brighten highlights** Drag the white point slider to the left to make the brightest pixels brighter. This time, Photoshop makes pixels located at the new slider position white, again reassigning other pixels accordingly.
- **Adjust midtones** Drag the midtones slider, also called the *gamma* control or *midpoint* control, to the left to brighten midtones. Drag to the right to darken them.

To maximize contrast, drag the black point or white point slider to the position where the histogram indicates at least a handful of pixels. For the sample image, for example, drag the white point slider to the position shown in Figure 9.7.

As you move the shadow or highlight slider, the midtones slider moves as well. You can adjust the midtones slider after setting the new black or white point if needed. For the example image, nudge the midtones slider to the left to produce the results shown in Figure 9.7.

7. **Click OK to close the dialog box.**

Because you applied the correction on an adjustment layer, you can refine the results using all the techniques outlined in Chapter 8. A quick recap:

- Double-click the dialog box thumbnail, labeled in Figure 9.5, to open the Levels dialog box and change the slider settings.
- Click the mask thumbnail, also labeled in the figure, and paint with black to hide the correction in certain areas of the image. (If you created a selection outline before creating the adjustment layer, the unselected areas already appear black in the mask.) Paint with white to restore the effect.
- Lower the opacity of the adjustment layer to lessen the impact of the filter without changing the filter settings.

As for the other Levels dialog box controls, most aren't terribly useful, allow you to do harm to your image, or are designed for making color changes, not exposure changes. See Chapter 10 for information on using Levels in color-correction projects.

Applying a Fading Exposure Correction

Consider the photo in Figure 9.8. Exposure is good at the bottom of the image but grows gradually too dark toward the top. To fix images like this, you must apply a gradual exposure change, fading the correction to full strength where the image needs the most help. The secret is to create a gradient mask, as explained in Chapter 7, before applying your correction.

The following steps show you how to apply the Levels filter with this technique, but you can translate the steps to any Photoshop filter as well as to the Screen/Multiply trick explained earlier in this chapter. Try it out using the sample image Garden.jpg.

Figure 9.8: This image needs a gradual exposure correction that grows stronger toward the top of the scene.

1. Press Q to enter Quick Mask selection mode.

2. Set the foreground color to black and the background color to white.

3. Select the Gradient tool and establish the tool options shown in Figure 9.9.

Choose the first gradient in the gradient picker, which will produce a black-to-white gradient. Also select the first Style icon, which creates a linear gradient.

4. Drag to create a gradient mask.

Drag from the edge of the image that's properly exposed to the point where you want the exposure change to occur at full strength. In the example, drag from the bottom of the image upward to about the top of the saw, as shown in Figure 9.9.

5. Press Q again to exit Quick Mask mode and return to normal selection mode.

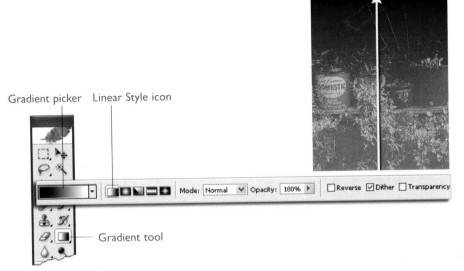

Gradient picker Linear Style icon

Gradient tool

Figure 9.9: Set the endpoint of the gradient at the point where you want the correction to be at full strength.

6. Create a Levels adjustment layer.

Just click the Adjustment Layer icon, labeled in Figure 9.10, and choose Levels from the pop-up list. Shoot for Levels settings that result in a proper exposure in the problem areas, but realize that you probably need to strike a compromise to get good results. In the Garden.jpg photo, for example, if you bring the very top of the image entirely out of

Mask thumbnail

Adjustment Layer icon

Figure 9.10: Your original gradient mask is converted to a layer mask after you create the adjustment layer.

the shadows, you overexpose the saw area. Keep in mind, too, that you can always apply a second correction just to the stubborn areas if needed.

For the example image, drag the midtones Levels slider left until your results look similar to what you see in Figure 9.10.

7. **Click OK to close the Levels dialog box.**

Because you created a selection outline before applying the correction, the adjustment layer's mask thumbnail shows a black-to-white gradient, as shown in Figure 9.10. If needed, you can use the tricks discussed in Chapter 8 to refine the mask. Or, if you want to redraw the gradient entirely, click the mask thumbnail, grab the Gradient tool, and have at it. You don't need to go back to Quick Mask mode and re-create the selection outline.

Gaining More Control with Curves

Figure 9.11: This image appears flat because most of the pixels fall in a narrow range of brightness values.

Capable as it is, the Levels filter limits you to manipulating just three brightness points: the black point, white point, and midpoint. With the Curves filter, you can tweak as many as 14 different points along the brightness spectrum. What's more, you can specify which brightness values you want to adjust. For example, you can brighten pixels that have a brightness value of 240 (on that famous 0-to-255 scale) and darken pixels that have a brightness value of 50.

The following steps show you how to apply a Curves correction as an adjustment layer. To work along with the steps, open the Corn.jpg photo, shown along with its original histogram in Figure 9.11. This image is a perfect candidate for a Curves adjustment. Although the image contains pixels along the entire span of the histogram, the majority huddle in the medium to medium-dark brightness range. You can improve the image by using Curves to make some of those clustered pixels darker and others lighter.

A word of encouragement before you begin: If you grasp the Curves concept completely on the first go-round, you're a rare bird. Work through the steps to get the gist of things, and then read the subsequent tips for a better understanding of how to harness the power of this filter.

1. In the Layers palette, click the topmost layer that you want to correct.

If your image contains just one layer, skip this step.

2. Select the area that you want to adjust (optional).

If you don't create a selection outline, the adjustment will affect all pixels on the current layer and any underlying layers. For the example, don't select anything.

3. Click the Adjustment Layer icon and select Curves from the pop-up menu.

(Refer to Figure 9.10 to see the icon.) You see the Curves dialog box, shown in Figure 9.12.

The meat of the dialog box is the grid and the diagonal line that runs through it. This line represents the range of possible brightness values, 0 (black) to 255 (white), and is officially known as the *tone curve*. Black is at the lower left end of the line; white, at the top right. This setup, however, assumes that the little grayscale bars to the left and below the grid look like the ones in the figure—

black at the left and bottom, and white at the top and right. If your bars are reversed, click the little double-triangle in the middle of the bottom bar to set things straight. Also be sure the point mode icon, labeled in Figure 9.12, is selected, and turn on the Preview check box.

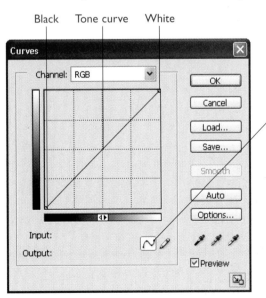

Figure 9.12: The diagonal line represents the range of possible brightness values, from 0 (black) to 255 (white).

> **Remember**
>
> After creating an adjustment layer, you can easily apply the same correction to another image. Just drag the adjustment layer from the Layers palette into the other image window.

4. **Click on the tone curve to add control points.**

My, that was helpful, no? Here's the deal. To apply your correction, you turn that diagonal line into a curve—hence the filter name—by dragging control points that correspond to the brightness values you want to adjust. Look closely, and you can see that two control points already exist, one at each end of the diagonal line, which represent black (0 brightness value) and white (255 brightness value). You add additional control points by clicking the line. As you pass your cursor over the line, the Input number under the grid shows you the brightness value at the current cursor position.

Time Saver

If you're not sure exactly where to place a control point, move your cursor into your image window. Place the cursor over a pixel that has the brightness value you want to change and then CTRL-click (Windows) or ⌘-click (Mac). Photoshop automatically places a control point at the position that corresponds to that brightness value.

For the sample image, click in the grid at the three locations shown in Figure 9.13. (The middle control point in the figure is black because it's the active control point, ready to be moved.)

Figure 9.13: Click on the line to add control points corresponding to the brightness values you want to adjust.

5. **Move your cursor over a control point.**

6. **When you see the four-headed arrow cursor, drag the control point to adjust the corresponding brightness value.**

Drag a point up to brighten corresponding areas of the image; drag down to darken them. You also can press the arrow keys to move points. (Click the control point first to make it the active control point.)

As you drag points, the originally straight diagonal line becomes a curve. The Output value underneath the grid shows you the new brightness value for the active point. For the example, drag the three points to the approximate positions shown in Figure 9.14. Your results should look something like the image in the figure.

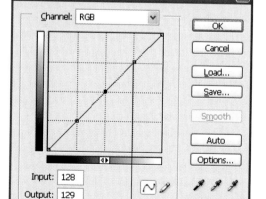

Control point

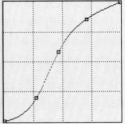

Figure 9.14: Create an S-shaped curve to increase contrast.

7. **Keep adding and manipulating points until you're happy with the correction.**

Watch Out!

Although you can create as many as 14 control points, limit yourself to a handful. With too many points, you can create pretty ugly results. And watch for signs of posterization when you're creating your curve. (You can see an example of this defect in Chapter 2.) The problem usually occurs when you make your curve too extreme or complex.

To delete a curve point, click it to make it the active point. Then just press DELETE.

8. **Click OK to close the dialog box.**

If necessary, you can adjust the filter effect as you can with any adjustment layer; see Chapter 8 for details.

Remember

To restore settings that were in force when you first opened a dialog box, ALT-click (Windows) or OPTION-click (Mac) the Cancel button.

Now that you've done a trial run with Curves, here are a few more details:

- **Adjusting contrast** To increase contrast, create an S-shaped curve like the one in Figure 9.14. To decrease contrast, create a backwards S.
- **Making overall exposure changes** If you place just one point on the tone curve, you can drag that point up to lighten the entire image or drag down to darken the image. Try using this technique to fix the sample image Boat.jpg, shown in its original, overexposed state on the left in Figure 9.15. The right image shows the photo after the application of the tone curve.
- **Locking a brightness value** To prevent a particular brightness value from being moved when you adjust other areas of the curve, add a point at that brightness value.
- **Solving unwanted color shifts** If Curves produces unwanted color shifts, try changing the adjustment layer's blending mode to Luminosity. Also give Overlay, Hard Light, and Soft Light a shot.

Figure 9.15: After adding a single point to the tone curve, drag down to darken the image without adjusting black and white pixels.

To set the blending mode of an adjustment layer *before* you create the layer, press the ALT key (Windows) or OPTION key (Mac) as you click the Adjustment Layer icon and select the layer type. Photoshop displays the New Layer dialog box, where you can select the blending mode.

Dodging and Burning

Photoshop's Dodge and Burn tools take their names from traditional darkroom exposure techniques. Dodging lightens an image; burning darkens it. However, these two tools don't really supply the same results as you get in the darkroom.

Dodge and Burn do lighten and darken pixels, but they also desaturate colors. If you drag over medium blue pixels with the Burn tool, for example, you don't get navy pixels but a darker, grayish blue. Similarly, Dodge would give you a brighter, but also grayish, shade of blue, not the pure, light blue you may expect.

That's not to say that these tools are useless, however. First, if you're working on a grayscale image, all the pixels are already desaturated, so the tools produce good results. Just dab at your image with the Dodge tool to make pixels lighter and swab with the Burn tool to make them darker. (See the next section for advice regarding tool options.) In the color world, Dodge makes an excellent teeth-whitener when you're retouching portraits, and Burn can emphasize eyes. The next sections show you these techniques.

Watch Out!

Unlike Levels and Curves, you can't apply Dodge and Burn corrections as an adjustment layer. So before you pick up either tool, copy the problem area to a new layer and then do your editing on that layer. See Chapter 8 for the full story on layers.

Whitening Teeth with the Dodge Tool

Although the Dodge tool isn't terribly useful for general exposure corrections, it comes in handy for portrait retouching work. You can use it to whiten teeth, as outlined in the following steps. If you don't have a photo of your own choppers, work along with the sample image Teeth.jpg. Figure 9.16 shows before and after views to give you an idea of the results you can achieve.

Remember

To preserve independent layers between editing sessions, save the image in the PSD or TIFF format, with the Layers option enabled.

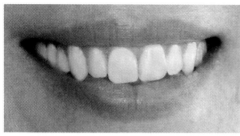

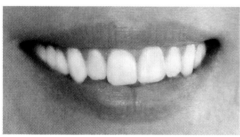

Figure 9.16: Use the Dodge tool to brighten and whiten teeth.

1. **Select the teeth.**

2. **Copy the selection to a new layer by pressing CTRL-J (Windows) or ⌘-J (Mac).**

3. **Select the Dodge tool, shown in Figure 9.17.**

4. **Choose a small, slightly soft, round brush.**

Try a brush hardness value of about 90 percent. Also turn off the Airbrush option; the icon should appear as in Figure 9.17. (If you need help with this step, see Chapter 5.)

5. **Set the Range control to Midtones.**

The Range control determines whether the Dodge and Burn tools affect shadows, highlights, or midtones. Normally, Midtones is the best lead-off hitter.

6. **Limit the tool impact by lowering the Exposure value.**

The Exposure value determines how much change you get from a single click or drag with the tool. The default value, 50 percent, is too high in most cases; try

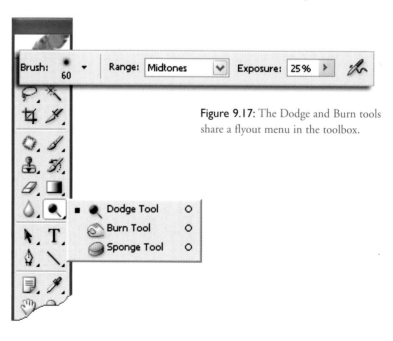

Figure 9.17: The Dodge and Burn tools share a flyout menu in the toolbox.

25 percent or even lower. You can apply the tools repeatedly to the same area to make the pixels progressively lighter or darker.

7. **Drag over dark areas in the teeth to lighten and whiten them.**

If any very dark areas remain, try using the tool with the Range option set to Shadows. Don't use the Highlights setting; you'll blow out subtle details in the teeth.

8. **Merge the lightened layer with the underlying layer, as covered in Chapter 8.**

You can use this same trick to brighten the whites of someone's eyes. Don't go overboard, or your edits will be obvious.

Emphasizing Eyes with the Burn Tool

With the Burn tool, you can add a little extra "pop" to eyes by darkening eyebrows, eyelashes, and pupils, as illustrated in Figure 9.18. To produce the right image, I just dragged over the brows and lashes and then clicked a few times on the pupil.

To try this technique, open the sample image Eyes.jpg. Follow the steps outlined in the preceding section, but select the Burn tool instead of the Dodge tool in Step 3. Again, start with the Range control set to Midtones, and then follow up with the tool set to Shadows if necessary. For the lashes, drag outward from the eye to the tip of a lash, just as if you were applying mascara. When darkening the pupil, take care not to alter the catch light (that little white highlight caused by reflecting light).

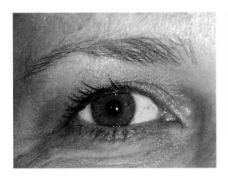 

Figure 9.18: Draw attention to the eyes by using the Burn tool to darken lashes, brows, and pupils.

Saving Time with the Shadow/Highlight Filter

| CS | Photoshop CS offers a new filter, Shadow/Highlight, that may save you time when you're correcting certain types of images. The filter enables you to lighten shadows, making it well-suited for dealing with subjects that were underexposed due to strong backlighting. Alternatively, if your subject is too strongly lit, such as when shot at too close a range with a flash, you can use the filter to tone down the highlights.

Watch Out!

Realize, though, that you can make dramatic exposure shifts easily with this filter, so keep an eye out for posterization—large areas of flat color where you should have a smooth gradation of many different tones. Second, Shadow/Highlight can't be applied as an adjustment layer. So always duplicate the problem area to a new layer and apply the filter to the duplicate.

Figure 9.19: I used the Shadow/Highlight filter to bring the sunflower out of the shadows.

With those caveats in mind, take these steps to try out the filter. The sample image Sunflower.jpg, shown on the left in Figure 9.19, offers a good example for putting the filter through its paces. The right image shows the post-filter sunflower.

1. Copy the problem area to a new layer.

If you want to correct the entire image in a single-layer photo like the sample image, just duplicate the Background layer.

Figure 9.20: Initially, the Shadow/Highlight filter offers just two controls.

2. **Choose Image | Adjustments | Shadow/Highlight to display the dialog box shown in Figure 9.20.**

By default, the dialog box offers you just two sliders, one for adjusting shadows and one for highlights. Initially, the Shadows slider is set to a value of 50 percent, which results in an immediate brightening of the darkest parts of your photo, as shown in Figure 9.20. The default Highlights value is 0, which produces no change to the brightest pixels.

3. **Adjust the Shadow and Highlights values as needed.**

- Raise the Shadow value to brighten the shadows more. Reduce the value to 0 to eliminate any change to the shadows.
- Raise the Highlights value to darken the brightest pixels.

If you can't get the results you want by using these sliders, select the Show More Options box to display the additional dialog box controls shown in Figure 9.21. These controls enable you to fine-tune the shadow and highlight adjustments (the list following the steps tells you what each option does). I used the settings shown in Figure 9.21 to produce the right image in Figure 9.19.

4. Click OK to apply the filter.

The additional controls that become available when you expand the filter dialog box work as follows:

- **Tonal Width** This control determines the brightness range that Photoshop manipulates when adjusting shadows or highlights. If you use a low value for the Shadows tonal width, Photoshop tweaks the darkest pixels only. Similarly, a low Highlights tonal width restricts changes to the brightest pixels. At 100 percent, all pixels are fair game, but Photoshop applies the adjustment on a sliding scale. For a Shadows adjustment, the darkest pixels receive the greatest lightening; midtones get half that amount; and the brightest highlights remain untouched. For a Highlights adjustment, the reverse occurs. The upshot: If you want to affect just the darkest or lightest areas of the picture, use a low Tonal Width value.

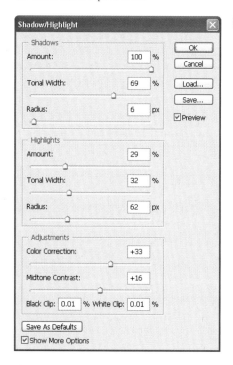

Figure 9.21: To gain access to all the filter options, select the Show More Options box.

Watch Out!

When raising the Tonal Width value, monitor the parts of the image where light pixels meet dark. A very high value sometimes causes halos at those edges.

- **Radius** This control affects the formula that Photoshop uses when determining whether a pixel should be considered a shadow or highlight. The correct setting depends on image content, so you need to experiment. At a high value, you tend to get overall image darkening or brightening.
- **Color Correction** This control really should be named Saturation; it affects the intensity of colors in the areas where you adjusted highlights or shadows. The impact you can make with this option depends on the Amount value you used when applying the shadow or highlight adjustment. The higher the Amount value, the more you can affect the colors. Keep in mind that you can always adjust saturation by applying the Hue/Saturation filter, covered in Chapter 10, after you finish using the Shadow/Highlight filter.

- **Brightness (Grayscale images only)** You get this option only when working on a grayscale photo. Use it to adjust the overall brightness of the image.
- **Midtone Contrast** Raise this value to increase contrast in the image midtones. Doing so tends to deepen shadows and brighten highlights as well, however. A negative value here reduces contrast.
- **Black Clip and White Clip** These options control the range of brightness values that Photoshop can change to black or white when you apply the filter. At a high value, dark pixels turn black, and very pale pixels turn white. Obviously, this destroys details in the shadows and highlights. I suggest that you don't stray too far from the default value (.01 percent) for most images. Inspect the image carefully as you adjust the clipping values to make sure that you're improving, and not ruining shadow and highlight details.

Time Saver

If you need to correct a batch of images that all suffer from similar shadow/highlight problems, take advantage of the Save button in the Shadow/Filter dialog box. After correcting the first image, click the Save button to save the settings. (Give the settings a name that will help you identify their purpose later, such as BacklightFix.) Open the next image, open the Shadow/Highlight filter, and click the Load button. Select your saved file, and Photoshop automatically dials in the saved settings in the filter dialog box.

When Good Colors Go Bad

Compared with exposure corrections, tweaking colors in Photoshop is child's play. Well, young adult's play, at the least. With tools discussed in this chapter, you can remove color casts, play with color balance, adjust saturation, and even repair red-eye with surprising ease.

Before doing any color work, however, calibrate your monitor so that you can evaluate your pictures on a neutral canvas. Chapter 14 walks you through the process and explains Photoshop's color-management options, which also affect on-screen colors.

Removing Red-Eye

The top image in Figure 10.1 suffers from an all-too-common problem: red-eye. Photoshop doesn't offer an automated red-eye removal tool—and for good reason.

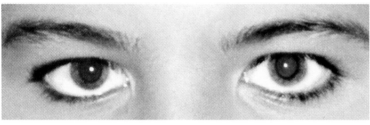

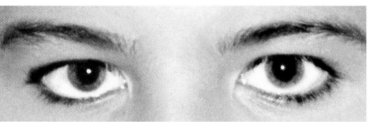

Figure 10.1: Red-eye removal takes only seconds.

Automated tools rarely produce natural results, and the "manual" fix is incredibly easy. To try it out, open the image RedEye.jpg and work through these steps:

1. Select the Brush tool, labeled in Figure 10.2.

Choose a small, round, slightly soft brush—about 90 percent Hardness works well. Set the other options as shown in Figure 10.2 and turn off Brush Dynamics. (See Chapter 5 for a review of these brush settings.)

2. Set the Foreground color to match the desired pupil color.

> **Time Saver**
>
> To get a good match quickly, ALT-click (Windows) or OPTION-click (Mac) on a pupil pixel that isn't red. If you can't grab a pupil pixel, look for a dark pixel somewhere else in the eye.

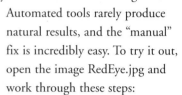

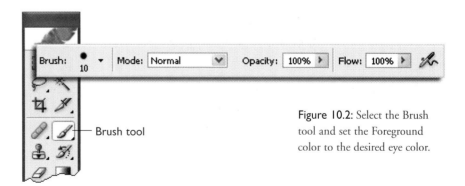

Brush tool

Figure 10.2: Select the Brush tool and set the Foreground color to the desired eye color.

3. Create a new, empty layer and set the layer blend mode to Color.

Open the Layers palette (F7) and click the New Layer icon, labeled in Figure 10.3. Set the Blending Mode to Color as shown in the figure. Create the new layer directly above the layer that contains the red-eye pixels.

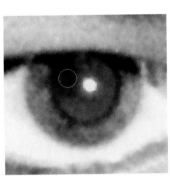

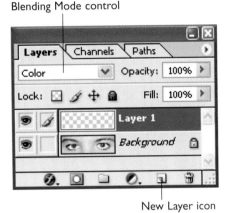

Blending Mode control

New Layer icon

Figure 10.3: Paint on a new layer set to the Color blending mode.

4. Paint over the red pixels, working on the new layer.

Photoshop uses the color information from the Color layer—your paint layer— but takes the shadow and highlight information from the underlying layer, which contains the original eyes. This setup retains the natural tonal details in the eyes. You may need to dab on a few different paint colors to get good results, depending on how much of the eye is red.

5. Merge the paint layer with the underlying layer by choosing Layer | Merge Down.

For animal pictures, you may need to vary this technique. If the eyes are white instead of red, the Color blending mode doesn't work. Instead, use the Normal blending mode and lower the paint layer's opacity as needed.

Neutralizing Color Casts with the Levels Filter

Did you ever visit Louisiana in July? While you were there, did you leave some unexposed film outside for a few hours in the 325-degree heat? And when you returned home to Indianapolis, did you totally space that incident, load one of those rolls in your camera, and shoot some local landmarks?

Just me? Well, if you ever do parboil your film, your photos may exhibit a lovely sunburn, as shown on the left in Figure 10.4. Fortunately, you can remove color casts by using either the Levels or Curves filter. Both offer a color-correction tool in addition to their exposure-correction features, covered in Chapter 9.

Figure 10.4: Applying the color-correction tool found in the Levels dialog box greatly improves this sunburned image.

Try the technique on the sample photo IndyMonument.jpg.

1. **Press F7 or choose Window | Layers to open the Layers palette.**

2. **If your image contains multiple layers, click the topmost layer that you want to correct.**

3. **Create a Levels adjustment layer.**

Click the Adjustment Layer icon at the bottom of the Layers palette, shown in Figure 10.5, and select Levels from the pop-up menu. The Levels dialog box opens.

4. **In the Levels dialog box, click the gray eyedropper, labeled in Figure 10.5.**

5. **In the image window, click a pixel that should be medium gray.**

For the sample image, click at the spot indicated in Figure 10.6. Photoshop finds all the pixels that match the one you click and recolors them medium gray, which should eliminate most, if not all, of your color cast.

Figure 10.5: Start your correction by creating a Levels adjustment layer.

Black point slider   Midtones slider   White point slider   Gray eyedropper

Adjustment Layer icon

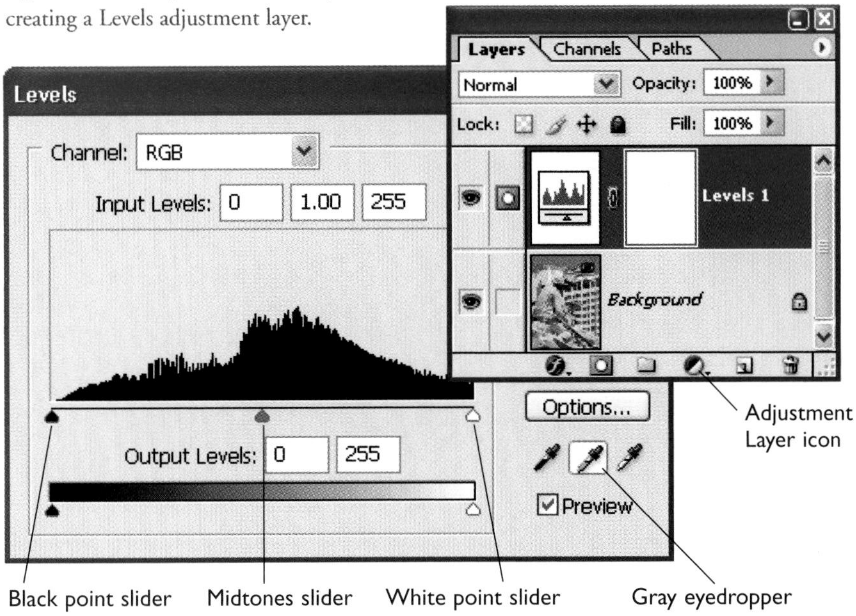

Watch Out!

If you don't get good results, hold down the ALT key (Windows) or OPTION key (Mac), which changes the dialog box Cancel button to a Reset button. Then click that Reset button to restore the original color values and try again. Don't simply keep clicking with the eyedropper—repeated manipulation of the color values isn't a good thing.

Figure 10.6: Click with the gray eyedropper on a pixel that should be medium gray.

Click with gray eyedropper

6. **Drag the histogram sliders to adjust exposure if necessary.**

Figure 10.5 labels the sliders, explained fully in Chapter 9. Drag the midtones slider left to lighten the image; drag right to darken it. Drag the black point slider right to make the darkest pixels darker. Drag the white point slider left to make the brightest pixels brighter.

7. **Click OK to close the Levels dialog box.**

If you want to use the Curves filter instead of Levels for your exposure correction, the process is the same. The gray eyedropper in the Curves dialog box works exactly as it does in the Levels dialog box.

Whether you use Levels or Curves, you can adjust the correction at any time by editing the adjustment layer as explained in Chapter 8. But don't spend *too* much time trying to achieve perfection with this technique; just eliminate as much of the color cast as possible. You can use other color and exposure filters to fine-tune the image.

Remember

Adjustment layers affect all underlying layers. To correct one layer *without* changing underlying layers, duplicate that layer and then apply the filter directly from the Image | Adjustments menu.

Shifting Color Balance

Although the gray eyedropper in the Levels and Curves dialog boxes is a great tool, it's effective only for neutralizing a color cast. To manipulate color with more flexibility—for example, to tone down reds and play up blues—investigate the Variations, Color Balance, and Selective Color filters.

Variations: The Simple Approach to Color Balancing

If you read Chapter 2 before coming here, you may recall the concept of the *color wheel,* a graph used to plot out the color spectrum. Figure 10.7 shows the color wheel.

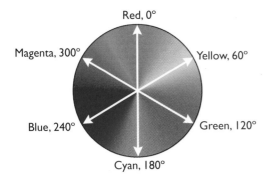

Red, 0°

Magenta, 300°

Yellow, 60°

Blue, 240°

Green, 120°

Cyan, 180°

Figure 10.7: The Variations and Color Balance filters are based on the color wheel.

Both the Variations filter and its cousin, Color Balance, are based on the wheel. By introducing more of one color, you reduce the amount of the color that's directly opposite on the wheel, as indicated by the arrows in Figure 10.7. This process is called *color balancing*.

The following steps show you how to apply the Variations filter. As a sample image, work with FallColor.jpg, shown in its original state on the left in Figure 10.8. This image leans a little too much to the red/magenta/yellow half of the spectrum for my taste. Adding a bit of cyan, green, and blue produces the more balanced palette shown in the right image.

1. Copy the area you want to alter to a new layer.

For the sample photo, the entire image needs help, so just duplicate the Background layer by dragging it to the New Layer icon in the Layers palette. (Refer to Figure 10.3.)

2. Choose Image | Adjustments | Variations to display the Variations dialog box, shown in Figure 10.9.

The dialog box features three groups of thumbnails:

- The top pair of thumbnails show the original image and a preview of the image with the current filter settings applied (the preview thumbnail is labeled Current Pick).
- The color-shift thumbnails, labeled in Figure 10.9, serve as the color-balancing controls. Clicking a perimeter thumbnail adds more of that color and decreases its opposite. For example, clicking More Magenta

Figure 10.8: A small shift in color balance can make a big difference.

adds magenta and reduces green. The center thumbnail is a duplicate of the Current Pick thumbnail.

- The three thumbnails running down the right side of the dialog box enable you to adjust image brightness. Ignore these options and instead rely on the more capable tools covered in Chapter 9.

3. Select a range button (Shadows, Midtones, Highlights).

With Variations, you adjust shadows, midtones, and highlights separately. Specify the range you want to alter by clicking one of the three buttons at the top of the dialog box (see Figure 10.9). For the sample image, start with the Midtones button.

Watch Out!

Bypass the Saturation button; it enables you to tweak saturation, but with less control than you get with the Hue/Saturation filter, explained later in this chapter.

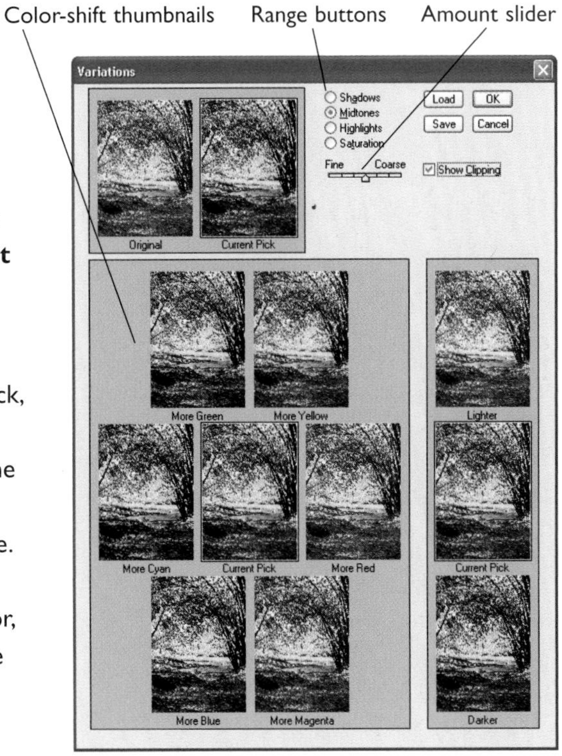

Color-shift thumbnails   Range buttons   Amount slider

Figure 10.9: Click a thumbnail to add more of that color and subtract its opposite.

4. **Click the color-shift thumbnails to adjust the image.**

A few notes:

- Each time you click, the color-shift thumbnails and the Current Pick thumbnails update.

- If you add too much of one color, click the opposite thumbnail. For example, if your image becomes too red, click More Cyan.

- To change the impact of each click, drag the Amount slider, labeled in Figure 10.9. Drag the slider toward Coarse to produce bigger shifts in color; drag toward Fine to make more subtle changes.

Watch Out!

When the Show Clipping option is selected, random, neon-colored spots may appear in the thumbnails when you adjust the Shadows or Highlights ranges. Those spots warn you that pixels that originally were slightly different in color will all become either black or white. If the preview indicates large clipped areas, back off; you're destroying detail.

For the sample image, drag the slider all the way to the Fine end of the bar. Click four times each on the Blue and Green thumbnails, and click twice on the Cyan thumbnail.

5. **Adjust the remaining two brightness ranges as needed.**

Again, click the Shadows, Midtones, or Highlights button at the top of the dialog box, depending on which range you want to adjust. Then click the color-shift thumbnails as before. For the sample image, apply the same changes as you did in Step 4 to the shadows and highlights.

At any time, you can restore the image to its original appearance by clicking the Original thumbnail.

6. **Click OK to close the dialog box.**

7. **When you're satisfied with the image colors, choose Layer | Merge Down to merge the corrected layer with the original.**

When you're just getting started in the digital darkroom, Variations is a nice tool because the thumbnails provide you with visual reminders about the inverse relationships between red/cyan, green/magenta, and blue/yellow. The thumbnails also help you determine which direction the colors need to go if you're unsure.

But Variations has some important drawbacks. First, you can't apply Variations as an adjustment layer. Second, you can't preview the results of your changes in the image window—you have to rely on the thumbnails within the dialog box. Third, the Amount slider is a little cumbersome; finding the right position to get the degree of color shift you want can take time. So after you get comfortable with the whole notion of color balancing, you may want to shun Variations in favor of the Color Balance filter, explained next.

Color Balance: The Professional's Tool

Unlike Variations, Color Balance offers live image previews, adjustment layer application, and more precise control over the strength of the color shifts you make. For these reasons, most professionals prefer this filter to Variations.

To put the Color Balance filter through its paces, open the image Totem.jpg, shown on the left in Figure 10.10. The settings suggested in the steps produce the slight warming effect shown in the right image.

1. **In the Layers palette, click the topmost layer you want to alter.**

For single-layer images, you can skip this step.

2. **Select the area to be changed (optional).**

If you don't create a selection outline, all pixels on the active layer and any underlying layers will be affected by the filter.

3. **Create a Color Balance adjustment layer.**

Figure 10.10: Boosting reds and yellows produced
an effect similar to a traditional warming filter.

You can accomplish this in two ways:

- Choose Layer | New Adjustment Layer | Color Balance. When the
  New Layer dialog box opens, click OK.
- Click the Adjustment Layer icon at the bottom of the Layers palette
  (see Figure 10.5) and select Color Balance from the pop-up menu.

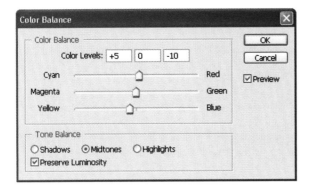

Either way, the Color
Balance dialog box
opens, as shown in
Figure 10.11. Select the
Preview check box to
preview the filter effect.

Figure 10.11: The Color Balance
filter offers live image previews.

4. **Select the Preserve Luminosity check box (optional).**

When you enable this option, Photoshop tweaks colors in a way that preserves the tonal relationships in the image. For the sample image, keep the option turned on, but with your own photos, experiment to see which setting produces the results you like best.

5. **Select a Tone Balance option (Shadows, Midtones, Highlights).**

You adjust shadows, midtones, and highlights separately. Select the range you want to adjust by clicking the corresponding Tone Balance button. For the sample image, start with Midtones.

6. **Drag the color sliders to adjust the color balance within the selected range.**

As you move a slider toward one color, you increase that color and decrease the opposite color. You also can enter values into the Color Levels boxes: the left box corresponds to the Cyan/Red slider; the middle box, to the Magenta/Green slider; and the right box, to the Yellow/Blue slider. A positive value moves the slider to the right; a negative value moves it to the left. Values can range from −100 to 100. (You don't need to enter the plus sign for positive values, but you do need to enter a minus sign for negative values.)

> **Time Saver**
>
> To make precision adjustments, double-click a Color Levels box to activate it. Then press the down arrow key to lower the value by one. Press the up arrow key to raise the value by one. Press SHIFT plus the arrow key to change the value by 10.

For the sample image, set the Cyan/Red value to 5 and the Yellow/Blue value to −10, as shown in Figure 10.11.

7. **Adjust the remaining two brightness ranges (Shadows, Midtones, or Highlights).**

To complete the sample color correction, use the same values as before for the Shadows and Highlights.

8. **Click OK to close the dialog box.**

If necessary, you can refine the color change later by editing the adjustment layer. See Chapter 8 for specifics.

Remember

You can reduce the impact of a filter applied via an adjustment layer by lowering the layer opacity.

Remixing Colors with Selective Color

Selective Color takes you one step beyond the capabilities of either Variations or Color Balance. Whereas Variations and Color Balance enable you to rebalance colors by changing the amounts of the six primary colors—red, green, blue, cyan, magenta, and yellow—Selective Color enables you to *reblend* those color ranges. You can add some yellow to your reds, for example, or some magenta to your blues. You're still adjusting color balance, but for just a single color component. In addition, you can adjust blacks, whites, and neutrals (grays).

Figure 10.12 shows a perfect candidate for Selective Color. As with any hand that hasn't been retouched, this one has some ruddy areas. With Selective Color, you can pull out those reds quickly and easily, as shown in Figure 10.13. (The background didn't change because I selected the hand before applying the filter.)

The following steps show you how to apply Selective Color as an adjustment layer—which, if I haven't hammered home the point enough yet, is the best option for applying exposure or color corrections. Try out the filter on the sample image HennaHand.jpg, shown in Figure 10.12.

1. In the Layers palette, click the topmost layer you want to correct.

You need to take this step only if your photo contains more than one layer.

Figure 10.12: Unretouched skin normally has some ruddy or reddish areas.

Figure 10.13: The Selective
Color filter enables you to
even out the skin tones.

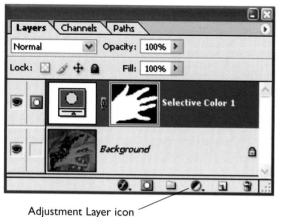

Adjustment Layer icon

2. Select the area that you want to correct (optional).

For the sample image, select the hand. If you don't create a selection outline,
the filter will affect all pixels on the active layer and any underlying layers.

3. Create a Selective Color adjustment layer.

You can do this quickly by clicking the Adjustment Layer icon, labeled in Figure
10.13. Or choose Layer | New Adjustment Layer | Selective Color and then click
OK after the New Layer dialog box opens. Whichever method you use, you see
the Selective Color dialog box,
shown in Figure 10.14.

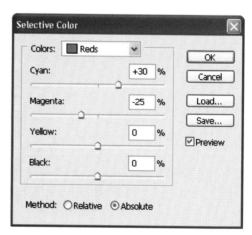

Figure 10.14: Use Selective
Color to manipulate
individual color ranges.

4. **Select the Preview check box.**

5. **Select a color range from the Colors drop-down list.**

You can choose from Reds, Yellows, Greens, Cyans, Blues, and Magentas. But wait, there's more! You also can choose Whites, Neutrals, and Blacks.

Watch Out!

Keep in mind that these options refer to a color *range*, not precise, pure hues. Photoshop applies the color shift proportionally based on how closely pixels match the color you select. For example, if you select Reds, pink pixels get less adjustment than full-on reds. And when you select Blacks, Whites, or Neutrals, your changes *aren't* limited only to pixels that are absolute black, white, or gray. Selecting Neutrals, in fact, often produces a strong, overall change to image colors.

For the sample image, choose Reds, as shown in the figure.

6. **At the bottom of the dialog box, select a Method button.**

These two options determine the formula Photoshop uses when applying the color shift. Absolute usually produces more pronounced effects, but experiment to see which setting works best for your image. If you want to recolor whites, you must use Absolute.

For the sample image, choose Absolute.

7. **Drag the sliders to adjust the selected color range.**

Because the Selective Color filter was originally designed for pre-press technicians working in the CMYK color model, the dialog box contains sliders for adjusting the amount of cyan, magenta, yellow, and black—the four standard ink colors for commercial printing. However, as with the Color Balance and Variations filters, changing the amount of any one color also changes the strength of the opposite color. So remember:

- To add red, lower the Cyan value. To reduce red, increase cyan.
- To add green, lower the Magenta value. To reduce green, add magenta.
- To add blue, lower the Yellow value. To reduce blue, add yellow.
- To add black, drag the black slider to the right. Decreasing the black value subtracts black and adds white.

For the sample image, your first step is to adjust the Reds range. So raise the Cyan value to 30 and lower the Magenta value to –25. These changes eliminate the red patches, but they take too much warmth out of the rest of the hand. To restore a better overall skin color, select Neutrals from the Colors drop-down list. Then lower the Cyan value to –5 and increase the Yellow value to 5.

8. Click OK to close the dialog box.

Of course, because you applied the filter as an adjustment layer, you can use all the techniques covered in Chapter 8 to refine the correction later if needed.

Figure 10.15: Colors in this market image are a little lackluster.

Time Saver

Also note the Save and Load buttons in the Selective Color dialog box. By clicking the Save button, you can create a special type of Photoshop file that stores the current filter settings. On your next trip to the dialog box, you can click the Load button and select that file to automatically establish the same settings. This feature can save you time if you need to correct a batch of images that exhibit the same color flaw—multiple portraits of the same subject, for example.

Adjusting Saturation

Saturation refers to color purity or intensity. A fully saturated pixel is pure, undiluted color, containing not a hint of white, gray, or black. A completely desaturated pixel can be only white, black, or gray.

Increasing saturation can sometimes improve the impact of a photo, as illustrated by the examples in Figures 10.15 (original) and 10.16 (corrected). Color is the important story in this image, and making those colors bolder emphasizes that characteristic.

That's not to say that boosting saturation is always the way to go, however. Some images may call for a more subtle color palette, and thus a slight decrease in saturation. Reducing color strength also sometimes allows subtle tonal details to emerge.

Either way, Photoshop gives you two capable tools for adjusting saturation: the Hue/Saturation filter, which you can apply via an

Figure 10.16: A quick trip to the Hue/Saturation dialog box gives colors some oomph.

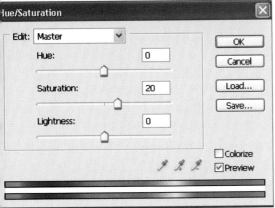

adjustment layer, and the Sponge tool, which enables you to "brush on" saturation changes as if you were working with a magical paint brush.

Applying the Hue/Saturation Filter

Adjusting saturation via the Hue/Saturation filter is one of the easiest things you'll ever do in Photoshop. To prove it to yourself, open the sample image Market.jpg, shown in Figure 10.15, and play along:

1. Select the area that you want to adjust (optional).

If you want to affect an entire, single-layer image—as is the case with the sample image—bypass this step. In a multilayer image, open the Layers palette and click the topmost of the layers you want to change. You also can draw a selection outline to limit the filter to just some pixels on affected layers.

2. Create a Hue/Saturation adjustment layer.

You can get there two ways:

■ Choose Layer | New Adjustment Layer | Hue/Saturation and click OK when the New Layer dialog box opens.
■ Click the Adjustment Layer icon at the bottom of the Layers palette (see Figure 10.13) and select Hue/Saturation from the pop-up list.

Photoshop displays the Hue/Saturation dialog box, shown in Figure 10.16.

3. Select the Preview check box.

4. **Deselect the Colorize check box.**

This option enables you to desaturate your entire image and then add a color tint. Chapter 11 discusses this and other color effects.

5. **Select the range of colors you want to adjust from the Edit drop-down list.**

For the sample image, choose Master. When Master is selected, as in Figure 10.16, all colors receive the saturation adjustment. But you also can adjust the reds, yellows, greens, cyans, blues, and magentas individually. Just select the color range you want to affect from the Edit drop-down list.

Note that like Selective Color, this filter does not limit the saturation change to the pure form of the selected color, but also adjusts closely related colors.

6. **Drag the Saturation slider to adjust saturation.**

Drag right to increase saturation; drag left to decrease saturation. You also can enter a specific value in the box above the slider. Acceptable values range from −100, which completely desaturates the image, to 100, which is well beyond the limits of polite society and the capabilities of most printers.

For the sample image, drag the slider to the right to raise the value to about 20.

7. **Click OK to close the dialog box.**

If you later want to tweak saturation further, see Chapter 8 to find out how to edit your Hue/Saturation adjustment layer.

Watch Out!

One additional point: The options that appear at the bottom of the dialog box when you select a color range from the Edit drop-down list enable you to modify the range of colors that will be affected. I don't recommend that novices fool with these options, because you can introduce banding—noticeable color breaks where you should have smooth, subtle color transitions. If you want to know more, however, the program Help system details the options.

Figure 10.17: Increasing saturation
of the butterfly helps set it apart
from the similarly colored plant.

Applying Saturation Changes with a Sponge

For saturation adjustments to small areas, consider the Sponge tool. With this tool, you click on or drag over pixels to adjust saturation. To try it out, open the sample image Butterfly2.jpg, shown on the left in Figure 10.17. In the original image, the orange plant competes with the butterfly for attention. Increasing the saturation of the butterfly brings the eye more strongly to it, as shown in the right image.

If you wanted to make this change via the Hue/Saturation filter, you would need to select the butterfly or add a layer mask after applying the filter—both time-consuming operations. But with the Sponge tool, you can just dab at the butterfly to get the job done.

Feel free to agree or disagree with the aesthetic choice here, by the way. Although the butterfly becomes more prominent because of the saturation boost, the original version is interesting, too—there's a nice visual surprise when your eye figures out what's what. Just understand that the Sponge tool provides a good option should you decide to play with saturation in a limited area, whichever direction you want to go.

Follow these steps to use the tool:

1. Copy the area that you want to adjust to a new layer.

> **Watch Out!**
>
> Don't ever apply this or any of the editing tools directly to your original image—you lose flexibility and risk permanently damaging your photo. Instead, use the Lasso or one of the other selection tools to draw a rough outline around the area that you want to edit. Then choose Layer | New | Layer via Copy or press CTRL-J (Windows) or ⌘-J (Mac) to copy the selection to a new layer.

2. Select the Sponge tool, labeled in Figure 10.18.

The tool shares a flyout menu with the Dodge and Burn tools.

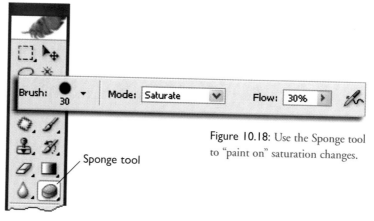

Sponge tool

Figure 10.18: Use the Sponge tool to "paint on" saturation changes.

3. Set the brush size, shape, hardness, and other options.

The Sponge tool is a brush-based tool, which means that you can customize the brush size, shape, hardness, and all the other characteristics explained in Chapter 5. For the sample image, choose a 30-pixel round brush and set the Hardness value to 100 percent. Also turn off the Airbrush option (the icon should look like the one in Figure 10.18). Disable Brush Dynamics, which are controlled via the main Brushes palette at the right end of the options bar (not shown in the figure).

4. Select a Mode option (Saturate or Desaturate).

Select Saturate to boost saturation; select Desaturate to suck out color. Sorry, didn't mean to insult your intelligence.

5. Set the Flow value to adjust the tool impact.

For the Sponge tool, the Flow value determines how much impact you make with each click or drag. Set this one according to your personal taste, keeping in mind that your clicks and drags are cumulative. I usually start with a relatively low set-ting—say, 30 percent—and then just keep swabbing those pixels until I reach the saturation I want.

6. Click on or drag over the image areas you want to tweak.

That's all there is to it. When you're happy with your image, merge the corrected layer with the underlying image by choosing Layer | Merge Down or using one of the other techniques outlined in Chapter 8.

Tool Tricks

When using the Sponge tool, press the number keys to raise or lower the Flow value, which controls the tool's impact. Press 0 for 100 percent, 9 for 90 percent, and so on.

More Color Tricks

When you're taking pictures, you may use filters or special films to emphasize a part of the color spectrum. Most portrait photographers put a warming filter on the lens to give skin a golden glow, for example, while landscape photographers often work with films that render highly saturated blues and greens.

For times when you forget to load your camera bag—or just don't want to lug all those bits and pieces around—this chapter shows you how to create a variety of color effects in the digital darkroom. You'll also find out how to convert color pictures to black-and-white images and produce the look of a hand-tinted photo.

In This Chapter:

- ☐ Easy ways to change the color of an object

- ☐ Warming and cooling filters, the digital way

- ☐ How to replace a distracting background

- ☐ Three techniques for creating black-and-white images

- ☐ Recipes for creating hand-tinted and antiqued photo effects

Replacing the Color of an Object

Chapter 10 introduces you to filters that enable you to make subtle color adjustments—slightly reducing red tones or boosting blues, for example. To completely replace the color of an object, use the techniques described in the next two sections. If you're not sure what color you want the object to be, try the first method; to apply a specific color, opt for technique number two.

Recoloring Pixels with the Hue/Saturation Filter

The easiest way to change the color of an object is to use the Hue control provided with the Hue/Saturation filter. This control is based on the *color wheel*. As discussed in Chapter 10, a color wheel is a circular graph that plots out the color spectrum. Red occupies the 0-degree position on the wheel; yellow, 60 degrees; green, 120 degrees; cyan, 180 degrees; blue, 240 degrees, and magenta, 300 degrees. The top color bar in the bottom section of the Hue/Saturation dialog box, shown in Figure 11.1, is a linear representation of the wheel.

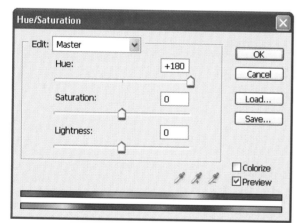

Figure 11.1: Drag the Hue slider to shift selected pixels around the color wheel.

Changing the Hue value in the dialog box spins pixels around the color wheel. For example, if you enter +180 as the Hue value, red pixels move from 0 degrees to 180 degrees and become cyan. In Figure 11.2, setting the Hue value to +180 changed the image on the left to the version on the right.

To try the Hue color-spinning technique, take the following steps, working along with the sample image Brooch.jpg. The steps apply the Hue/Saturation filter as an adjustment layer, a concept you can explore in detail in Chapter 8.

1. In a multilayered image, open the Layers palette (F7) and click the topmost layer that you want to recolor.

The sample image contains just one layer, so you're good to go.

2. Select the area that you want to recolor (optional).

If you don't select anything, all pixels on the active layer and any underlying layers will be changed. For the sample image, skip this step.

Original

Hue, +180

Figure 11.2: I created the variation of the brooch on the right by raising the Hue value to +180.

3. Create a Hue/Saturation adjustment layer.

Choose Layer | New Adjustment Layer | Hue/Saturation and then click OK in the resulting dialog box. Or click the Adjustment Layer icon in the Layers palette and choose Hue/Saturation from the pop-up menu. Either way, you see the Hue/Saturation dialog box, shown in Figure 11.1.

4. Select a color range from the Edit drop-down list.

To affect all colors, choose Master. Alternatively, you can manipulate a specific color range by selecting it from the list. For the sample image, choose Master.

5. Deselect the Colorize option and select the Preview box.

6. Drag the Hue slider to adjust the colors.

Drag right to move pixels clockwise around the color wheel. Drag left to move pixels counterclockwise. You also can enter a specific value in the box at the right end of the slider bar. (You don't have to enter the plus sign for positive values, but you need a minus sign for negative values.)

7. Use the Saturation and Lightness controls to fine-tune the colors if needed.

Both controls affect the range you selected from the Edit drop-down list.

8. Click OK to close the dialog box.

After closing the dialog box, use the adjustment layer techniques explained in Chapter 8 to alter the filter effect if needed.

The Hue technique does have two shortcomings: First, it doesn't work on grays, whites, or blacks. Second, because Hue/Saturation shifts all shades within a particular color range by the same degree, you can't easily convert a range of hues to a single color. The solution to both problems lies in the technique outlined next.

Painting on New Colors

To produce a color shift you can't achieve via Hue/Saturation, you can simply paint on the desired color. However, there's a secret to getting natural results instead of a flat, unnatural blob of paint like what you see on the top lip in Figure 11.3. Try it out with the sample image Teeth.jpg, shown in the figure.

1. Create a new layer above the pixels that you want to recolor.

Just click the New Layer icon in the Layers palette, labeled in Figure 11.3.

2. Set the layer blending mode to Color, as shown in Figure 11.3.

3. Add the paint to the new layer.

- For small areas like the lips in the sample image, use the Brush tool or, if you need precise, sharp lines, the Pencil. See Chapter 5 to find out how to choose a brush tip and paint color.

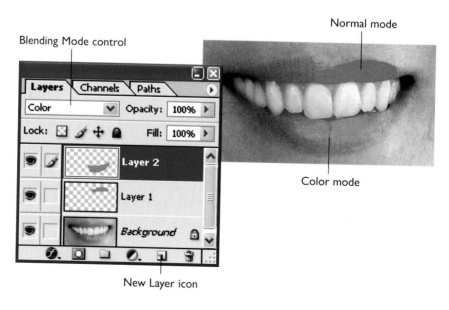

Figure 11.3: To create natural color shifts, set the blending mode of the paint layer to something other than Normal.

- For larger areas, create a selection outline as explained in Chapters 6 and 7. Set the foreground color to the desired paint color and then press ALT-DELETE (Windows) or OPTION-DELETE (Mac).

4. Experiment with other blending modes.

Each blending mode produces different results, and the best mode depends on your ultimate color goal. I used the Color mode for the bottom lip in Figure 11.3. In Figure 11.4, I set the mode to Hue for the top lip and Overlay for the bottom lip.

Hue mode

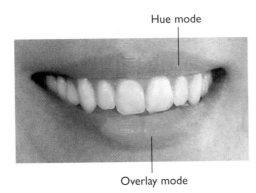

Overlay mode

Figure 11.4:
Changing the
layer blending
mode produces
different results.

Try these tricks if you can't achieve the color mix you want by simply changing the blending mode:

- Vary the paint layer's opacity, using the Opacity control in the Layers palette.
- To recolor white and black pixels, change the blending mode back to Normal but reduce the Opacity value.
- Use the Hue control in the Hue/Saturation dialog box to nudge the colors on the paint layer around the color wheel. Apply the filter directly to the paint layer by choosing Image | Adjustments | Hue/Saturation.
- Use the Levels filter to lighten or darken the paint layer color. Again, apply the filter directly to the paint layer, choosing the Levels command from the Image | Adjustments menu. See Chapter 9 to find out how to use the Levels filter.

Applying Virtual Warming and Cooling Filters

Time Saver

Using the Variations and Color Balance filters, discussed in Chapter 10, you can warm or cool shadows, highlights, and midtones independently. For a faster way to apply an overall warming or cooling effect, however, bypass those filters and opt for the techniques explained in the next two sections.

Using the CS Photo Filter

CS Photoshop CS users can take advantage of the new Photo Filter command, which produces effects similar to what you can achieve with traditional lens filters. These steps explain how to apply the filter as an adjustment layer. Try it out with the Iguana.jpg sample image, shown on the left side of Figure 11.5. I added the warming effect in the image on the right using Photo Filter.

1. Select the area that you want to alter (optional).

For a multilayer image, open the Layers palette (F7) and click the top layer that you want the filter to affect. You can limit the filter to specific pixels on the affected layers by creating a selection outline.

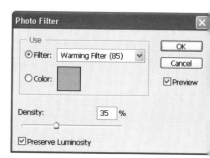

Figure 11.5: Add a virtual warming filter via the Photoshop CS Photo Filter.

Remember

Play with the Opacity and Blending Mode controls in the Layers palette to vary the impact of an adjustment layer.

In a single-layer image, skip this step if you want to apply the filter to the entire image, as is the case with the sample photo.

2. **Create a Photo Filter adjustment layer.**

Either choose Layer | New Adjustment Layer | Photo Filter and then click OK in the resulting dialog box, or click the Adjustment Layer icon at the bottom of the Layers palette and choose Photo Filter from the pop-up menu. You see the Photo Filter dialog box, shown in Figure 11.5.

3. **Select the Preview check box.**

4. **Select a filter from the Filter drop-down list.**

The list offers four filters that mimic specific lens filters: 81 and 85 warming filters along with 80 and 82 cooling filters. For the sample image, choose Warming Filter (85). In addition, the list offers a choice of specific colors. You also can click the Color swatch and choose a custom color from the Color Picker, explained in Chapter 5.

5. **Adjust the Density and Preserve Luminosity options as needed.**

Raise the Density value to produce a stronger effect. Turn the Preserve Luminosity option off to give Photoshop permission to adjust image brightness as it adjusts colors. Experiment with both options; the correct settings depend on the look you want. For the sample image, select the Preserve Luminosity box and set the Density value to 35%.

6. **Click OK to close the dialog box.**

The standard tips and reminders about editing adjustment layers apply; see Chapter 8 for the full story.

Creating Filter Effects the Old-Fashioned Way

Although the Photo Filter is undeniably convenient, don't feel too badly if your budget doesn't allow you to upgrade to CS—at least, not with regard to that particular enhancement. You can add a warming or cooling effect or any other tint quite easily without the filter. The following steps show you how; try the technique with the Iguana.jpg sample image, shown on the left in Figure 11.5. Your results should look similar to the photo in Figure 11.6.

These steps assume that you want to apply the effect to your entire image. If not, first select the area that you want to tint.

1. Create a new, empty layer above the layer(s) you want to alter.

You can do this quickly by clicking the New Layer icon, labeled in Figure 11.6.

2. Set the blending mode for the filled layer to Soft Light, as shown in Figure 11.6.

3. Set the foreground paint color to the tint color you want to apply.

Just click the foreground color swatch in the toolbox to open the Color Picker, shown in Figure 11.7 and explained in Chapter 5. To produce the look of a warming filter, set the Hue (H) value in the 30 to 45 range. Adjust the Saturation (S) and Brightness (B) values as you see fit. For a cooling filter, try a Hue value in the 200 to 215 range.

For the sample image, enter these HSB values: Hue (H), 30; Saturation (S), 82; and Brightness (B), 86, as shown in Figure 11.7. Click OK to close the Color Picker.

4. Fill the new layer with the foreground color.

Blending Mode control

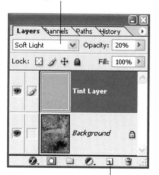

New Layer icon

Figure 11.6: To add a tint, fill a new layer with color and adjust layer opacity and blending mode as needed.

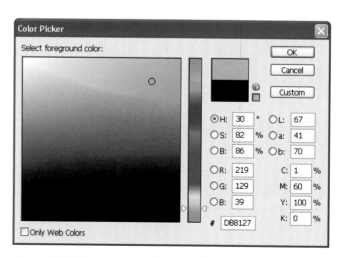

Figure 11.7: Select a tint color from the Color Picker.

Or choose Edit | Fill to open the Fill dialog box. Select Foreground Color from the Use drop-down list; set the Mode option to Normal; leave the Opacity value at 100 percent; and turn off the Preserve Transparency box. Click OK to dump the color into the new layer. (Really, it's so much easier to use the keyboard shortcut.)

5. Lower the layer Opacity value to adjust the strength of the tint.

For the sample image, set the Opacity value to 20 percent.

The only difficult aspect of this technique is predicting what tint color will produce the results you want. If the first color you chose doesn't work, try different blending modes or simply change the color of the paint layer via the Hue/Saturation filter, explained at the beginning of this chapter. Also try the other tricks given in the earlier section "Painting on New Colors." Merge the tint layer with the original when you find a look you like.

Replacing a Backdrop

When circumstances prevent you from catching your subject against a flattering background, you can create a new, more appropriate backdrop in Photoshop. Figure 11.8 offers an example of the dramatic impact you can make by swapping out the background. The colors in the new backdrop fade from dark green to pale green in a circular pattern, creating the illusion of a spotlight behind the chop (Chinese stamp). Imaging experts refer to a fading circle of color like this as a *radial gradient blend,* by the way.

The following steps walk you through the process of creating a backdrop like the one in Figure 11.8. To work along with the steps, open the sample image Chop.jpg.

1. Loosely select the original background.

For the sample image, use the Magnetic Lasso to draw a rough outline around the chop. Then choose Select | Inverse to deselect the chop and select the background instead. Your selection outline doesn't have to be perfect; you can clean things up later.

Figure 11.8: Replacing the original background with a color gradient makes the subject pop.

Image thumbnail   Mask thumbnail

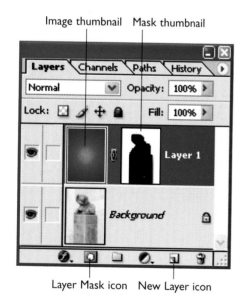

Layer Mask icon   New Layer icon

Figure 11.9: Use a layer mask to prevent the new backdrop from covering the subject.

2. **Create a new empty layer by clicking the New Layer icon, labeled in Figure 11.9.**

This layer will hold your new backdrop. Position the layer on top of the layer that contains the background area you want to replace.

3. **Click the Layer Mask icon, labeled in Figure 11.9.**

Photoshop creates a layer mask, and a mask thumbnail appears in the Layers palette, as shown in the figure. Black areas in the mask thumbnail represent unselected pixels—areas where you'll ultimately see your subject and not the new backdrop. (Your mask won't be as precise as the one in the figure yet.)

4. **Click the image thumbnail, labeled in Figure 11.9.**

Note that in the figure, the image thumbnail appears as it does after you create the gradient. Your image thumbnail appears as a checkerboard pattern at this stage, indicating that the layer is empty.

5. **Establish the backdrop colors by setting the foreground and background colors.**

For the sample image, set the foreground color to pale green and the background color to a darker shade of the same hue, as shown in Figure 11.10. (If you need help with this step, see Chapter 5.)

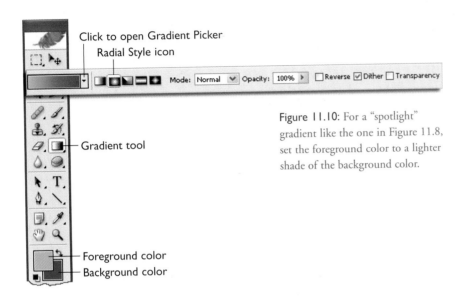

Click to open Gradient Picker

Radial Style icon

Gradient tool

Foreground color

Background color

Figure 11.10: For a "spotlight" gradient like the one in Figure 11.8, set the foreground color to a lighter shade of the background color.

6. Select the Gradient tool, labeled in Figure 11.10.

7. Select the Foreground to Background gradient from the Gradient Picker.

To open the picker, click the arrow labeled in Figure 11.10. By default, the foreground-to-background gradient is the first one in the picker.

8. On the options bar, select the Radial Style icon, labeled in Figure 11.10.

9. Set the other options as shown in Figure 11.10.

10. Drag from the center of the image outward to any corner.

Photoshop fills the new layer with the gradient. Wherever the mask thumbnail is black, however, you see the underlying image.

11. Edit the layer mask to hide and reveal the new background where needed.

Because I told you that it was okay to be a little sloppy when you selected the background in Step 1, the new background may cover up some portions of the subject. In other areas, some of the original background may be visible.

To remedy either problem, first click the mask thumbnail, labeled in Figure 11.9. Now, select the Brush tool and paint with white in areas where you want to extend the background over the original image. Paint with black in areas where you need to hide the new backdrop and reveal the subject. (Chapter 8 provides you with more direction in the art of working with layer masks.)

12. Click the image thumbnail (see Figure 11.9) to exit mask-editing mode and return to editing the image.

13. Add a shadow behind the subject (optional).

This step creates additional separation between subject and background, often producing a more realistic image. The next section tells you how to add the shadow.

If you *don't* want to add a shadow, merge the new background with the underlying layer by choosing Layer | Merge Down. Don't merge if you plan to add a shadow; retaining the new backdrop layer with its layer mask makes that task easier.

Casting a Shadow

Adding a shadow behind the subject can make a faux background more realistic—assuming that the subject cast a shadow in your original photo, of course. You can create the shadow by applying the Drop Shadow layer style effect. Follow these steps:

1. Select the subject.

Time Saver

If you previously followed the steps to produce a gradient backdrop, just CTRL-click (Windows) or ⌘-click (Mac) the mask thumbnail for the new backdrop layer. (Figure 11.11 shows the mask thumbnail.) Photoshop creates a selection outline that encompasses all white areas of the mask—the image background, in this case. Choose Select | Inverse to reverse the selection outline and select the subject instead of the background.

2. In the Layers palette, click the layer that contains the subject.

If you're continuing with the chop example, click the Background layer. In a single-layer image, you can skip this step.

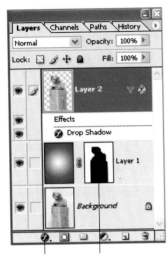

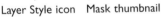

Layer Style icon   Mask thumbnail

Figure 11.11: Copy the subject
to a new layer and then apply
the Drop Shadow layer style.

3. **Choose Layer | New | Layer via Copy or press CTRL-J (Windows)
or ⌘-J (Mac).**

Photoshop copies the subject onto a new layer.

4. **Drag the new layer to the top of the layer stack, as shown in
Figure 11.11, if it's not already positioned there.**

5. **Click the Layer Style icon, labeled in Figure 11.11, and choose
Drop Shadow from the pop-up menu.**

You see the Layer Style dialog box, with the drop shadow options at the foreground.
Chapter 8 explains the specifics of adjusting the shadow effect, so I won't repeat
it all here. Suffice it to say: Just play with options in the Structure section of the
dialog box to customize the effect. Make sure that Drop Shadow is the only Styles
box selected in the column on the left side of the dialog box.

6. **Click OK to close the Layer Style dialog box.**

When you're satisfied with the new backdrop and its shadow, use the techniques
covered in Chapter 8 to merge the layers.

Figure 11.12: Textured and patterned backdrops are also easy to create.

Creating Textured and Patterned Backdrops

Bored with simple gradient backdrops? Figure 11.12 shows two variations on the theme. In the image to the left, I applied a texture filter to a solid color backdrop; in the other image, I created a patterned backdrop. (I didn't take the step of adding a shadow behind the subject in either example.)

Both effects are easy to create. Follow the steps provided for creating a gradient backdrop, but replace Steps 5 through 10 with the following:

- **To create a textured backdrop** Set the foreground paint color to the desired backdrop color. Then choose Edit | Fill and select Foreground Color from the Use list in the Fill dialog box. Set the Mode to Normal; set the Opacity to 100 percent; and deselect the Preserve Transparency option. Click OK. Next, choose Filter | Texture | Texturizer and experiment with the filter options to produce a texture you like.

- **To create a patterned backdrop** Choose Edit | Fill to open the Fill dialog box. This time, however, choose Pattern from the Use list. Click the arrow labeled in Figure 11.13 to open a palette that houses an assortment of patterns. To display additional patterns, click the palette menu arrow, also labeled in the figure, and select a pattern collection from the bottom of the resulting pop-up menu. When you find a pattern you like, click it. (Don't worry if you like a texture but not its color—you can adjust the color later.)

Leave the other Fill dialog box options at their default settings. (Mode, Normal; Opacity, 100 percent; Preserve Transparency, Off.) After clicking OK to close the dialog box, you can tweak the look of the pattern by using the layer's Opacity and Blending Mode controls. Use the Hue/Saturation technique outlined at the start of the chapter to adjust the pattern color.

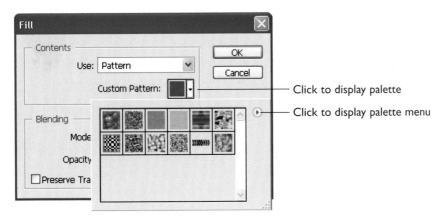

Click to display palette

Click to display palette menu

Figure 11.13: The Edit | Fill command gives you access to an assortment of patterns that can serve as backdrops.

Converting Color Photos to Grayscale Beauties

Photoshop gives you several ways to create grayscale versions of color photos. Before getting into specifics, however, I need to clarify some terminology:

- In the photography world, the term *black-and-white* refers to non-color images. But in digital imaging circles, a black-and-white picture is one that contains just those two colors. Photos that also contain shades of gray are known as *grayscale* images. I go with *grayscale,* mostly because I find traditional photography enthusiasts more easy-going about such things than digital imaging wonks, who spend too much time with uncooperative computers and so are usually a bit on the edge.

- To complicate the issue, Photoshop enables you to convert an image to the official Grayscale color model. A color model, as explained in Chapter 2, is a formula for defining a spectrum of colors. In the Grayscale model, an image can contain just 256 colors: white, black, and shades of gray. (You do not have to make this conversion to produce a non-color image, however.)

To avoid confusion, I use the term *Grayscale* with a capital *G* only when referring to an image that has been converted to the official Grayscale color model. I use a lower-case *grayscale* when I use the term in a general descriptive sense.

With that bit of administrative business covered, the following sections explain the three best color-to-gray techniques. For important images, try all three methods because each produces slightly different results.

Converting to the Grayscale Model

The fastest way to produce a grayscale image is to convert it to the 256-color Grayscale color model. To try this technique, open the sample image Anemone.jpg, shown on the left in Figure 11.14, and take these steps:

1. Save a copy of your color original.

Watch Out!

Don't skip this step! After you apply the command and save the image, you can't get your original colors back.

Original RGB   Image | Mode | Grayscale

Figure 11.14: I used
the Image | Mode |
Grayscale command
for this conversion.

2. **Choose Image | Mode | Grayscale.**

What happens next depends on your image:

- If your image contains just one layer, you see an alert box asking for permission to discard the original color information; click OK to move forward.
- If your image contains multiple layers, you instead see an alert box that gives you the option of flattening (merging) the layers or keeping them independent. If you opt not to flatten the image, some types of adjustment layers are discarded, and the look of layers that you blended with certain blend modes may also change. An alert box notifies you of this issue. (You can always use Edit | Undo if you don't like the results of your choice.)

3. **Save your image under a new name.**

Otherwise, you overwrite your color original. See Chapter 4 for help on saving files.

For casual work, Image | Mode | Grayscale produces acceptable results and is quick and easy. The image on the right in Figure 11.14 shows the full color Anemone.jpg image converted with this command. With some images, however, you can lose tonal details because of the formula Photoshop uses to convert the original color values to gray values. It's a one-size-fits-all approach that sometimes doesn't fit as well as one of the other, custom techniques.

Going Gray from a Single Channel

As explained in Chapter 2, every color image in Photoshop consists of three or four color channels, depending on the color model. An RGB image contains three channels, one each for the red, green, and blue brightness values.

When viewed by itself, a color channel is nothing more than a grayscale image— and that image may contain just the tonal values you have in mind for your grayscale picture. For example, the first three images in Figure 11.15 show the red, green, and blue channels for the full-color RGB Anemone.jpg sample image (see Figure 11.14).

Red Channel

Green Channel

Blue Channel

Lightness Channel

Figure 11.15: A single color channel often provides the basis for a nice grayscale image.

By trashing the other channels, you can create a grayscale image using the contents of the channel you like. Here's the process:

1. Save your original image.

2. If your image contains multiple layers, merge all layers by choosing Layer | Flatten Image.

This technique works only on single-layer images. However, the end result produces a brand new image file, so don't fret about merging the layers. Your original image will have all its independent layers the next time you open it.

3. Choose Window | Channels to open the Channels palette, shown in Figure 11.16.

Click to open palette menu.

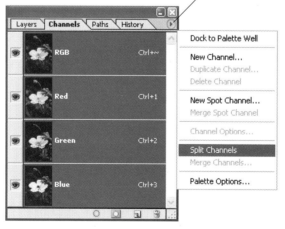

Figure 11.16: Choose Split Channels from the palette menu to create a new Grayscale image out of each channel.

4. Open the palette menu and choose Split Channels, as shown in Figure 11.16.

Photoshop closes your color image and creates a new, separate Grayscale-model image from each channel. (You can change the color model later if needed.) Each image appears in its own window, as shown in Figure 11.17. This enables you to easily compare the channel images. Just drag the windows by their title bars to arrange them side by side.

Figure 11.17: After splitting the channels, compare the resulting images side by side.

5. Save the channel image that produced the version you like best.

Watch Out!

Be sure to give the image a different name than your color original! See Chapter 4 for details on saving your file. Close the other two channel images without saving them.

In addition to surfing channels in the RGB or CMYK models—the two most common color models for digital images—try converting your color original to the Lab color model. The Lightness channel in Lab images sometimes contains another great grayscale rendition. Choose Image | Mode | Lab Color and then split the channels as outlined in the steps. (The images produced from the other two Lab channels, A and B, won't be of any use, so just close those windows.) I used this technique to produce the final variation in Figure 11.15.

Channel Mixer

Image | Mode | Grayscale

Creating Custom Grayscale Blends with the Channel Mixer

Recapping your color-conversion options so far: Image | Mode | Grayscale converts colors to the 256-color Grayscale model by mixing the original pixel values from all the color channels, using a standard formula determined by Photoshop. The Channel Splitter command, available via the Channels palette, enables you to create a Grayscale-model image using the contents of a single color channel.

With the Channel Mixer filter, you enjoy the best of both worlds. You can draw from all the original color channels but control the amount of each channel that goes into your final image. In this case, the color model does not change—an RGB image remains an RGB image, for example.

Even better, you can apply the filter as an adjustment layer, which enables you to retain the original color values and the grayscale values *in the same image file,* assuming that you save the file in the PSD or TIFF format with the Layers feature enabled. So if you apply the Channel Mixer one day and decide the next to emphasize different details in the grayscale version, all you have to do is edit the adjustment layer. You don't have to start over from scratch.

I used the Channel Mixer to produce the first Anemone variation in Figure 11.18. Just for easy comparison, the second image shows the version from Figure 11.14, which I produced using the Image | Mode | Grayscale command. Note that neither is right or wrong—which one you like best is a subjective matter.

Figure 11.18: Using the Channel Mixer filter often allows you to pull out different tonal details than you may get with a Grayscale mode conversion.

Apply the Channel Mixer filter as follows, using the original Anemone.jpg sample image if you want to work along with the steps:

1. **Make sure that no selection outline is active.**

Otherwise, only the selected pixels will go gray. To quickly get rid of an active selection outline, press CTRL-D (Windows) or ⌘-D (Mac).

2. **In a multilayer image, open the Layers palette and click the top layer.**

Again, this step ensures that you want your entire image to receive the grayscale effect. If your image contains just a single layer (the Background layer), you can skip this step.

3. **Create a Channel Mixer adjustment layer.**

Click the Adjustment Layer icon at the bottom of the Layers palette and choose Channel Mixer from the pop-up menu. Or choose Layer | New Adjustment Layer | Channel Mixer and click OK when the New Layer dialog box appears.

You then see the Channel Mixer dialog box, shown in Figure 11.19. The dialog box contains sliders representing each channel in your image—in an RGB image, you get Red, Green, and Blue sliders, as shown in the figure.

4. **Select the Monochrome and Preview options.**

The Preview option enables you to preview the results of the filter in the image window. Checking the Monochrome box tells Photoshop that your goal is a grayscale (monochrome) image. Accordingly, the Output Channel option at the top of the dialog box automatically changes to Gray.

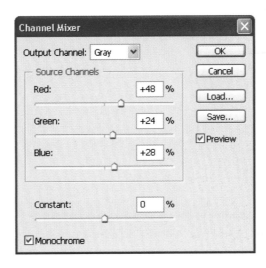

Figure 11.19: Drag the sliders to custom-blend your grayscale image.

5. **Drag the sliders to custom-mix your grayscale image.**

The Source Channels sliders determine the weight given to each channel in the grayscale conversion. For most images, you should aim for percentages that add up to 100 percent, but let your eyes be your guide. I used the values shown in Figure 11.19 to produce the first image in Figure 11.18.

The Constant slider increases or decreases the amount of white and black in the image, which of course affects image brightness. I suggest that you instead adjust brightness and contrast after applying the filter by using the Levels or Curves filters, both covered in Chapter 9.

6. **Click OK to close the dialog box.**

Remember that your grayscale effect exists as an adjustment layer, so you can use all the tips outlined in Chapter 8 to refine the effect if necessary. If you want to create a version of the image in the official, 256-color Grayscale color model, first flatten the image by choosing Layer | Flatten Image. Then choose Image | Mode | Grayscale. When doing the Grayscale model conversion, Photoshop retains the gray values you assigned with the Channel Mixer. Be sure to save your image under a different name than the color original.

Creating Antiqued and Hand-Tinted Effects

Want to give your photo that antiqued, sepia tone without waiting a hundred years for the process to occur naturally? You can add the sepia tint—or any other tint color—in a flash. In Figure 11.20, I created a sepia version of the Anenome image. Just for fun, I also made a purple-tinted version.

Watch Out!

For both effects, your image must be in a full-color model—RGB, CMYK, or Lab. If you want to tint or "hand-paint" an image that has been converted to the Grayscale model, first choose Image | Mode | RGB Color to convert it to the RGB color model.

Here's the tinting process:

1. **Create a Hue/Saturation adjustment layer.**

Just click the Adjustment Layer icon at the bottom of the Layers palette (see Figure 11.21), and choose Hue/Saturation from the pop-up menu.

Figure 11.20: I used the Colorize option in the Hue/Saturation dialog box to produce these variations of the full-color original shown in Figure 11.14.

2. In the Hue/Saturation dialog box, select the **Colorize** option.

3. Drag the Hue slider to specify the tint color, and adjust the Saturation and Lightness values if desired.

If you're playing along with the home version of our game, featuring the Anemone.jpg sample image, set the Hue values to 41 and 340, respectively. Raise the Saturation value to 30 to produce the variations shown in Figure 11.20.

4. Click **OK** to close the dialog box.

See Chapter 8 to find out how to refine the effect if needed by editing the Hue/Saturation adjustment layer. When you're happy with your results, flatten the image and save the file under a name that's different from your original.

If you care to go even further, you can produce hand-painted effects like the ones shown in Figure 11.22 in several ways:

- **Lower the image saturation** For a color photo, one easy trick is to simply create a Hue/Saturation adjustment layer and reduce the image saturation. (Be sure to turn off the Colorize box.) I produced the image on the left in Figure 11.22 by lowering the Saturation value to -70.

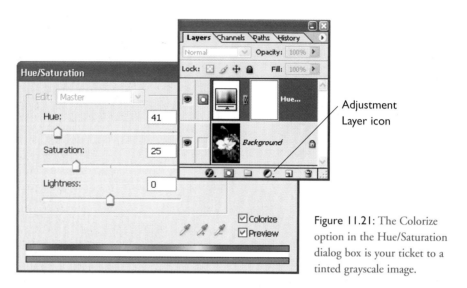

Figure 11.21: The Colorize option in the Hue/Saturation dialog box is your ticket to a tinted grayscale image.

- **Desaturate and then paint on a Color layer** Alternatively, choose Image | Adjustments | Desaturate to completely desaturate the image. (You don't have to take this step if you're starting with a grayscale photo.) Then create a new, empty layer at the top of the layer stack and set the layer blending mode to Color. Now you can paint on the image using the Brush tool or any other paint tools. The section "Painting on New Colors," earlier in this chapter, offers more specifics.

- **Set the Channel Mixer to hand-painting mode** If you're not good with a paintbrush and want more color flexibility than you get when you simply lower saturation, the Channel Mixer can provide a solution. This technique works only for color images in the RGB or CMYK color models, however.

  First, create a Channel Mixer adjustment layer, as outlined in the preceding section. In the Channel Mixer dialog box, click the Monochrome box once to turn on the option and then click again to turn it off. Your clicks tell Photoshop that you want to produce a hand-painted effect.

  Now select a color channel from the Output Channel drop-down list and drag the sliders to shift the image colors. You'll have to experi-

Reduced Saturation   Channel Mixer

Figure 11.22: You can mimic a hand-painted effect by decreasing saturation
(left) or by using a secret Channel Mixer technique (right).

ment to see which channels and slider positions produce the effect
you want. To replicate the flower version shown on the right in Figure
11.22, use these settings for the Red Output Channel: 70 Red, 20
Blue, and 10 Green. For the Green Output Channel, set the values to
30 Red, 60 Green, and 10 Blue. For the Blue Output Channel, set the
values to 20 Red, 55 Green, and 20 Blue.

Spot Removal and Other Touch-Up Work

Every photographer knows the disappointment of "almost perfect" pictures—the would-be stunners spoiled by small imperfections. Lens flare pierces a brilliant blue sky. Blown highlights mar a poignant portrait. A stray candy wrapper distracts the eye from a skateboarder caught flying down the street.

With techniques presented in this chapter, you can eradicate these and other picture-wrecking problems. You'll find out how to use the Clone tool and Healing Brush to remove small blemishes, apply the Patch tool to hide larger defects, remove digital camera noise, and more.

In This Chapter:

- [ ] Fast cover-ups for scratches, blemishes, and other flaws

- [ ] Step-by-step guides to the Clone, Patch, and Healing Brush tools

- [ ] How to create a custom patch to hide large defects

- [ ] The secret to repairing blown highlights

- [ ] Tips for softening digital camera noise and film grain

Covering Up Problem Areas

Cropping can eliminate flaws around the perimeter of an image. But what do you do when the problem occurs in the middle of subject matter you don't want to crop? Depending on the photo, you may be able to duplicate untainted pixels from another part of the image and use the copies to cover the bad spots—sort of like performing a photographic skin graft.

The upcoming sections introduce you to tools for doing this kind of repair work: the Clone tool, Healing Brush, and Patch tool. Investigate the Clone tool first— it's the most difficult to master but will be your workhorse retouching weapon. The Patch tool and Healing Brush are variations of the Clone tool, so getting acquainted with cloning will help you better understand those tools.

Figure 12.1: I cloned sea pixels from the left side of the image over the tent and post.

Cloning over Defects

One of the most useful Photoshop tools, the Clone tool "paints" with existing image pixels, enabling you to easily copy and paste good areas over bad. In Figure 12.1, I cloned sea pixels from the left side of the photo over the white tent and post, for example. Then I covered the tent support in the lower-left corner with surrounding sand pixels.

Because the Clone tool has no real-life equivalent, it can be perplexing at first. So instead of diving right into specifics, the next section explains the general concept and one important tool option.

Getting Familiar with Cloning

Working with the Clone tool involves two basic steps:

1. First, establish the initial clone source.

The *clone source* refers to the pixels that you want to copy and paste over the problem pixels. To set the initial clone source point, you hold down the ALT key (Windows) or OPTION key (Mac) to display a target cursor, as shown in Figure 12.2. Then you click the initial pixels you want to copy.

2. Click or drag to paint copies of the source pixels over the problem pixels.

If you click, you lay down one cursor's worth of copied source pixels. If you drag, Photoshop lifts a swath of source pixels as wide and long as your brushstroke. A crosshair cursor appears to show you the position of the pixels currently being cloned. The crosshair cursor moves in tandem with your tool cursor, so as you move the tool cursor, you clone a different part of the photo.

For example, in Figure 12.3, I set the initial clone source at the position indicated in Figure 12.2. Then I dragged down over the white canvas, as indicated by the white arrow in Figure 12.3. The circle is the Clone tool cursor. As I dragged down, the crosshair cursor moved the same distance and direction, following the path indicated by the yellow arrow, cloning a continuous strip of sea pixels onto the canvas.

What happens with your second click or drag depends on the Aligned control on the options bar:

- **Aligned on** Photoshop continues cloning from the current position of the clone source cursor. This option prevents you from cloning

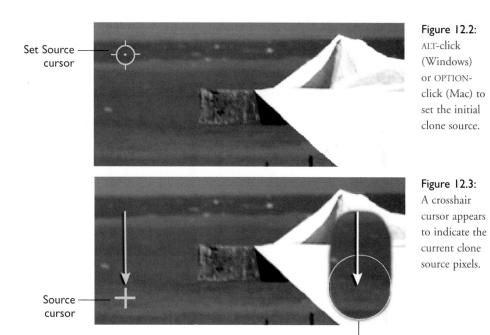

Set Source
cursor

Source
cursor

Tool cursor

Figure 12.2:
ALT-click
(Windows)
or OPTION-
click (Mac) to
set the initial
clone source.

Figure 12.3:
A crosshair
cursor appears
to indicate the
current clone
source pixels.

the same area each time you click or drag with the Clone tool.

■ **Aligned off** After each click or drag, the clone source cursor returns
to the initial clone-source position you set when you ALT- or OPTION-
clicked. This option allows you to reclone the same pixels repeatedly.

Figure 12.4 illustrates this difference. Suppose that you set your initial clone
source at the position shown in the left image. If you drag three times across
your image with the Aligned option on, you get the result shown in the top-
right example. Turn the option off, and you duplicate the same strip of pixels
three times, as shown in the lower-right example.

There's no right or wrong setting—which way you should go depends on your
cloning project. Sometimes you need to clone the same area repeatedly, and sometimes you don't. Either way, you can reset the clone source at any time by ALT- or
OPTION-clicking again.

Now that you have a better idea of how cloning works, the next section gives you
specifics on using the Clone tool.

Initial clone source

Aligned on

Aligned off

Figure 12.4: Turn off the Aligned option to clone the same source pixels repeatedly.

To switch from icon-based tool cursors to a brush size or crosshair cursor, visit the Display and Cursors panel of the Preferences dialog box. Chapter 1 has details.

Remember

Applying the Clone Tool

In a practiced hand, the Clone tool can remove almost any unwanted object from a photo. Practice, however, is the operative word. You can't get good cloning results without it. So open the sample image Dresses.jpg and work along with the steps.

1. Create a new layer to hold your cloned pixels.

Just click the New Layer icon in the Layers palette (F7), shown in Figure 12.5. Place the new layer above the layer that contains the problem pixels.

2. Select the Clone tool, labeled in Figure 12.6.

The official tool name is Clone Stamp, but nearly everyone in the Photoshop world drops the "Stamp." Whatever you call it, the tool shares a flyout menu with the Pattern Stamp tool. (The Pattern Stamp has little practical use in everyday photographic projects, so I don't cover it.)

3. Set the brush options.

The tool offers the full complement of brush settings, detailed in Chapter 5. For normal cloning, use the Mode, Opacity, Flow, and Airbrush settings shown in Figure 12.6, and turn off Brush Dynamics (accessible via the main Brushes palette).

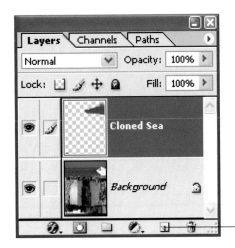

Figure 12.5: Always do your cloning on a separate layer.

New Layer icon

PART 4 | RETOUCHING TECHNIQUES

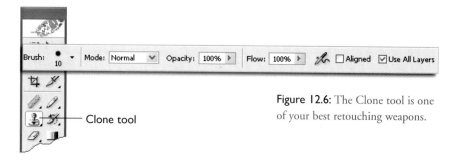

Clone tool

Figure 12.6: The Clone tool is one of your best retouching weapons.

If the area you're fixing is in soft focus, a soft brush helps your cloning strokes blend with the surrounding area. In areas that feature sharp focus, try a Hardness value of around 90 percent. At 100 percent, clone strokes tend to be more noticeable because they have distinct edges. For the sample image, set the Hardness value to 70 percent.

4. Set the Aligned option.

As explained in the preceding section, this option affects what happens on your second click or drag during a cloning session. A quick recap:

- **On** You continue cloning from the point where you left off, picking up new source pixels as you move your tool cursor.
- **Off** You clone from the same source pixels each time you click or drag.

For the sample image, turn the option on.

5. Turn on the Use All Layers check box.

This option allows the Clone tool to see through the new, empty cloning layer and grab the pixels from all underlying layers. If you don't want to clone pixels from a particular layer, hide the layer by clicking its eyeball icon in the Layers palette.

6. ALT-click (Windows) or OPTION-click (Mac) to set the initial clone source.

Your click tells Photoshop what pixels you want to clone. For the sample repair job, use an empty area of the sea as the clone source.

7. Click on or drag over the area you want to hide.

The cloned pixels appear underneath your tool cursor. If necessary, you can clone from another area of the image by simply resetting the clone source. Change the brush size and hardness as needed as you go.

Watch Out!

Be careful not to introduce a noticeable pattern into areas that should be random. In Figure 12.7, for example, the whitecap area repeats several times, providing a giveaway to the repair. You can avoid this by cloning from several different source points.

Figure 12.7: Avoid introducing visible patterns into an area that should be random.

8. When you're satisfied with the repair, merge the cloning layer and underlying layer as explained in Chapter 8.

A few final cloning tips:

- For some repairs, allowing the original pixels to remain partially visible produces a smoother result, so experiment with adjusting the opacity of the cloned pixels. The Opacity control on the options bar affects your next cloning stroke. To change the opacity of the entire cloning layer, use the Opacity control in the Layers palette.

- Adjusting the brightness or color of the cloned pixels is sometimes necessary. See Chapters 9 and 10 for help.

- You can use the Eraser tool to rub out cloned pixels that don't look right, as explained in Chapter 8. Or just trash the cloning layer and try again.
- If you can't find any good pixels to clone in the current image, check your archives; you can clone from one photo to another. Open both photos, arrange the image windows side by side, and set the clone source in the window that contains the usable pixels.

Dabbing Out Spots with the Healing Brush

Like the Clone tool, the Healing Brush copies pixels from one area of the image and paints them on the pixels under your tool cursor. But the Healing Brush adjusts the texture, opacity, and brightness of the cloned pixels to match the surrounding pixels. This adjustment can be good or bad, depending on what you're trying to do. If you want the copied pixels to retain their original appearance, the Healing Brush isn't your tool; use the Clone tool instead.

PHOTO COURTESY HEIDI P. MIELKE

I rely on the Healing Brush most for repairing small skin blemishes, getting rid of scanner dust, and eliminating negative scratches. Try it out with the sample image Portrait.jpg, shown in Figure 12.8. I used the Healing Brush to remove the scratch underneath the lip and the strands of hair that wrap around the neck. Figure 12.9 shows the result.

v.7 **1. In Photoshop 7, copy the blemish and the area you want to use to hide it to a new layer.**

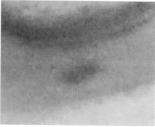

Figure 12.8: Small facial blemishes call for an application of the Healing Brush.

Figure 12.9: I used the Healing Brush to remove the blemish and some hair that blew across the neck.

- In a single-layer image like the sample photo, just drag the layer to the New Layer icon in the Layers palette (refer to Figure 12.5).
- In a multilayer image, copy both the problem and repair pixels to the same new layer. Select those areas and press CTRL-J (Windows) or ⌘-J (Mac). Position the new layer above the original layer that contains the blemish.

CS **2. In CS, create a new layer to hold the Healing Brush strokes.**

The CS Healing Brush tool can see through layers, so just create a new, empty layer to hold the Healing Brush strokes by clicking the New Layer icon in the Layers palette (refer to Figure 12.5).

3. Select the Healing Brush tool, shown in Figure 12.10.

The tool shares a flyout with the Patch tool and, in CS, the Color Replacement tool. The figure shows the tool options available for CS. In Version 7, you don't get the Use All Layers check box.

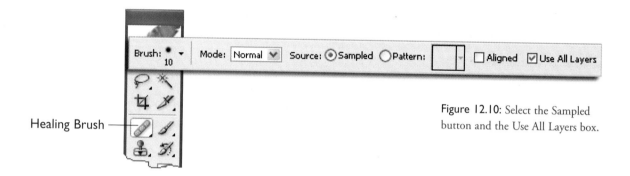

Healing Brush

Figure 12.10: Select the Sampled
button and the Use All Layers box.

4. **Set the brush options.**

Unlike other brush-based tools, the Healing Brush offers only a handful of brush
options. Access them via the palette at the left end of the options bar, as shown
in Figure 12.11.

- Leave the Spacing, Angle, and Roundness values at their default settings
(shown in the figure).
- The appropriate brush size and hardness depend on your image.
As with the Clone tool, use a softer brush in areas where the picture
focus is soft. For the sample image, use a 10-pixel brush and set the
Hardness value to 50 percent. (You can change brush size and hardness between tool strokes if needed.)
- The Size option relates to pressure-
sensitive tablets; it enables you to
vary brush size by adjusting pen
pressure or moving the stylus
wheel. Until you're experienced
with your Photoshop tools, select
Off and change the brush size in
the normal ways. Otherwise, predicting the behavior of the tools
is more difficult.

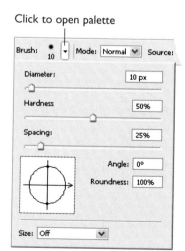

Click to open palette

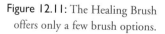

Figure 12.11: The Healing Brush
offers only a few brush options.

5. Set the Mode control to Normal and select the Sampled button, as shown in Figure 12.10.

6. Set the Aligned option.

This check box has the same impact as for the Clone tool; see the earlier section "Getting Familiar with Cloning" for an explanation. For the sample repair, turn the option off.

CS **7.** In CS, select the Use All Layers check box.

8. ALT-click (Windows) or OPTION-click (Mac) the pixels that you want to use to "heal" the blemish.

Your click does the same thing as when you use the Clone tool: It tells Photoshop what pixels to use as the *source pixels*—the pixels to copy and paste over the problem pixels. As with the Clone tool, you see the target cursor when you hold down ALT or OPTION.

For the sample portrait, click at the location shown in the image on the left in Figure 12.12.

9. Click on or drag over the blemish.

Photoshop paints the source pixels over the pixels underneath your cursor and then adjusts the color and brightness of the copied pixels to match their surroundings.

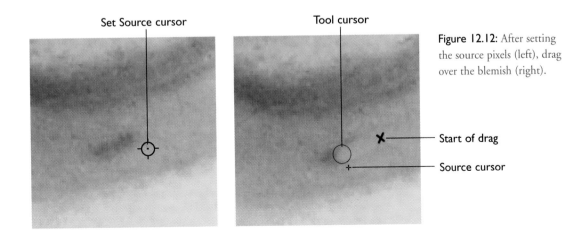

Set Source cursor

Tool cursor

Start of drag

Source cursor

Figure 12.12: After setting the source pixels (left), drag over the blemish (right).

In addition to your tool cursor, you see a crosshair cursor, as shown in Figure 12.12. The crosshair indicates what pixels are currently being used as the source pixels, just as with the Clone tool. If you drag with the Healing Brush, the crosshair cursor moves in tandem with your tool cursor. In the figure, the black X indicates the spot where I began dragging with the Healing Brush.

10. Keep clicking and dragging until the blemish disappears.

For a large blemish, you usually get a more natural result if you reset the source target several times as you go, using pixels from different sides of the blemish as the source pixels.

Figure 12.13: The Healing Brush doesn't work well when the area surrounding the problem pixels is significantly brighter or darker.

11. When the repair is done, merge the healed layer with the underlying layer as discussed in Chapter 8.

After you repair the chin blemish in the sample image, give the Healing Brush another whirl, this time working on the stray hairs on the neck. Notice, though, what happens if you try to cover the hairs very close to the shirt. The hairs disappear, but because Photoshop adjusts the edges of the copied area to match the neighboring area, the resulting skin patch is too dark, as shown in Figure 12.13. To fix this area, return to the Clone tool.

Saving Time with Patchwork

When you need to hide a large defect, you may be able to save time by creating a patch instead of using the Clone tool or Healing Brush. You have two options: First, try the Patch tool, explained next. This tool automates part of the process and, in the right circumstances, does the job well and quickly. If the Patch tool fails you, the subsequent section shows how to create your own patches.

Applying the Patch Tool

Flaws that occur in an area that's relatively free of detail, such as the lens flare that ruins the upper-left corner of Figure 12.14, respond well to the Patch tool.

The following steps show you how to use the Patch tool; experiment with the sample image Swamp.jpg, shown in Figure 12.14. Note that the steps assume that your image contains just one layer. If your image contains multiple layers, copy the flawed region and the area that you want to use for patching to a new layer instead of duplicating the Background layer in Step 1.

Figure 12.14: Because it falls in an area of flat color, this example of lens flare is the perfect candidate for the Patch tool.

1. Duplicate the Background layer.

Do this by dragging the Background layer to the New Layer icon in the Layers palette (refer to Figure 12.5).

2. Select the Patch tool, labeled in Figure 12.15.

The tool shares a flyout menu with the Healing Brush and, in Photoshop CS, the Color Replacement tool.

3. On the options bar, select the Source button as shown in Figure 12.15.

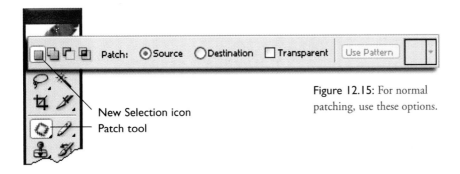

New Selection icon
Patch tool

Figure 12.15: For normal patching, use these options.

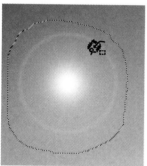

Figure 12.16: Drag with the Patch tool to enclose the defect in a selection outline.

CS **4.** In CS, select the New Selection icon and turn off the Transparent option, as shown in the figure.

5. Drag around the defect, as shown in Figure 12.16.

As you drag, a solid outline trails your cursor, as shown in the top image in Figure 12.16. For best results, make your selection outline as precise as possible. When you release the mouse button, a selection outline appears and your cursor looks like the one in the lower image.

6. Move your cursor inside the selection outline.

7. Drag the outline over the area that you want to use as the patch.

As you begin dragging, a second outline appears, as shown on the left in Figure 12.17. In CS, the pixels inside that second outline appear inside the first outline, giving you a preview of how the patch will look—sort of. Photoshop will adjust the patch to blend it with the surrounding pixels, so the color or brightness may initially look wrong, as in the figure.

For the sample image, use the area right below the lens flare as the source of the patch.

Figure 12.17: Drag the outline over the patch pixels.

8. Evaluate the patch.

When you release the mouse button, Photoshop adjusts the patch pixels to match their new neighbors, as shown on the right in Figure 12.17. The second selection outline disappears, but the initial outline remains. To get a better view of the patch results, hide the selection outline by pressing CTRL-H (Windows) or ⌘-H (Mac).

If the patch doesn't look right, press CTRL-Z (Windows) or ⌘-Z (Mac) to undo it and then redisplay the selection outline by pressing CTRL-H or ⌘-H again. Then drag the outline to another area that might provide better source pixels. Be careful not to click or drag outside the outline, or it disappears and you must start over.

9. **When you're happy with the patch, merge the patched layer and Background layer as discussed in Chapter 8.**

Now that you've got the basics down, here are a few additional tips:

- If you prefer, you can select the patch pixels first and drag them over the defect. To work in this mode, choose the Destination button on the options bar.

- You can expand and contract the Patch tool outlines as you do when working with selection tools. See Chapter 6 for the full story.

- You also can apply the Select | Feather command after drawing a Patch tool outline. The Feather command creates an outline that fades gradually around the perimeter, as explained in Chapter 6. Sometimes, this trick creates a more invisible patch.

- The Transparent option provided in CS creates a more translucent patch. This option is usually best left turned off.

- If you have trouble creating a good outline with the Patch tool, instead select the defect using the regular selection tools. Then grab the Patch tool, click the Source button, and drag the selection outline onto the patch pixels.

- Finally, if you don't get good results after one or two tries, the repair likely doesn't lend itself to this tool. Try the technique explained next instead.

Creating Your Own Patches

For simple repairs like the lens flare example used in the preceding section, the Patch tool is a magical, fast-acting spot remover. However, when the problem area contains lots of detail or has precise borders, the patch may not blend well with the surrounding area despite Photoshop's best efforts. And in some cases, you may not *want* Photoshop to adjust the opacity, texture, and brightness of the patch— you may want those patch pixels to retain their original appearance.

In this scenario, use the method we old-timers relied on before the invention of the Patch tool: Simply select an area to use as a patch, feather the selection and copy it to a new layer, and drag the copied pixels over the problem area. Try using this technique to cover up the white scoop in the Market2.jpg sample image, shown on the left in Figure 12.18. The right image shows the patched photo, offering a new twist on the phrase "from scoop to nuts."

Figure 12.18: I created a "hand-made" patch to cover up the white scoop in the lower-right corner.

I. Select the area that you want to use as a patch.

For the example project, select the Lasso tool, turn off the Anti-aliased option, and set the Feather value to 4. Then drag around the area shown in Figure 12.19.

Figure 12.19: Select an area to use as a patch.

As explained in Chapter 6, feathering creates a selection outline that fades gradually at the edges. For the sample image, slight feathering will help the patch blend in with the surrounding nuts. For your own photos, you'll need to experiment to see whether a feathered or unfeathered patch works best. Ditto for anti-aliasing.

If you draw your selection outline with a tool that doesn't offer a Feather control on the options bar, you can feather the outline via the Select | Feather command.

2. **Copy the selection to a new layer by pressing CTRL-J (Windows) or ⌘-J (Mac).**

Or choose Layer | New | Layer via Copy. The copied selection will serve as your patch. Make sure that the new layer is above the layer that contains the problem pixels, as shown in Figure 12.20. If not, drag it up the layer stack in the Layers palette.

3. **Press v to select the Move tool and then turn off the Auto Select Layer and Show Bounding Box controls on the options bar.**

4. **Drag the copied selection over the problem pixels.**

You also can nudge the patch into place by pressing the arrow keys. Press an arrow key to move the patch one pixel in the direction of the arrow. Press SHIFT plus an arrow key to move the patch 10 pixels.

5. **Refine the patch as needed.**

Use these techniques:

- If the patch doesn't cover the entire area, create a second patch and drag it over the remaining problem pixels. You can simply duplicate the patch layer or create an entirely new patch.

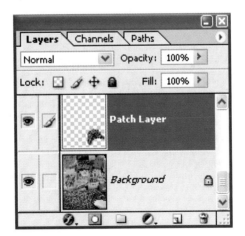

Figure 12.20: Copy the selected area to a new layer.

- You can rotate, scale, and otherwise manipulate the patch via the Edit | Free Transform command, explained in the next chapter.
- Experiment with different layer blending modes and opacity settings.
- Adjust the color and exposure of the patch by using the techniques discussed in Chapters 9 and 10. Apply the correction directly to the layer, via the commands on the Image | Adjustments submenu rather than using an adjustment layer. That way, your changes affect only the patch pixels.
- Use the Eraser to rub away any excess patch pixels. Chapter 8 covers the Eraser tool.

6. When the patch looks good, merge the patch layer with the underlying layer, as explained in Chapter 8.

SPEED KEYS: Retouching Tool Shortcuts

Tool	Shortcut
Brush tool*	B
Clone tool*	S
Eraser*	E
Eyedropper	I
Healing Brush or Patch tool*	J
Move tool	V

*Shares shortcut with other tools; press SHIFT plus the shortcut key to cycle through the tools.

Fixing Blown Highlights

Using the techniques discussed in Chapter 9, you can fix portions of a photo that are slightly overexposed. But no exposure tool can repair *blown highlights*—areas that are so overexposed that they're completely white, devoid of any detail. A few of the stems and the front seed pod in the image on the left side of Figure 12.21 suffer from this problem.

You can take two approaches to repairing blown highlights:

- Use the Clone tool to copy properly exposed pixels over the problem pixels. The first section in this chapter shows you how.
- Use the Brush tool to paint in the missing color.

Figure 12.21: You can repair blown highlights (left) with the Clone tool or simply paint on the missing color and then add some texture (right).

I prefer the second approach for fixing areas such as the stems in the sample photo. Staying within the bounds of such a narrow area with the Clone tool requires using a very small tool brush, which means a tedious, time-consuming repair. In most cases, painting enables you to produce good results, as shown in the image on the right in Figure 12.21, in less time. Painting is also the way to go when you can't find any good pixels to clone.

The following steps show you how it's done. Experiment on the sample image Lanterns2.jpg.

1. **Create a new layer above the layer that holds the blown highlights.**

2. **Select the Brush tool and set the tool options as shown in Figure 12.22.**

For the sample project, work with a small, round brush, and set the Hardness value to 90 percent. Other repair jobs may call for a different brush size or Hardness value.

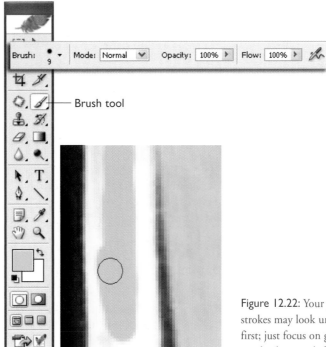

Figure 12.22: Your paint strokes may look unnatural at first; just focus on getting a good color match for now.

While you're first learning this technique, also turn off Brush Dynamics, controlled in the main Brushes palette at the right end of the options bar. After you understand how the technique works, however, you may want to enable dynamics so that you can vary paint opacity on the fly if you use a pressure-sensitive tablet. (Chapter 5 details all these options.)

3. Set the foreground paint color to the color you want the object to be.

Time Saver

If the color exists elsewhere in the image, press ALT (Windows) or OPTION (Mac) to temporarily access the Eyedropper and then click the color. For the sample image, click a green stem near one of the problem stems to set the color to light green, as shown in the figure.

To select a color that's not in the image, use the Color Picker as described in Chapter 5.

4. Paint over the blown highlights, as shown in Figure 12.22.

As you paint near the edges of the blown highlights, lower the tool Opacity value to better blend the paint with the surrounding area. If you spill paint on surrounding pixels, use the Eraser to remove it. (Chapter 8 shows you how.)

> **Tool Tricks**
> Press a number key to adjust the opacity of the next stroke you paint with the Brush tool or Clone tool. Press 0 for full opacity, 9 for 90 percent opacity, 8 for 80 percent opacity, and so on. To adjust opacity in increments smaller than ten, type the specific value: 85, 23, or whatever.

5. Study the painted area to see whether a texture fix is needed.

When you finish, your painted highlights may look something like what you see on the left in Figure 12.23. The color is correct, but something's missing: texture. Compare the left stem in the figure, which is the one I painted, with the right stem, which was properly exposed. The unpainted stem contains subtle variations of color, while the repaired stem is a flat strip of solid color—definitely not natural.

If the repaired area is small, this problem may not be noticeable, in which case you can skip to Step 7. Otherwise, move on to Step 6.

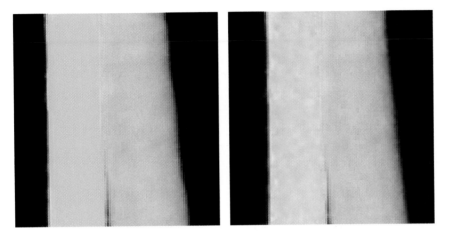

Figure 12.23: The painted stem looks flat compared to its neighbor (left); an application of the Grain filter adds texture (right).

6. Apply the Grain filter to add texture to the painted area (optional).

Choose Filter | Texture | Grain. In Photoshop CS, you see the Filter Gallery dialog box, shown in Figure 12.24; in Version 7, your dialog box shows just the filter controls plus a small preview.

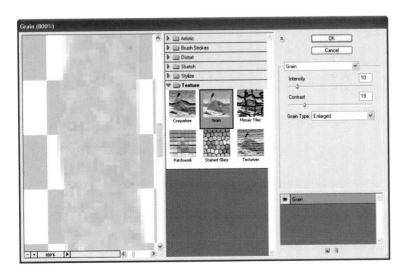

Figure 12.24: Experiment with the Grain Type option to see which setting produces the best texture match.

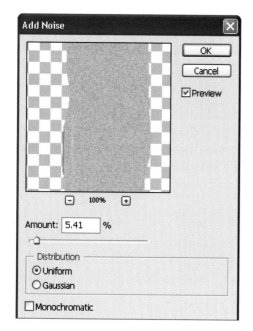

Figure 12.25: To add small-grain texture, try the Add Noise filter.

Experiment with the filter settings to find the right texture match for the image. For the Grain Type setting, Enlarged usually works well; use this option for the sample image. The other two options control the strength and contrast of the grain effect. For the sample image, set the Intensity to 10 and the Contrast to 19. Click OK to apply the effect and close the dialog box.

After closing the filter dialog box, you can adjust the opacity of the paint layer if needed by using the Opacity control in the Layers palette.

7. **Merge the paint layer with the underlying image as described in Chapter 8.**

For paint jobs that require small-grain texture, also try the Add Noise filter in Step 6. This filter simulates a defect called noise, discussed in the next section. Choose Filter | Noise | Add Noise to display the dialog box shown in Figure 12.25. The Amount value controls the strength of the effect. Experiment with the Distribution options; Uniform produces a more subtle effect than Gaussian. Select the Monochromatic box to create noise based solely on tones of the paint color, without introducing any other colors.

Softening Noise, Grain, and Compression Artifacts

Noise refers to a defect that sometimes occurs when you shoot with a digital camera in low light. Noise makes an image look as though it has been dusted with colored sand, as shown in Figure 12.26. The effect is similar to excess grain in a film print or slide.

Although you usually can't completely eradicate the level of noise found in the example picture, you can soften it by applying a blur effect. You can use the same approach to reduce the appearance of film grain or compression artifacts, a defect caused by too much JPEG compression. (Chapter 15 details this problem.)

Photoshop offers you several blurring options. Try them out using the sample image Noise.jpg, featured in the figure.

Figure 12.26: Noise gives your photo a speckled look, similar to film grain.

- **Despeckle filter** This filter looks for *edges*—areas where significant color changes occur—and then blurs everything but those edges. The effect is subtle, and you don't get any control over the intensity of the blur. In fact, you don't even see a dialog box. Choose Filter | Noise | Despeckle to apply the filter.
- **Gaussian Blur filter** Discussed in the next chapter, this filter enables you to specify exactly how much you want Photoshop to blur the image. Try this filter if Despeckle isn't strong enough. Choose Filter | Blur | Gaussian Blur and use the Radius value inside the filter dialog box to adjust the blurring amount.
- **Blur tool** Use this tool to rub on the blurring effect as if you were painting Vaseline on a lens. The next chapter details the tool, which is ideal for getting into small nooks and crannies.

Watch Out!

The problem, of course, is that you lose details when you apply a blur, so you have to find a balance between removing the defect and retaining details. Fortunately, noise, grain, and artifacts usually are most noticeable in areas that don't contain much detail, such as the sky in the sample image, making blurring an acceptable solution. You can prevent the detail areas from being affected by creating a selection outline, as discussed in Chapters 6 and 7, before applying the blur. And as with any edit, be sure to duplicate the area you want to blur to a new layer, and apply the blur on the duplicate layer.

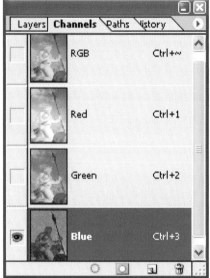

Figure 12.27: Click a channel name to view it without its companion channels.

Here's one other trick that may enable you to hold onto important details:

1. Choose Window | Channels to display the Channels palette, shown in Figure 12.27.

Chapter 2 covers this palette and explains channels, if you're new to the term.

2. Inspect each channel by clicking its name in the palette.

Often, one channel will be significantly noisier than the others, as shown in Figure 12.28. Typically, the Blue channel is the culprit in an RGB image, as here. If you're really lucky, this channel won't also be the sole container of the most important image details.

Note that if your image contains adjustment layers, you must visit the Layers palette and make the Background layer (or another regular image layer) active in order to display the channels individually.

3. Apply the blur to the noisiest channel only.

Just click the channel's name in the Channels palette and apply the blur using any of the three techniques I just mentioned. Note that the blur will affect only the

Red Channel   Green Channel   Blue Channel

Figure 12.28: Try applying the blur just to the noisiest image channel.

Figure 12.29: Although the noise isn't completely gone, the situation is much better.

active image layer, even if you're working with the Blur tool and select the Use All Layers option.

4. Click the composite channel name to return to the full-color view.

In an RGB image, click the RGB channel name. Or just press CTRL- ~ (tilde) in Windows or ⌘- ~ (tilde) on a Mac.

Often, this single-channel blur does the trick. If not, you can apply a less intense blur to each of the other channels or return to the composite image and do more work to all three channels at once.

To produce the image in Figure 12.29, I blurred the Blue channel significantly and then applied a lesser blur to the composite image. I used a combination of all three blurring methods—Despeckle, Gaussian Blur, and the Blur tool—as you may need to do for many photos. For detail areas, such as the hand, I worked with the Blur tool, concentrating the tool in the areas between the edges. The noise isn't gone completely, and some detail has been lost, but the image is much improved.

Lens Work: Perspective and Focus Adjustments

13

In This Chapter:

When you consider that everything that occurs in Photoshop is the result of a mathematical calculation, some of its features become even more amazing. Filters and tools in this chapter are a case in point.

With the techniques presented here, you can alter perspective and focus, creating the illusion that you shot a picture with a completely different lens than you actually used. Imagine how many formulas and pieces of computer code must be involved in that bit of digital manipulation! On second thought, don't—it will only boggle your mind, and we're all boggled enough already. Instead, just take advantage of these lens-related features and join me in a 20-click salute to the Adobe wizards who make them possible.

Straightening the Horizon Line

Unless you're purposely trying to convey the idea that the world is off balance, a tilting horizon line like the one shown in Figure 13.1 is problematic. Fortunately, you can correct the situation easily by using the Free Transform command to rotate the image. Try it using the sample photo Harbor.jpg.

Watch Out!

These steps assume that you're working with a single-layer image. If your photo contains multiple layers, open the Layers palette and click the name of the layer you want to rotate before moving forward. To rotate multiple layers, link them as discussed in Chapter 8.

1. Display the rulers by pressing CTRL-R (Windows) or ⌘-R (Mac).

2. Press V to select the Move tool.

3. Drag from each ruler to display horizontal and vertical guidelines.

Position the horizontal guide near the horizon line, and put the vertical guide next to a structure that should be vertical, as shown in Figure 13.2. The guides will help you gauge how much to rotate the photo. (If guides don't appear when you drag from a ruler, choose View | Show | Guides.)

Figure 13.1: A tilting horizon line calls for an application of the Free Transform command.

Guide

Figure 13.2: Position guides at the horizon line and next to a structure that should be vertical.

Handle

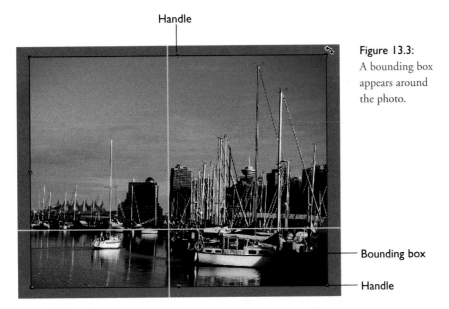

Figure 13.3:
A bounding box
appears around
the photo.

Bounding box

Handle

4. **Choose Select | All or press CTRL-A (Windows) or ⌘-A (Mac).**

Unlike most other commands, Free Transform requires this step, which selects
the whole image.

5. **Choose Edit | Free Transform.**

Time Saver

Or save time by pressing CTRL-T (Windows) or ⌘-T (Mac).

A solid outline called a *bounding box* surrounds your image, as shown in Figure 13.3.
Little squares known as *handles* appear around the perimeter. Don't see the handles?
Drag a corner of the window to enlarge it, and they should become more apparent.

6. **Move your cursor outside a corner handle to display the curved
rotate cursor, as shown in Figure 13.4.**

7. **Drag up or down to rotate the image and level the horizon line.**

As you drag, the image updates to preview the rotated photo, as shown in Figure 13.5.
In addition, the value in the Rotate box on the options bar changes to reflect the
degree of rotation. Figure 13.4 labels this control.

When the Rotate control is active—the number in the box appears highlighted—
you can press the up and down arrow keys to change the rotation angle one-tenth

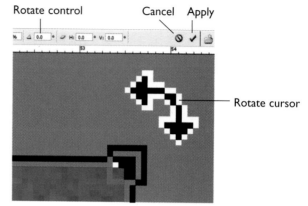

Rotate control   Cancel   Apply

Rotate cursor

Figure 13.4:
Position your
mouse outside
a corner handle
to display the
rotate cursor.

of a degree. Press SHIFT plus an arrow key to increase or decrease the value one degree. This technique makes precision rotating easier. Double-click the box to activate the control if it's not highlighted.

8. Press ENTER or click the Apply button on the options bar, labeled in Figure 13.4.

(Press ENTER twice if the Rotate control is active.) Photoshop applies the rotation, and the bounding box and related options bar controls disappear. To get rid of the selection outline, choose Select | Deselect or press CTRL-D (Windows) or ⌘-D (Mac). To lose the guidelines, choose View | Clear Guides.

Figure 13.5: Rotating
moves part of the
image off the canvas
and reveals the canvas
in some areas.

Figure 13.6: After a counterclockwise
rotation, the horizon is level and
vertical structures tilt no more.

9. Crop the image as needed.

Rotating the image moves some parts of the photo off the canvas and exposes
empty areas of canvas, as shown on the previous page in Figure 13.5. Crop the
image as explained in Chapter 4 to trim away empty canvas. Figure 13.6 shows
the final rotated and cropped sample image.

Watch Out!

Try to make this repair with one application of the Free Transform command. Each
time you rotate, Photoshop rebuilds the image, which can cause a slight loss of picture
quality. Obviously, you also should rotate the horizon line before doing any cropping
since the rotation process itself involves some cropping.

Figure 13.7: When you shoot with the lens pointing up, vertical lines may appear to lean inward, or converge.

Correcting Convergence

Convergence is a photographic phenomenon that creates the illusion that vertical structures lean either away from each other or toward each other, as shown in Figure 13.7. Also known as *keystoning,* the problem occurs when the camera lens isn't level with the horizon line.

Once again, the Free Transform command is the solution. In addition to its rotation function, this command enables you to distort the image in a way that alters perspective. Experiment with the sample image Boston.jpg, featured in Figure 13.7.

Watch Out!

Always apply this correction *before* cropping your photo. You lose some areas around the perimeter of the photo as a result of the transformation, so you want to start with as much of the original scene as possible. As with rotating, try to perform the entire correction with one application of the Free Transform command to retain as much picture quality as possible.

1. Choose View | Show | Grid to display gridlines over your image.

The grid, visible in Figure 13.8, enables you to easily monitor the vertical alignment of structures throughout the image.

2. Choose Image | Canvas Size and enlarge the image canvas by 40 percent.

When the Canvas Size dialog box opens, select the Relative check box and set the unit of measurement to Percent. Enter 40 into the Width and Height boxes, and click OK. You'll need the extra canvas when you distort the photo.

3. Choose Select | All or press CTRL-A (Windows) or ⌘-A (Mac) to select the entire image.

This instruction assumes that you're working with a single-layer image. To transform one layer in a multilayer image, click the layer name in the

Layers palette instead of choosing Select | All. To transform multiple layers, link them as explained in Chapter 8.

4. **Choose Edit | Transform or press CTRL-T (Windows) or ⌘-T (Mac).**

In Figure 13.8, you see the transformation bounding box and handles, introduced in the preceding section. If you don't see the handles, enlarge the image window.

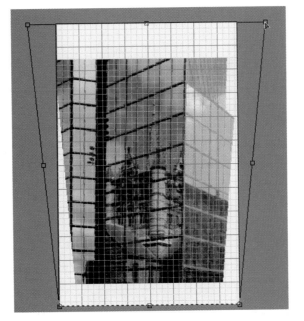

Figure 13.8: To adjust perspective, press CTRL-ALT-SHIFT (Windows) or ⌘-OPTION-SHIFT (Mac) as you drag a corner handle.

5. **Hold down the CTRL-ALT-SHIFT keys (Windows) or the ⌘-OPTION-SHIFT keys (Mac) as you drag a corner handle horizontally.**

When you drag, you apply a perspective change. As you move one handle, the opposite handle moves in tandem.

- Drag outward to tilt vertical structures away from each other. Go this direction for the sample image, tugging one of the top corner handles as shown in Figure 13.8.
- Drag inward to tilt structures toward the center of the image.

You may not be able to fix all structures with this one transformation, so release the mouse button when the most visually dominant structures no longer lean. In the sample image, focus on the thick black strip in the left half of the photo.

6. Apply further distortions as needed to complete the correction.

Depending on your photo, you may need to make further adjustments. For the sample image, drag the top center handle up to increase the height, as shown in Figure 13.9. (This step is often necessary after a large perspective shift.) Then

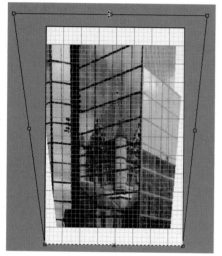

CTRL-drag (Windows) or ⌘-drag (Mac) the corner handles to the positions shown in Figure 13.10. By CTRL- or ⌘-dragging, you can move one handle without shifting the others, enabling you to distort the image freely.

For other adjustments, use the handle-dragging techniques listed in the upcoming Speed Keys table. Or enter values into the Width, Height, Rotate, and Skew controls on the options bar, labeled in Figure 13.11. Click the Proportional icon to resize the image without distorting its width-to-height ratio.

Figure 13.9: Drag up on the top center handle to increase image height as necessary after a perspective shift.

Figure 13.10: Dragging the handles to the positions shown here squared up the rest of the image.

If you don't like the results of your last handle-drag, press CTRL-Z (Windows) or ⌘-Z (Mac) or choose Edit | Undo to undo it. To undo everything and start over, press ESC.

Width Proportional icon Height   Rotate   Horizontal Skew   Vertical Skew

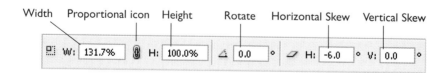

Figure 13.11: Instead of dragging handles, you can enter specific transformation values.

Figure 13.12: Expect to lose some original image area as the result of the transformation.

7. Do a final alignment check.

When you think you have things squared up, choose View | Show | Grid to hide the grid so that you can see your image more clearly. Then pull out a few guides to do a final alignment check at various points across the image, as shown in Figure 13.10.

Watch Out!

If critical areas of the photo have moved off the canvas, drag inside the bounding box to reposition the image on the canvas. Or cancel the transformation (press ESC) and enlarge the canvas more. Any pixels off the canvas will be lost after you apply the transformation in the next step.

8. When you're happy with the image, press ENTER or click the Apply button.

The Apply button, which looks like a check mark, lives at the right end of the options bar. (Refer to Figure 13.4, earlier in the chapter.)

9. Crop away any excess canvas.

Your corrected photo will have an irregular shape that no longer fills the entire canvas. Crop the image as explained in Chapter 4. Figure 13.12 shows the final sample image.

SPEED KEYS: Free Transform Shortcuts and Techniques

Action	Windows	Mac
Select the entire image	CTRL-A	⌘-A
Display the transformation handles	CTRL-T	⌘-T
Rotate the horizon line	Drag outside a corner handle	Drag outside a corner handle
Adjust perspective	CTRL-ALT-SHIFT-drag a corner handle	⌘-OPTION-SHIFT-drag a corner handle
Adjust height	Drag a top or bottom center handle	Drag a top or bottom center handle
Adjust width	Drag a side center handle	Drag a side center handle
Adjust size proportionately	SHIFT-drag a corner handle or click the Proportional icon and just drag	SHIFT-drag a corner handle or click the Proportional icon and just drag
Skew the image	CTRL-SHIFT-drag a center handle	⌘-SHIFT-drag a center handle
Distort the image freely	CTRL-drag any handle	⌘-drag any handle
Distort relative to the center point of the bounding box	ALT-drag a handle	OPTION-drag a handle
Move the image around the canvas	Drag inside the bounding box	Drag inside the bounding box

Sharpening Focus

No photo-editing program, even one as capable as Photoshop, can pull an extremely blurry image into sharp focus—no matter what you've seen people do in Hollywood spy thrillers. But when an image is only slightly soft, such as the flower in Figure 13.13, you can improve it through a process called *sharpening*. Figure 13.14 illustrates the results you can achieve.

You can approach sharpening in two ways:

- To sharpen an entire photo or a large region, rely on the Unsharp Mask filter.
- To sharpen very small areas, such as someone's eyes, try the Sharpen tool.

The next two sections walk you through both techniques. But before you try either, it's important to understand that

Figure 13.13: Camera shake caused a slight case of the blurs.

Figure 13.14: Sharpening creates the illusion of better focus.

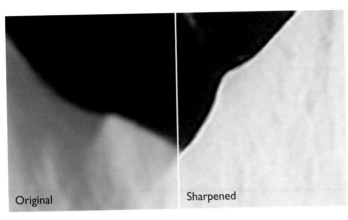

Original   Sharpened

Figure 13.15: Sharpening tricks the eye by increasing contrast in areas where one color meets another.

a sharpening filter doesn't really adjust focus. Instead, it increases contrast along the border where one color meets another, which tricks the eye into thinking that the picture is in sharper focus.

Figure 13.15, which features a magnified view of the flower petals, gives you a close-up look at the effect. The left half of the image is untouched; the right half was sharpened. Notice the light and dark halos that appear between the white petal and the green background in the right half? That's sharpening. Pixels on the light side of a color boundary get lighter; pixels on the dark side get darker.

Figure 13.16: Oversharpened photos have a sandpaper-like texture, with visible sharpening halos.

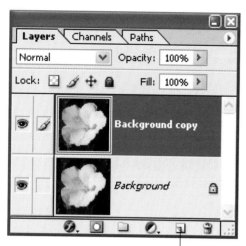

Figure 13.17: Always apply sharpening on a duplicate layer.

New Layer icon

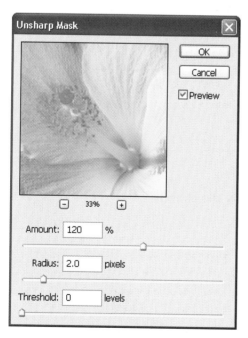

Figure 13.18: Click the plus and minus buttons to zoom the dialog box preview.

Applying the Unsharp Mask Filter

Click open the Filter | Sharpen submenu, and you'll find four sharpening filters: Sharpen, Sharpen More, Sharpen Edges, and Unsharp Mask. But only Unsharp Mask gives you control over how the effect is applied, so ignore the others.

The following steps explain the technique that I use for applying the Unsharp Mask filter, which involves sharpening on a duplicate image layer and then creating a layer mask. By painting on the layer mask, you then can vary the impact of the correction as needed throughout the image. To try the technique, open the sample image Hibiscus2.jpg, which is the blurry original from Figure 13.13.

1. Copy the area that needs sharpening to a new layer.

If your image contains just one layer and you want to sharpen the entire photo, drag the Background layer to the New Layer icon in the Layers palette, labeled in Figure 13.17. Go this route for the sample image. Otherwise, select the area you want to sharpen and then choose Layer | New | Layer via Copy or press CTRL-J (Windows) or ⌘-J (Mac).

2. Choose Filter | Sharpen | Unsharp Mask.

You see the Unsharp Mask dialog box, shown in Figure 13.18.

3. Select the Preview check box so that you can preview the effect in the image window.

Remember

Magnify the view in
the image window
by pressing CTRL-+
(Windows) or
⌘-+ (Mac). Zoom
out by pressing the
minus key instead
of the plus key.

You can preview the effect both in the image window and in the small preview inside the dialog box. Zoom the dialog box preview by clicking the plus and minus buttons underneath the preview; drag inside the preview to view a different part of the image.

If you set the dialog box preview to a magnified view, as shown in Figure 13.18, keep the view in the image window zoomed out. This enables you to keep an eye on both the overall image and the close-up details while you're sharpening.

4. **Use the Amount, Radius, and Threshold controls to adjust the sharpening effect.**

These controls work as follows:

- **Amount** The higher the value, the stronger the effect.
- **Radius** This value determines the thickness of the sharpening halos discussed in the preceding section. For print photos, values under 2.0 usually do the trick. On-screen images generally need narrower halos; anything more than 1.0 is typically too much.
- **Threshold** If you leave this set to 0, the sharpening is applied anywhere a color change occurs. Raise the value to limit the effect to areas of high contrast—*edges,* in Photoshop lingo. In portraits, try a value in the 3 to 5 range to sharpen without adding unwanted texture to skin. Also bump up the Threshold value if sharpening starts to bring out noise, grain, or compression artifacts in areas of flat color.

Don't worry if you have to slightly oversharpen some areas in order to get others into decent focus; you can tone down the oversharpened regions later. For the sample image, use the settings shown in Figure 13.18.

5. **Click OK to close the dialog box and apply the effect.**

6. **Evaluate the image.**

First, view the image at its intended output size. For a screen image, choose View | Actual Pixels; for a print image, choose View | Print Size. (Note that the latter view is just an approximation of the print size.) Then zoom in to inspect details. Look for areas that are oversharpened, exhibiting noticeable texture or obvious sharpening halos. For print images, you may want to make a test print to see how the image translates to paper. If everything looks fine, you're done.

Remember

After sharpening or blurring a layer, you can lessen the impact of the change by lowering the layer's Opacity value.

7. If necessary, use a layer mask to tone down oversharpened areas.

Chapter 8 details this process, but here's the quick story: Click the Layer Mask icon, labeled in Figure 13.19, to create the mask. Then select the Brush tool and paint with black on areas where you want to remove the sharpening effect. Set the tool opacity lower than 100 percent to simply make the sharpening effect more subtle. (Areas painted at a lower opacity appear gray in the mask thumbnail.)

In the sample image, paint with black around the perimeter of the flower, which has some too-obvious sharpening halos as a result of the Unsharp Mask settings I recommended in Step 4. Then dab with medium gray or black on parts of the flower petal that appear too rough. (If you see paint on the image itself, click the Mask thumbnail, labeled in Figure 13.19.) To restore the Sharpening effect, paint with white.

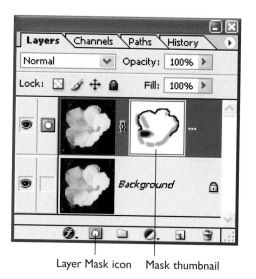

Figure 13.19: Paint with black on the layer mask to remove the effect from oversharpened areas.

Layer Mask icon   Mask thumbnail

The beauty of this technique is that you can concentrate on the softest areas when applying the filter, knowing that you can always lessen the sharpening in other areas by painting on the mask. And as long as you retain the sharpening layer and mask, you can revisit the image and adjust the effect by simply painting anew on the mask.

As an alternative, you can create a fading selection outline before applying the sharpening filter; use the technique outlined in the upcoming section "Creating a Graduated Blurring Effect." However, I find the layer mask option easier for sharpening because it's difficult to tell what areas need how much sharpening before you actually apply the filter.

Either way, when you're satisfied with the sharpening effect, merge the sharpened layer with the underlying image using the techniques discussed in Chapter 8.

Heightening Focus with the Sharpen Tool

With the Sharpen tool, labeled in Figure 13.20, you can sharpen simply by dragging over or clicking on the area you want to alter. I'm not terribly fond of this tool; I find its impact too unpredictable, which means a lot of trial and error to get the right amount of sharpening. The tool also doesn't offer the same range of control you get with Unsharp Mask—you can adjust the sharpening amount, but you don't get a Radius or Threshold option.

That said, I do regularly use the Sharpen tool for one bit of portrait retouching. I click once or twice on the eyeballs to make eyes "pop." I used this technique to create the lower example in Figure 13.21. This small change has a big impact; when the eyes are sharp, the entire photo appears more focused.

Using the Sharpen tool is simple:

1. Create a new layer above the layer you want to sharpen.

Just click the New Layer icon in the Layers palette (refer to Figure 13.17).

2. Select the Sharpen tool, labeled in Figure 13.20.

The tool shares a flyout menu with the Blur tool and Smudge tool.

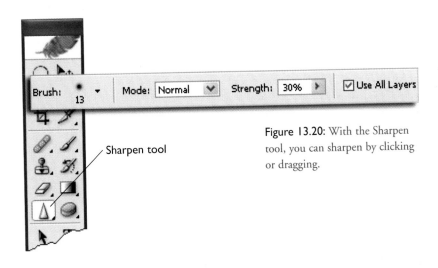

Sharpen tool

Figure 13.20: With the Sharpen tool, you can sharpen by clicking or dragging.

3. Set the brush options.

The Sharpen tool is a brush-based tool, so all the options covered in Chapter 5 apply. For eye sharpening, set the brush size just larger than the eyeball, and work with a slightly soft brush.

Set the Mode control to normal and lower the Strength value to 30 percent, as shown in Figure 13.20. The Strength value determines how much impact you make with each click or drag of the tool; the default setting of 50 percent typically produces too much change.

Figure 13.21: Sharpening the eyes makes the entire face seem more in focus.

Figure 13.22: Center
the Sharpen brush
over the eyeball and
click once or twice.

Tool Tricks

To sharpen or blur in a horizontal or vertical line, SHIFT-drag with the tool. To
sharpen or blur in a straight line at any other angle, click once at the start of the
line and then click again at the end. These same tricks work for any brush-based tool.

4. **Select the Use All Layers option.**

This step is critical; when the option is turned off, the Sharpen tool can't reach
pixels outside the new layer.

5. **Click or drag on the area you want to sharpen.**

If the sharpening effect isn't strong enough, click or drag again. For eyeball
sharpening, center the brush over the eye, as shown in Figure 13.22, and click
once or twice.

6. **Merge the sharpened layer with the underlying image as
explained in Chapter 8.**

Figure 13.23: I used the Gaussian Blur filter to soften the background, creating a shortened depth of field.

Blurring Focus

Whereas sharpening increases contrast along color boundaries, blurring reduces contrast to create the illusion of softer focus. By blurring a picture background, you can produce the effect of a reduced depth of field. Blurring also works wonders for softening laugh lines and diminishing digital camera noise, film grain, and compression artifacts.

The next three sections introduce you to three blurring techniques. If you use Photoshop 7, skip the third section, which discusses a filter found only in Photoshop CS.

Blurring Large Areas with Gaussian Blur

When you want to blur a large area, apply the Gaussian Blur filter as outlined in the following steps. I used this technique to produce an apparent shortening of depth of field in the sharpened flower image shown earlier, in Figure 13.14. Figure 13.23 shows the result.

1. Select the area that you want to blur, using the techniques outlined in Chapters 6 and 7.

2. Copy the selection to a new layer, as shown in Figure 13.24.

Just press CTRL-J (Windows) or ⌘-J (Mac). Or choose Layer | New | Layer via Copy.

3. Choose Filter | Blur | Gaussian Blur.

You see the Gaussian Blur dialog box, shown in Figure 13.24.

4. Use the Radius control to set the amount of blurring.

Select the Preview check box so that you can preview the effect in the image window as well as in the dialog box.

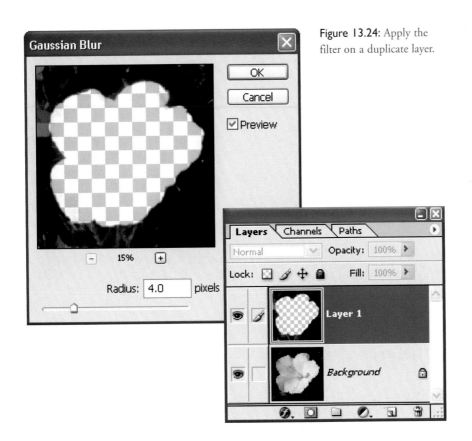

Figure 13.24: Apply the filter on a duplicate layer.

5. **Click OK to close the dialog box and apply the blur.**

6. **Evaluate and refine.**

The one hang-up with this and most blurring filters is that the effect often spills a little beyond the boundaries of your selection outline. To remedy the problem, use the Eraser tool on the blur layer, rubbing away areas where you don't want the blur effect. Or create a layer mask as outlined in the earlier section related to the Unsharp Mask filter. (Chapter 8 explores the Eraser and layer masks in detail.)

7. **Merge the blurred layer with the underlying layer; see Chapter 8 for details.**

These steps assume that you want a consistent blur over the entire selected area. For an easy way to produce a varied blur, check out the next section.

Figure 13.25: Use a gradient layer mask
to increase the strength of the blur in
areas farther from the focusing point.

Creating a Graduated Blurring Effect

The flower image featured in the preceding section presents a pretty easy example
of how to shorten depth of field. All the leaves in the background are about the
same distance from the subject, so you can apply the blur consistently throughout
the selected area.

Suppose, though, that the background contains objects at varying distances from
the area that you want to keep in sharp focus, as in the Market.jpg example

image shown in Figure 13.25. To realistically mimic the effect of shortened depth of field, the blur needs to become stronger as the distance from that focusing point increases.

You can create this effect by using a gradient (fading) layer mask as outlined in the following steps. The technique is similar to the one used to apply the Unsharp Mask filter, explained earlier in this chapter, except that this time, you create the mask before applying the effect. (For the full story on layer masks, check out Chapter 8.) Try the technique with the Market.jpg sample image.

1. Duplicate the Background layer.

Just drag the layer to the New Layer icon in the Layers palette or press CTRL-J (Windows) or ⌘-J (Mac). This step assumes that your image contains just one layer; if not, copy the layer that contains the area you want to blur.

2. Click the Layer Mask icon, labeled in Figure 13.26.

You see a white thumbnail next to the image thumbnail, as shown in the figure. This thumbnail represents the layer mask.

3. Set the foreground and background paint colors to black and white, respectively.

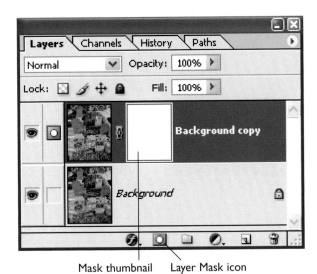

Figure 13.26: Add a layer mask as the first step in creating a fading blur effect.

Mask thumbnail   Layer Mask icon

Time Saver

When a layer mask is active, you can set the colors to black and white by pressing D and then X.

Figure 13.27: Use the Gradient tool to add a black-to-white gradient.

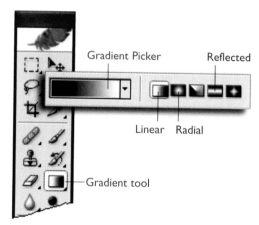

Gradient Picker

Reflected

Linear   Radial

Gradient tool

4. **Select the Gradient tool, labeled in Figure 13.27.**

5. **Open the Gradient Picker and select the foreground-to-background gradient.**

By default, this is the first gradient in the picker, which is labeled in Figure 13.27.

6. **Set the gradient style according to the fade pattern you want to produce.**

For the sample image, you want the blur to get stronger at the top of the image, so click the Linear icon, labeled in Figure 13.27. To create a blur that fades in a circular pattern, choose the Radial icon. To create a blur that fades in and out at the center of the image, click the Reflected icon.

7. **Drag to produce your gradient.**

Start your drag at the spot where you want the blur to begin fading in. Anywhere the gradient is black will not be blurred; anywhere the gradient is white will receive the full impact of the blur filter. Gray areas will receive a more subtle blur. (Don't worry about getting it perfect yet; you can refine the gradient later.)

For the sample image, drag from the bottom of the pink sign in the foreground to the top of the image, as shown in Figure 13.28. After you release the mouse button, a black-to-white gradient appears in the mask thumbnail, as shown in Figure 13.29.

8. **Click the image thumbnail next to the mask thumbnail.**

Your click tells Photoshop that you want to edit the image itself and not the mask.

Release mouse button

Figure 13.28: Drag in the image window to set the start and end points of the gradient mask.

9. Choose Filter | Blur | Gaussian Blur to open the Gaussian Blur dialog box.

You can see the dialog box in the preceding section, in Figure 13.24. Turn on the Preview check box so that you can preview the results of the blur.

Start of drag

Raise the Radius value as needed to produce the maximum amount of blur you want. For the sample image, set the value to 2.0. Again, don't worry now if the placement of the blur isn't right; just click OK to close the dialog box.

10. Adjust the layer mask if needed to refine the effect.

You can adjust the effect by editing the layer mask. First, click the mask icon (refer to Figure 13.26). Then paint on the mask with the Brush tool as follows:

- Paint with black to hide the blur. Lower the brush tool opacity to partially remove the blur. (Chapter 5 provides details about working with the Brush tool.)

Image thumbnail

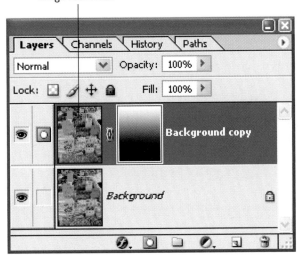

Figure 13.29: After you release the mouse button, your gradient mask appears in the Layers palette.

- Paint with white to reveal the blur. Again, if you lower the Brush tool opacity, you reveal the blur at a lower intensity.
- Redraw the gradient from scratch using the Gradient tool.
- You can even apply the Gaussian Blur filter to the mask, which softens the transition between blurred and unblurred regions.

To lessen the impact of the entire blur layer, reduce the Opacity value in the Layers palette. If you want to increase the maximum amount of blurring, click the image thumbnail and then reapply the Gaussian Blur filter. (Keep in mind that you can touch up small areas with the Blur tool later, which can be an easier solution in small areas.)

11. **When you're satisfied with the blur, merge the blur layer and underlying layer as discussed in Chapter 8.**

Time Saver

If you only want the blur to fade by a slight amount and you don't need precision, you also can opt to simply use a feathered selection outline instead of creating a layer mask. Create your outline, copy the area you want to blur to a new layer, and apply the filter. This technique is faster than creating a layer mask, but it may require a lot of experimentation with the feathering amount to get the effect you want. For that reason, I usually prefer the layer mask technique. For information about creating a feathered selection outline, flip back to Chapter 6.

Using the CS Lens Blur Filter

CS New to Photoshop CS, the Lens Blur filter is designed to simplify the job of producing a realistic reduction in depth of field. The filter provides you with more control than Gaussian Blur and also adds a few other related touches.

The best way to apply this filter is to first create a layer mask. You can use two approaches:

- **To produce a blur that becomes gradually stronger** Copy the area you want to blur to a new layer and then create a gradient layer mask as explained in the preceding section.
- **To produce a consistent blur** Copy the area you want to blur to a new layer and then click the Layer Mask icon in the Layers palette.

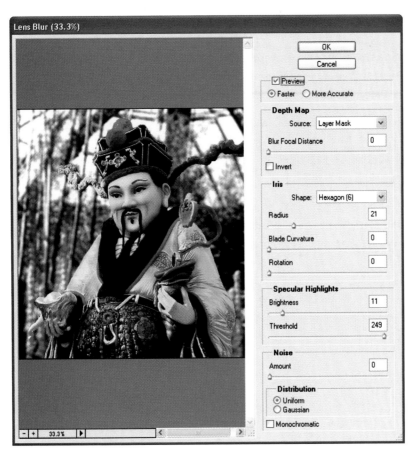

Figure 13.30: The CS Lens Blur filter offers features that can make shortening depth of field easier.

After creating your layer mask, click the image thumbnail (refer to Figure 12.29) and then choose Filter | Blur | Lens Blur. You then see the dialog box shown in Figure 13.30. Customize the blur effect as follows:

1. Select the Preview check box and the Faster option.

The previews in the dialog box take a *looong* time to update, especially with large image files, and the Faster option speeds things up.

2. Select Layer Mask from the Source drop-down list.

This option tells Photoshop to apply the blur according to the gradient mask you created (again, see the preceding steps for specifics). Leave the Blur Focal Distance at 0 for now and deselect the Invert box.

3. Use the Iris options to adjust the blur effect.

These options may make more sense if you understand that they're based on the iris of a real camera lens. If you're an experienced photographer, you may know that you get different depth-of-field effects depending on the iris design. Not much help? Just play with the different settings—there are no rights or wrongs. The Radius option controls the amount of the blur.

4. Adjust the focal point if needed.

Because you left the Blur Focal Distance value at 0 in Step 2, Photoshop applies the blur with respect to your layer mask. Black areas in the mask appear in sharp focus; white areas get the full blur effect; and gray regions (if any) receive a moderate blur. But if you click in the image preview, you move the focal point. Photoshop centers the zone of sharp focus over the spot you click. You can also move the Blur Focal Distance slider to adjust the effect.

5. Add specular highlights (optional).

Specular highlights—what some people refer to as blown highlights—are areas so bright that they're entirely white, with no tonal gradations. A real lens often produces specular highlights when you throw a bright area out of focus, so the Lens Blur filter offers you a way to fake this result. Nudge the Brightness value up and the Threshold value down until you get the highlights you want. Figure 13.31 shows an image blurred without (left) and with (right) the specular highlights effect.

6. Reintroduce noise (optional).

If your original image exhibited noticeable film grain, the blurred areas may look odd because blurring tones down that grain. To restore the texture match, add some grain to the blurred areas. You can do this with the Noise options, which are the same ones offered by the Add Noise filter introduced in the previ-

Figure 13.31: I blurred the background of the top image without adding any specular highlights; for the image below, I used the settings shown in Figure 13.30.

ous chapter. Experiment to see which options produce the best match with the surrounding image.

7. Click OK to close the dialog box.

You then can refine the effect by adjusting the layer mask; use the techniques presented in the preceding section and in Chapter 8.

8. Merge the blurred layer and the underlying image using the techniques covered in Chapter 8.

Softening Focus with the Blur Tool

When you click or drag with the Blur tool, you blur pixels underneath your cursor. Use this tool for making focus adjustments to small areas or when applying a blur filter would require lots of intricate selection or layer masking work.

The top image in Figure 13.32 offers an example of a perfect candidate for the Blur tool. Suppose that you wanted to shorten depth of field as shown in the bottom image. You could spend hours perfecting a selection outline or layer mask to precisely blur all the openings between the spokes. But you can make quick work of the job by simply

Figure 13.32: Use the Blur tool to soften focus in areas where drawing a selection outline or layer mask would be too time-consuming.

dragging over those areas with the Blur tool. The tool offers the full complement of brush options, so you can work with as small and soft a brush as necessary to get into nooks and crannies. You can also adjust the tool opacity as you work to make the blur weaker or stronger as needed.

The following steps show you how to use this tool. To work along with the steps, open the sample image Wheel.jpg.

1. Create a new layer by clicking the **New Layer** icon in the **Layers palette.**

Or choose Layer | New | Layer and click OK when the New Layer dialog box opens.

2. Select the **Blur tool,** shown in **Figure 13.33.**

The tool shares a flyout menu with the Sharpen and Smudge tools.

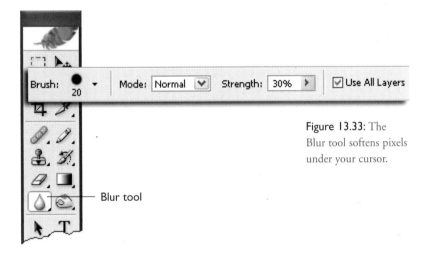

Blur tool

Figure 13.33: The Blur tool softens pixels under your cursor.

3. Set the brush options.

Establish the brush size, shape, and hardness as explained in Chapter 5. For the sample project, work with a small, round brush and set the Hardness value to 80 percent.

Until you understand how the Blur tool works, turn off Brush Dynamics (accessible via the main Brushes palette at the right end of the options bar). After you get familiar with the tool, you may want to turn the option back on if you work with a pressure-sensitive tablet. You then can vary the tool opacity just by adjusting pen pressure, as explained in Chapter 5.

4. Set the Mode option to Normal.

5. Set the Strength value to 30 percent.

Figure 13.34: Just drag over the area you want to blur.

As with the Sharpen tool, the Strength value determines how much change you produce with each click or drag. Start low—you can always apply the tool multiple times to the same pixels if needed.

6. **Turn on the Use All Layers check box.**

This option enables the Blur tool to see through your new layer, which will hold the blur information, and access pixels on underlying layers.

7. **Click on or drag over the pixels you want to blur, as shown in Figure 13.34.**

As you work, you can adjust the Strength value as needed to create more or less blurring with each swipe of the tool.

8. **When you finish blurring, merge the blur layer with the underlying image as discussed in Chapter 8.**

In addition to creating depth-of-field effects, you can use the Blur tool to soften small image defects such as digital camera noise, film grain, or compression artifacts. The Blur tool also acts as a great wrinkle-reducer when you're retouching portraits. For that use, try changing the tool Mode to Darken or Lighten:

- Use the Darken mode to soften light creases amid darker skin.
- Use the Lighten mode to reduce dark lines amid paler skin.

Try it out using the sample image LaughLines.jpg, shown in Figure 13.35. For the sake of experimentation, set the tool to Normal mode and dab at the laugh lines near the left eye. You merely get blurrier lines, not less noticeable lines, as shown on the left in Figure 13.36. Now switch to Lighten mode and work on the right eye. As shown in the right example of Figure 13.36, this mode does a much more capable job of fading dark lines in light skin. (Again, use the Darken mode if the lines are lighter than the surrounding skin.) The same trick works for removing dust, scratches, and other small defects.

Remember

If you mess up while editing a photo, press CTRL-Z (Windows) or ⌘-Z (Mac) to undo your last edit. See Chapter 4 for tips on undoing a series of blunders.

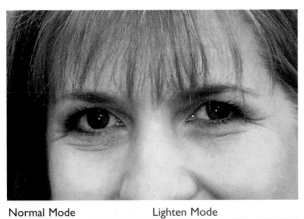

Figure 13.35: To try digital wrinkle-removal, open the sample image LaughLines.jpg.

Normal Mode   Lighten Mode

Figure 13.36: In Lighten mode, the Blur tool does a better job of softening dark wrinkles in light skin.

Tool Tricks

To quickly adjust the Strength value for the Sharpen and Blur tools, press the number keys. Press 0 for 100 percent, 9 for 90 percent, and so on.

Color Management Demystified

If you've read Chapter 2, you may recall that digital cameras, scanners, and monitors can generate colors beyond the printable spectrum, which is one reason why printed colors rarely match on-screen colors. To complicate matters, each monitor and printer puts its own spin on color. Display the same photo on 10 monitors, and you'll see 10 different renditions. Feed the same image to several printers, and no two prints will be exactly alike.

All this color confusion creates a dilemma: How do you make reasonable decisions when retouching your pictures if their appearance is subject to the whims of the output device? Keeping in mind that perfection isn't possible, you can improve color consistency significantly by implementing *color management*. This chapter explains how color management works and how to set it up in Photoshop.

Getting a Grip on Color Management

As explained in Chapter 2, every color in a digital photo is represented by a numeric value. The actual hue, brightness, and saturation you get from a particular value, however, depends on the device—monitor, printer, scanner, or digital camera. Each device has different capabilities, so the same value can produce a variety of colors. For example, the two images in Figure 14.1 offer an approximation of how colors shift when they move from my monitor to my inkjet printer.

The goal of a *color management system,* or CMS, is to find common ground so that colors remain as consistent as possible from input to output. A color management system involves two main components:

Figure 14.1: On-screen colors (left) appear more vivid than printed colors (right).

- ■ **Color Profiles** A color profile is a data file that describes the color characteristics of a device, using a universally accepted color reference standard. The International Color Consortium developed the standard, which is why profiles are known as *ICC profiles.*

Remember

With personal photo printers, severe color problems may indicate a depleted ink supply, clogged print heads, or incorrect printer settings. See Chapter 15 for specifics on setting up your print job.

- **Color Engine** Sometimes referred to as the *color management module,* or CMM, the color engine serves as the color translator. When an image moves from one device to another, the color engine looks at the profiles for both devices. Then it decides the best way to translate the values from the first device to the second.

Photoshop offers a sophisticated color management system—it's *fully ICC-compliant,* in the lingo of the color community. To implement the system, you take the following approach:

- First, you create or install color profiles for every device in your imaging chain.
- Next, you give the color engine specific instructions on how to apply profiles when opening and displaying your images.
- Before putting the finishing touches on your photo, you preview it using the output profile. You then tweak the image as needed to suit the output device.
- When printing, you specify the input profile and the printer profile so that Photoshop knows how to translate the colors from screen to paper.

The rest of this chapter explains the first three pieces in the color management puzzle; Chapter 15 explains the final part.

Before I give you my input, however, you should know that entire books have been written on this subject alone. The information in this book is designed to give you a foothold from which you can explore more of the color management landscape. If you're interested in color science or continue to have serious color problems even after working your way through this chapter, I recommend studying the many other resources available, including the Photoshop Help system. Just be prepared for your head to spin around its axis and perhaps twist clean off your neck. Yes, color can be that complex—who'd a thunk?

Profiling Your Monitor

Take a look at the background of the Photoshop program window. It's supposed to be neutral gray. But your monitor may be adding a tint to that gray—and to everything else on the screen. Figure 14.2, for example, shows a display with a serious green bias.

Figure 14.2: This screen shot was taken on a monitor that added a green color cast.

Figure 14.3: On a properly calibrated monitor, the program background is neutral gray.

Most monitors don't allow you to tweak the machine itself to remove a color cast. Instead, you use a calibration tool to create a monitor profile. Photoshop uses the profile to automatically adjust on-screen colors to neutralize monitor-related tints. Figure 14.3 shows the post-calibration version of the screen from Figure 14.2.

Profiling your monitor is the first step in putting color management in place. But even if you decide not to go further into color management, take this step so that you'll be viewing your images on a neutral canvas. Monitor calibration is quick and easy—what's more, a free calibration tool is available. For Windows users, Photoshop provides a tool called Adobe Gamma. On the Mac side, the operating system includes a calibration feature.

These tools provide on-screen instructions for getting the job done, so I won't insult your intelligence by plodding through the process click by click. You do need to take one important precalibration step, however: Allow your monitor to warm up for at least 30 minutes. Then just launch the calibration tool as follows:

- **Windows (Adobe Gamma)** Adobe Gamma is installed in the Windows Control Panel when you install Photoshop. To run Adobe Gamma, click the Windows Start button, click Control Panel, and then double-click the Adobe

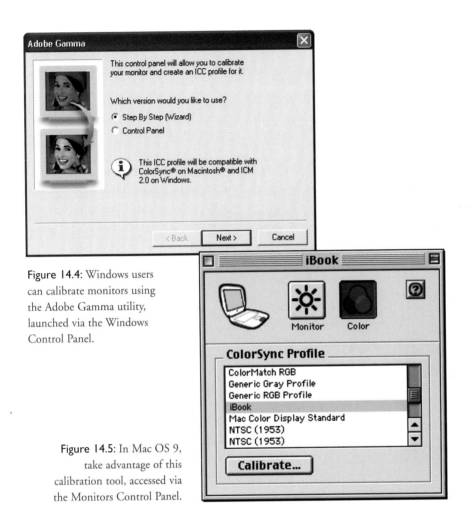

Figure 14.4: Windows users can calibrate monitors using the Adobe Gamma utility, launched via the Windows Control Panel.

Figure 14.5: In Mac OS 9, take advantage of this calibration tool, accessed via the Monitors Control Panel.

Gamma icon. You see the screen shown in Figure 14.4. Click Step By Step and then click Next.

- **Mac OS 9** Click the Apple menu, click Control Panels, and then click Monitors to display the dialog box shown in Figure 14.5. Click the Color icon, select your monitor type from the list, and click Calibrate.

- **Mac OS X** Click the Apple menu and then click System Preferences. In the resulting dialog box, click the Displays icon and then click the Color button to display the options shown in Figure 14.6. To simplify things, check the Show Profiles for This Display Only option. Then click the Calibrate button.

The drawback to these free utilities is that they depend on your eyes to make color, contrast, and brightness judgments during the calibration process. For a less subjective approach, you can purchase a device known as a *colorimeter*, which analyzes the display for you. Figure 14.7 shows a colorimeter from ColorVision.

Figure 14.6: In OS X, the System Preferences dialog box houses the calibration tool.

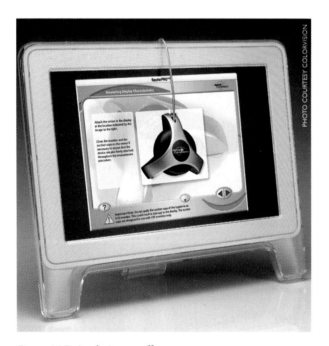

Figure 14.7: A colorimeter offers a more precise approach to monitor calibration.

Colorimeters start at about $150. In addition to ColorVision (www.colorcal.com), other respected manufacturers include X-Rite (www.xrite.com) and GretagMacBeth (www.i1color.com).

Watch Out!

Whichever calibration route you choose, repeat the process once a month. Displays drift over time, so your monitor profile can quickly become inaccurate. Also, if you build a Windows monitor profile with a colorimeter, consult the product manual to determine whether you should disable Adobe Gamma.

Profiling Your Printer

When you print an image, specifying a printer profile lets Photoshop best translate the image color information to the printer. Printer profiles also come into play when you use the program's soft-proofing feature, which enables you to preview printed colors.

Photoshop provides profiles for dozens of common printers, and many new printers add profiles when you install the printer software. To see what profiles are available, choose View | Proof Setup | Custom to display the Proof Setup dialog box and open the Profile drop-down list, as shown in Figure 14.8.

Depending on your printer, you may see several profiles, each specific to a type of paper (glossy, semigloss, watercolor, and so on). The paper stock impacts printed colors, so having paper-specific profiles is a good idea.

If you don't see profiles for your printer, you have several options:

■ Check the printer manufacturer's Web site. Some companies that sell photo

Figure 14.8: Ideally, you should install printer profiles for each type of paper you use.

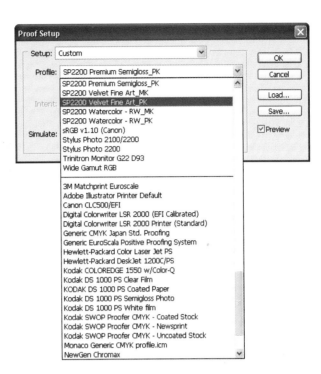

paper also make profiles available for using their products on certain printers. Follow the instructions on the Web sites for installing these profiles.

- If you're having your photo commercially printed, ask the company whether it provides profiles for its printer or press.
- Experiment with the generic profiles provided by Photoshop. The U.S. Web Coated (SWOP) v2 profile is a good all-around profile to try.
- Buy a profiling product such as Monaco EZColor, from Monaco Systems, or PrintFIX, from ColorVision. Although expensive—expect to pay $300 and up—these products enable you to create custom profiles, which usually provide more reliable results than the generic profiles from equipment manufacturers.

Again, Chapter 15 shows you how to specify a printer profile during the print process. You can read more about soft proofing and the Proof Setup dialog box at the end of this chapter. For now, just click Cancel to close the dialog box.

Profiling Your Scanner or Camera

If your digital darkroom includes a scanner, digital camera, or both, expert color management requires profiling them as well as your monitor and printer. The upcoming section "Color Management Policies" tells you how to pass on the profile information to Photoshop when you open files.

Many scanner and camera manufacturers don't provide profiles, however, so if you want a profile specific to your equipment, you'll have to purchase a profiling system such as those mentioned in the preceding section. As an alternative, you can use one of two generic RGB device profiles: sRGB or Adobe RGB. Some cameras and scanners enable you to "tag" image files with these profiles; if your equipment doesn't, you can simply add the tag when you open the file in Photoshop.

Here's what you need to know to choose between the two:

- **Adobe RGB** This profile is widely considered the best generic RGB profile because it defines a large spectrum, or *gamut,* of colors.
- **sRGB** This profile, which defines a smaller gamut than Adobe RGB, was developed as a joint effort by a variety of digital-imaging companies. The idea was to come up with a limited color palette that could be reproduced by all monitors and printers—the lowest common denominator, if you will.

Figure 14.9 gives you a look at the color variations that can occur between these two profiles. The image on the left is the Adobe RGB version; the image on the

right, sRGB. Of course, the differences you will see depend on the original subject colors. But Adobe RGB tends to deliver a broader, richer palette, which is why I prefer it. Some Web-only artists prefer sRGB because it increases the odds that everyone who views their work will see the same colors. The tradeoff is that sRGB does not encompass some printable colors. (Note that you can always create your original in Adobe RGB and then create an sRGB version for the Web.)

Figure 14.9: Adobe RGB (left) typically results in more vibrant colors than sRGB (right).

Watch Out!

One further caveat regarding digital camera profiles: As I mentioned in Chapter 1, many digital camera manufacturers include a color profile tag in the image metadata, sometimes referred to as EXIF metadata. Photoshop can read this tag when you open the image file. Unfortunately, the metadata tag often *does not* reflect the actual color profile used by the camera—many manufacturers just assign the generic sRGB tag. (There are technical reasons for this; manufacturers aren't purposely trying to screw you up.) So unless you're certain that the metadata tag is accurate, see Chapter 1 to find out how to tell Photoshop to ignore the tag. Then you can choose a profile when you open the file, as explained later in this chapter.

Figure 14.10: You can embed a profile when saving an image.

Embedding Profiles in Image Files

In Photoshop, you can select a color profile when you open an image. (Later sections in this chapter explain how.) When you save photos in certain file formats, including PSD, TIFF, and JPEG, you can store that profile as part of the image file. This is known as *embedding* the profile.

In Windows, simply check the ICC Profile box in the Save As dialog box, as shown in Figure 14.10. On a Mac, the option name is Embed Color Profile.

Embedding profiles is most helpful when you're sharing files with others. Everyone who opens the file then can use the same profile, thereby maintaining color consistency. But this assumes that people open the file in a program that supports color management. If not, the profile is simply ignored.

Even if you're not sharing files, embedding profiles is usually a good idea, although not absolutely necessary from a Photoshop perspective. If you embed the file, you'll be able to open an image five years from now and know exactly what color profile you used to create the image.

Watch Out!

There are some situations in which an embedded profile can screw up the works, however:

- Don't embed profiles in Web images. Profiles increase file size, and browsers can't take advantage of them anyway.
- If you're having your files commercially printed, ask the tech support contact whether or not to embed the file. This rule goes both for offset printers as well as for photo printers (such as a Fuji Pictography or Durst Lambda).

Establishing Color Management Settings

Understanding the concept behind color management is pretty simple—well, okay, not *simple* simple, but not quantum physics, either. Where things get miserably confusing is sorting through the options that Photoshop gives you for controlling its color management features.

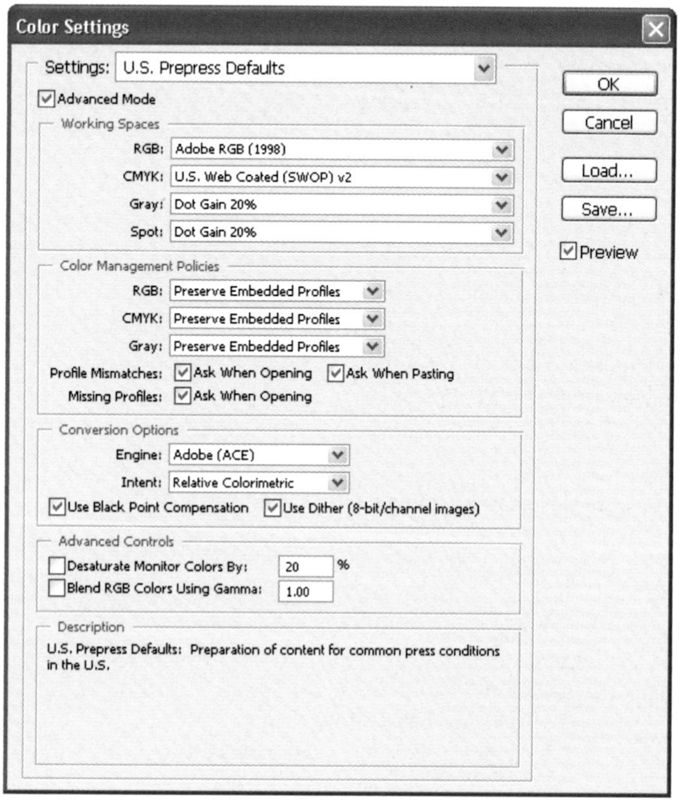

Figure 14.11: The Color Settings dialog box contains the primary color management options.

Command central is the Color Settings dialog box, shown in Figure 14.11. You access the dialog box via the Edit menu in Windows and in Mac OS 9; in OS X, choose Color Settings from the Photoshop menu. Select the Advanced Mode box to display all the options shown in Figure 14.11.

The next few sections discuss each option. But I want to take a quick detour here to let you know that this dialog box is the subject of intense debate, with very knowledgeable people disagreeing on which options provide optimum results. Before the dawn of digital imaging, photographers usually weren't involved in color management in a big way, so this stuff is pretty new to all of us. As everyone gains more experience, things should sort themselves out more definitively.

In the meantime, I'm recommending settings that I think provide the best combination of simplicity and good color for most users. The more you work with your own equipment, the more you'll be able to customize the settings to achieve a particular outcome.

Watch Out!

If you're part of a production workgroup, consult with the head honcho before adjusting *any* color management settings. Everyone in the workgroup needs to use the same settings, or the color train can jump radically off track.

The Settings Option

At the top of the dialog box, the Settings drop-down list simply enables you to select a predefined collection of color management settings.

- If you're working in the United States, choose U.S. Prepress Defaults.
- If you're working in Europe or Japan, choose the Defaults options for your country instead of the U.S. option.

Your dialog box should now show the options you see in Figure 14.11, which establishes a good starting base. In upcoming sections, I'll recommend tweaking a few of the options, after which the Settings control will change to Custom.

Working Spaces Options

The Working Spaces options, shown in Figure 14.12, determine the default profiles that Photoshop uses when no color profile is embedded or when you choose to forego color management. They also play a role in how the program converts an image from one color mode to another when you choose a command from the Image | Mode menu—for example, when you go from RGB to CMYK.

I recommend the following settings:

- **RGB** Choose Adobe RGB (1998). See my earlier description of this profile for more details.

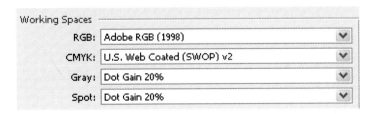

Figure 14.12: These Working Spaces settings work well for most folks.

- **CMYK** Stick with the default that appeared when you selected the Settings option. If you chose U.S. Prepress Defaults, for example, the CMYK option is U.S. Web Coated (SWOP) v2, as shown in Figure 14.12.
- **Gray and Spot** Use the defaults here as well unless you're working with a commercial printer. In that case, ask the printer rep for guidelines.

Color Management Policies

This section of the Color Settings dialog box, shown in Figure 14.13, determines what happens when you open an image file.

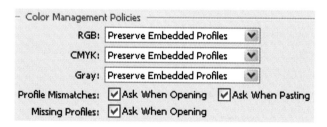

Figure 14.13: Choose these settings if you want Photoshop to alert you to missing or mismatched profiles when you open a file.

You can go in two directions: If you want to make a color profile decision every time you open a file, use the settings shown in Figure 14.13. Photoshop then uses embedded profiles *if* they match the profile you selected as your default working space. If the two don't match, you see the dialog box shown in Figure 14.14. You have the option of using the embedded profile, converting to the current working space, or discarding the profile and ignoring color management altogether.

If no profile exists, you instead see the dialog box shown in Figure 14.15. Again, you can forego color management, use the current working space, or assign some other profile. Choose the latter, and you also can choose to translate the colors from that assigned profile to your working space. You get these same choices if you try to paste a selection from one image to another and the images use different profiles.

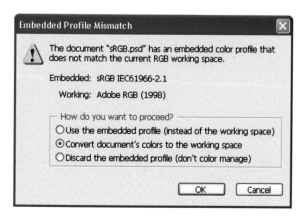

Okay, so now you know how you *should* do things. But if you're not sharing files with other people, going through this profile-picking rigmarole every time you open a file may be an unnecessary annoyance. You can save time by unchecking the Profile Mismatches and Missing Profiles boxes. Photoshop then automatically opens your files according to the settings in the three

Figure 14.14: You see this dialog box if the image profile is different from the default working space you selected.

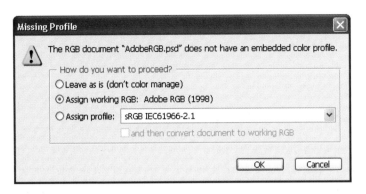

Figure 14.15: If no profile is embedded, you can assign one.

drop-down lists above the check boxes. You can specify a different policy for RGB, CMYK, and Grayscale photos. For each color model, you get three options:

- **Convert to Working (RGB, CMYK, or Gray)** Photoshop always uses the current working space, even if a different profile is embedded.
- **Preserve Embedded Profiles** Photoshop opens the image using the profile embedded in the image, if one exists. If not, the current working space takes hold.
- **Off** Photoshop doesn't apply any color management to the file.

Color Management Policies

RGB:	Convert to Working RGB
CMYK:	Preserve Embedded Profiles
Gray:	Off
Profile Mismatches:	☐ Ask When Opening ☐ Ask When Pasting
Missing Profiles:	☐ Ask When Opening

Figure 14.16: These settings are usually safe if you want Photoshop to open files without bugging you for profile information every time.

For most photographers who choose to go the automatic route, the settings shown in Figure 14.16 are appropriate.

Conversion Options and Advanced Controls

The final section of the Color Settings dialog box, shown in Figure 14.17, requires little discussion. (Thank goodness!) Change the Intent to Perceptual, and retain the default settings for everything else. I mean it, mitts off—you'll burn yourself.

Figure 14.17: Set the Intent to Perceptual, and leave everything else alone.

In case you're curious, the Intent option controls the *rendering intent,* which determines the exact method that Photoshop uses when translating color values between devices. You can read the description of each choice by pausing your cursor over the Rendering Intent option. Perceptual is the best choice for most photographic work.

Conversion Options

Engine:	Adobe (ACE)
Intent:	Perceptual
☑ Use Black Point Compensation	☑ Use Dither (8-bit/channel images)

Advanced Controls

☐ Desaturate Monitor Colors By:	20	%
☐ Blend RGB Colors Using Gamma:	1.00	

Soft Proofing: Previewing Output Colors

As you retouch your photographs, especially as you're doing color and exposure corrections, you should periodically *soft proof* the photo. Soft proofing adjusts the image display to approximate the colors as they'll appear when output to a specific printer. You also can preview how the image will look on a standard PC or Mac monitor that does not have your custom monitor profile—in other words, on most other people's screens.

The first step in soft proofing is to choose View | Proof Setup, which opens the submenu shown in Figure 14.18. Choose the option that corresponds to the machine on which the image will be printed or viewed.

- If you'll be converting your files to CMYK for output on a commercial press, choose Working CMYK. The soft proof then reflects the CMYK working space you set in the Color Settings dialog box. (Ask your printer for specifics on how to do the final file conversion.)
- For Web output, choose Windows RGB or Macintosh RGB to get an idea of how most Web viewers will see the image on a Windows PC or Macintosh computer. Check both previews; as you'll discover, images usually appear darker on a PC than a Mac, so you'll want to split the difference when correcting image brightness. (The Monitor RGB option uses your custom monitor profile, so it's not a good reference.)
- For output on a photo printer that works with RGB files—which includes your own office printer as well as the

Figure 14.18: Choose your final out-device (printer or monitor) from the Proof Setup submenu.

photo printers at some imaging labs—choose Custom to display the Proof Setup dialog box, shown in Figure 14.19. Choose your printer profile from the Profile drop-down list. Turn off the Preserve Color Numbers box, if it's available, and turn on the Preview box. (If you don't have a printer profile, just soft proof using the Working CMYK option.)

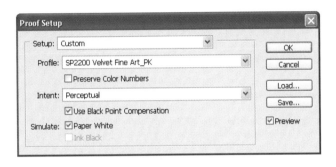

Figure 14.19: Be sure to turn on the Preview box when soft proofing your images.

Depending on which profile you choose, you have access to three additional options: Use Black Point Compensation, Paper White, and Ink Black. You'll need to experiment with some actual prints to see whether turning these options on or off provides a more accurate preview. But in general, it's best to turn them all on.

After establishing your settings, you can click Save to store them in a special Photoshop file. The file name then appears at the bottom of the Proof Setup submenu. This feature can save you time if you regularly print to many different printers or papers; you can simply select the proof options from the submenu instead of opening the Proof Setup dialog box.

Time Saver

After you select an option from the Proof Setup submenu, the Proof Colors option automatically becomes enabled. To toggle the soft proofing on or off quickly, choose View | Proof Colors or press CTRL-Y (Windows) or ⌘-Y (Mac). Photoshop displays the soft proof using the option currently selected in the Proof Setup submenu.

One final tip on soft proofing: If you choose an option from the Proof Setup submenu while no images are open, Photoshop uses that option as the default soft-proofing setting.

Print and Share Your Photos

For most of us, the real joy of photography comes with sharing pictures with others. And digital imaging makes it easier, cheaper, and faster than ever to get your photos out into the world. You can e-mail images to faraway clients or friends in minutes, and reach entirely new audiences through an online gallery. When you want prints to frame or sell, you can produce stunning results in your own studio or simply deliver your image files to a local lab for output. No more nasty darkroom fumes. No more wasting money on processing and printing those inevitable clunkers in every roll of film.

This chapter shows you how to prepare your best images for their journey to print or the Web. You'll also find information about Photoshop tools that simplify the job of creating contact sheets, picture packages, and online galleries.

Making Beautiful Prints

Whether you print your own photos or hand the job to someone else, you need to take a few steps to prepare your image files. The next few sections give you the low-down. If you haven't read Chapter 14, explore it as well to find out how to achieve more accurate screen-to-print color matching.

Setting Print Size and Resolution

As explained in Chapter 2, print quality is greatly affected by output resolution, which is measured in pixels per inch (ppi). How many pixels you need for good prints depends on the printer.

- If you're using your own printer, check your printer manual or the manufacturer's Web site for recommendations. Most home and office printers do their best stuff with about 300 ppi; some Epson printers suggest 360 ppi, however. Note, too, that most printers don't demand that you be spot on with resolution; you probably won't notice much difference between 300 ppi and 280 ppi, for example.
- If you're taking your files to a lab, consult with the service rep. Some labs ask for only 200 ppi. Be sure to follow the lab guidelines, or your order may not be output correctly.
- If you're submitting files for use in a publication, get resolution guidelines from the production artist. The norm is 300 ppi, but as we both know, not everyone is normal. You may need to submit a particular photo size as well.

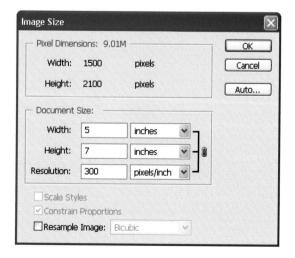

To establish output resolution and print dimensions, take these steps:

1. Choose Image | Image Size.

You see the Image Size dialog box, shown in Figure 15.1.

2. Uncheck the Resample Image box at the bottom of the dialog box.

Figure 15.1: Turn off the Resample Image check box to avoid altering the pixel count.

3. Enter the desired dimensions in the Width and Height boxes.

The Resolution value updates automatically to show you how many pixels per inch you'll get at the specified size.

- If the Resolution value is too low, you can either reduce the print dimensions or add pixels. Adding pixels won't improve print quality, however, and in fact may reduce it. See Chapter 2 for details.
- If the Resolution value is too high, you can eliminate excess pixels without doing much damage to the image. However, you may be able to skip this step if you're using your own printer; experiment to see whether print quality suffers noticeably when you send the printer an overage of pixels.

To adjust resolution by changing the pixel count, select the Resample Image box, turn on the Constrain Proportions box and, if available, the Scale Styles box (CS only). Finally, select Bicubic from the drop-down list next to the Resample Image box and then type the new Resolution value.

CS In CS, use Bicubic Smoother instead of Bicubic if you're adding pixels. Bicubic Sharper is designed for downsampling—eliminating pixels—but because it sometimes oversharpens, I suggest that you stick with plain old Bicubic.

4. Click OK to close the dialog box.

Watch Out!

If you resampled the photo in Step 3, save the resized image under a different name from the original. You may want the image at its original pixel count some day.

Printing from Photoshop

Follow these steps to print a photo on your own printer:

1. Choose File | Print with Preview to display the Print dialog box.

2. Select the Show More Options box and choose Color Management from the neighboring drop-down list.

You see the options shown in Figure 15.2. (When you select Output instead of Color Management, you get controls related to outputting images on a commercial press.)

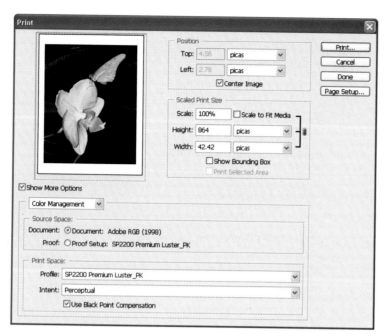

Figure 15.2: Select Document as the Source Space and choose your printer profile as the Print Space (in the Profile drop-down list).

3. **Click the Page Setup button to open the Page Setup dialog box and set the paper size and orientation.**

The dialog box differs depending on your operating system; you can see the Windows and Mac OS X versions in Figure 15.3.

Regardless of your system, you should be able to set the paper size and print orientation—Portrait (vertical) or Landscape (horizontal). On the Mac side, leave the Scale value (sometimes called Reduce or Enlarge) at 100 percent.

The Page Setup options reflect your currently selected printer. In OS X, you can select a printer directly from the Page Setup dialog box. In OS 9, you must select the printer via the Chooser. In Windows, click the Printer button to select a different printer.

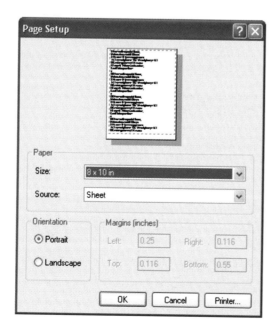

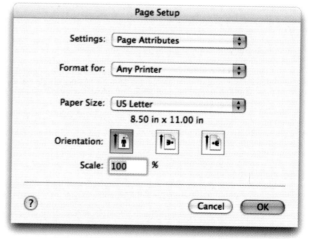

Figure 15.3: Choose paper size and print orientation from the Page Setup dialog box, shown here for Windows XP (left) and OS X (right).

4. Click **OK** to close the **Page Setup** dialog box and return to the **Print** dialog box.

5. Use the **Position** controls to position the image on the paper.

If you deselect the Center Image check box, you can access the Top and Left boxes to position the image precisely.

6. Deselect the **Scale to Fit Media** box (in the **Scaled Print Size** area).

This option and its adjacent controls adjust the print size to match a specific media size. You should instead set the output size (and resolution) as explained in the preceding section.

7. Set the **Color Management** options (**Source Space** and **Print Space**).

- ■ Choose Document as the Source Space.
- ■ Select your printer profile from the Profile drop-down list. Choose Perceptual from the Intent drop-down list and turn on the Use Black Point Compensation option.

These options provide the color profile information that Photoshop needs to best translate the on-screen colors to print. For the full story, see Chapter 14.

8. Click **Print** to display another **Print** dialog box.

Again, the dialog box depends on your operating system. Figure 15.4 shows the Windows version; Figure 15.5 shows the Mac OS X version.

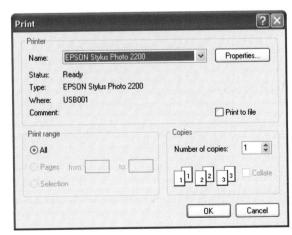

Figure 15.4:
In Windows, click the Properties button to access printer-specific options.

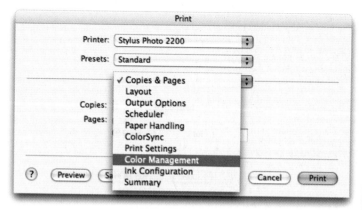

Figure 15.5: In OS X, all printer options are accessible via the Copies and Pages drop-down list.

Figure 15.6: Turn off printer color management and let Photoshop handle the job.

9. Specify your printer options.

Access the options as follows:

- **Windows** Click the Properties button.
- **Mac OS X** Open the Copies and Pages drop-down list and select a category of options, as shown in Figure 15.5.
- **Max OS 9** Check your printer manual; this step varies depending on your printer.

Every printer offers different options, so consult your manual to find out what each setting does and experiment to see what combination of options provides the best results. Figure 15.6 shows the multitude of controls available for an Epson 2200 as they appear in Windows.

Watch Out!

Two warnings apply regardless of your printer model:

- Turn printer color management *off*, if that control is available. Otherwise, both Photoshop and the printer try to color manage the image, which can lead to problems.
- Select the media setting that matches your paper stock. Most printers adjust printing based on that setting, and a mismatch usually leads to improper colors or saturation.

10. In Windows, click OK to close the Properties dialog box.

11. Click Print to send the image file to the printer.

HotelView2.JPG	PICT0100.JPG	PICT0105.JPG	PICT0107.JPG
PICT0108.JPG	PICT0111.JPG	PICT0122.JPG	PICT0131.JPG
PICT0137.JPG	PICT0142.JPG	PICT0149.JPG	PICT0152.JPG
PICT0185.JPG	PICT0219.JPG	StanleyParkSunset.tif	SuspensionBridge2...

Figure 15.7: Use the Contact Sheet utility to print thumbnails of a batch of images.

Printing Picture Packages and Contact Sheets

Photoshop offers two great print-related time-savers: Picture Package simplifies the job of printing the same picture at different sizes on a single piece of paper; and Contact Sheet enables you to print thumbnails for a group of images, as shown in Figure 15.7.

These features work the same way:

1. **Select the files that you want to include in the picture package or contact sheet.**

v.7 ■ In Version 7, place the files into a separate folder. You can do this in the File Browser. The folder should contain *only* the pictures that you want to include.

CS ■ In CS, open the File Browser and select the file thumbnails. Click the first thumbnail and CTRL-click (Windows) or ⌘-click (Mac) the others.

2. **Select the utility that you want to use.**

v.7 ■ In Version 7, choose File | Automate and then choose either Picture Package or Contact Sheet II.

CS ■ In CS, choose the commands from the Automate menu at the top of the File Browser.

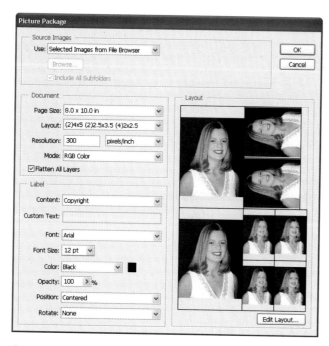

Figure 15.8: Use the Picture Package utility to print the same image at multiple sizes.

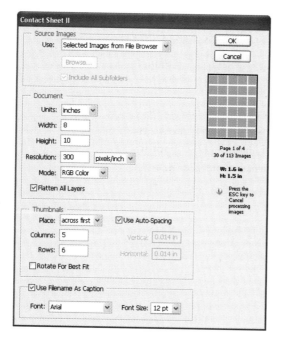

Either way, you see a dialog box in which you can customize the picture package or contact sheet. Figure 15.8 shows the Picture Package dialog box; Figure 15.9 shows the Contact Sheet II dialog box.

3. Use the dialog box options to customize the print layout.

I'm sure that someone with your smarts can figure out most options, but two may need explanation:

- Set the Resolution value to the optimum output resolution suggested by your printer manual. (See the earlier section "Setting Print Size and Resolution" for guidance.)

v.7

- In Version 7, click the Browse button (Windows) or Choose button (Mac) at the top of the dialog box to select the folder that contains your images.

4. Click OK.

Photoshop creates a new canvas and then opens each image and processes it to fit the picture package or contact sheet. Your original image files are *not* altered.

You can save and print the resulting contact sheet image in the usual ways. Both Picture Package and Contact Sheet create a two-layered image, so you may want to choose Layer | Flatten Image before saving the file. (The bottom layer is empty, so there's no point in holding on to it.)

Figure 15.9: To include filenames on contact sheets, select the Use Filename As Caption option.

Remember

Don't convert RGB images to CMYK if you're printing on your own photo printer. Although your printer uses CMYK inks, it's engineered to output RGB files.

Preparing Files for Commercial Printing

Before sending your photos to a lab or commercial printer, ask the service rep the following questions so that you can properly prepare your files:

- **What resolution (ppi) should I use?** Set the resolution and print dimensions as explained in the first section of this chapter.
- **Should I convert from RGB to CMYK?** Most photo labs request RGB, but for commercial presses, you'll probably need CMYK. If the printer wants CMYK, ask for guidelines in doing the conversion. For black-and-white printing, Grayscale may be the order of the day. See Chapter 2 for more about RGB, CMYK, and Grayscale.
- **What file formats can you accept?** Some printers accept Photoshop (PSD) files, but the most commonly used print format is TIFF. See the next section to find out how to save a TIFF version of your image.
- **Should I embed color profiles?** Some printers don't like profiles; others are happy to get them. If profiles are preferred, ask the rep whether you can get a printer profile so that you can soft proof your image accurately. (Head to Chapter 14 for details about color profiles.)

Finally, if you have a decent photo printer, it's a good idea to print a proof of your photo to give the printer a better idea of the colors you're after. Keep in mind that you shouldn't expect a perfect color match, however.

Saving TIFF Files for Publishing Use

Preparing a photo for publication in a newsletter, book, ad, or other document? You need to save the file in a format that's recognized by the program used to put the piece together. A few programs can work with the Photoshop (PSD) format, but TIFF is the safest bet. Even word processing programs accept TIFF files.

Watch Out!

The following steps show you how to save a TIFF copy of your photo. If your photo contains layers or alpha channels and you haven't yet saved the image in the PSD format, do so *before* you create your TIFF file. Choose File | Save As and select PSD as the file format. Be sure to select the Layers and Alpha Channels boxes. (See Chapter 4 for details about the other options in the Save As dialog box.)

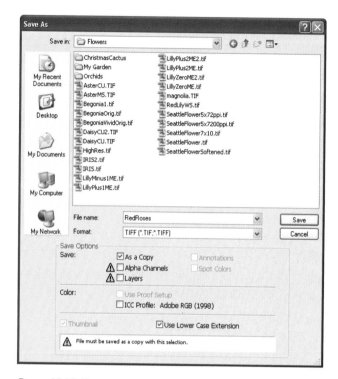

Figure 15.10: To ensure compatibility with other programs, turn off Alpha Channels and Layers when saving TIFF files.

With your PSD copy preserved, take these steps:

1. Choose File | Save As to display the Save As dialog box.

Figure 15.10 shows the Windows version of the dialog box. The Mac version contains the same basic options. (For details, see Chapter 4.)

2. Choose TIFF from the Format drop-down list and give the file a name.

3. Specify the other file-saving options.

Only a few programs—notably, those from Adobe—can work with files that contain layers and alpha channels. Presumably, you took my advice at the start of the steps and saved a PSD copy of the file that will preserve those features, so disable the Alpha Channels and Layers options here if they're available. The As a Copy box then automatically becomes selected.

Photoshop displays yellow warning triangles to remind you not to turn off that As a Copy box.

I'll leave the choice to embed the color profile up to you; for help in making the decision, see Chapter 14. (Some professional print applications can read profiles; most consumer programs can't.) On a Mac, you also can choose to include image previews and append the three-letter Windows file extension; Chapter 4 details these options.

4. Click Save to display the TIFF Options dialog box, shown in Figure 15.11.

Set the options as follows:

- **Image Compression** These options *compress* the image—which means to eliminate some data in order to shrink the image file. LZW compresses the file without harming image quality, but some programs gag on files that use this option. For maximum compatibility, choose None. (ZIP and JPEG aren't good choices in any circumstance.)

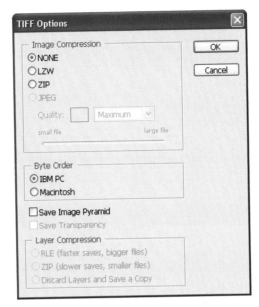

- **Byte Order** Don't worry about what this one means—just choose IBM PC if you'll be using the image on a Windows system and Macintosh if you're going the other way. Most programs can open files saved in either byte order, however.

- **Save Image Pyramid** This option stores the image in several resolutions within the same file. It's a Web-related feature, and most print programs can't deal with it.

5. Click OK.

Photoshop creates the TIFF version of your file. If you saved the file with the As a Copy option enabled, the PSD version of the file remains open and the TIFF file is stored in the folder you specified in Step 3.

Preparing Photos for the Web

To prepare an image for a Web page or any other on-screen use, don't follow the same approach as for printed pictures. You must set the image size differently and save the file in the JPEG format, not TIFF or PSD. The rest of this chapter walks you through the necessary screen-prep steps.

Setting the Display Size

Output resolution—ppi—is irrelevant for screen pictures. For reasons detailed in Chapter 2, the size at which a picture appears on-screen depends only on the image pixel dimensions and the monitor resolution. For example, at a monitor resolution of 800 x 600, an 800 x 600-pixel image fills the screen. You get the *exact same display size* whether ppi is 72 or 300 or 3000.

If you shot or scanned your photo at a high resolution, it will have way too many pixels for screen use. So you need to dump most of those pixels—*downsample,* in imaging lingo. Walk this way:

1. **Save a copy of the image in the PSD format.**

Watch Out!

Don't skip this step! You may need all your original pixels back some day. If your image contains layers or alpha channels, enable the appropriate check boxes in the Save As dialog box when you save your PSD file. Later, you'll need to save your file in the JPEG format, which can't retain those features.

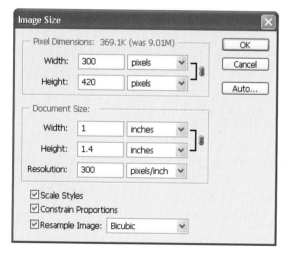

2. **Choose Image | Image Size to display the Image Size dialog box.**

3. **Select the Resample Image check box, as shown in Figure 15.12.**

4. **Choose Bicubic from the adjacent drop-down menu.**

This option determines the algorithm that Photoshop uses when downsampling the image. Bicubic typically produces the best results.

Figure 15.12: For screen pictures, set image size in pixels.

CS also offers Bicubic Sharper, which is designed to deliver a sharper downsampled image. The problem is that some areas may appear oversharpened. I usually stick with Bicubic and then apply the Unsharp Mask filter after setting the image size if needed. Chapter 13 discusses sharpening.

5. **Select the Constrain Proportions box and the Scale Styles box, if available.**

6. **Enter the new pixel dimensions.**

Use the top pair of Width and Height controls, in the Pixel Dimensions area of the dialog box.

7. **Click OK.**

After setting the image size, choose View | Actual Pixels to view the photo at the size it will appear on a screen that's using your same monitor resolution.

Time Saver

When you explore the next section, you'll discover that you can also change the pixel dimensions inside the Save for Web dialog box. This feature enables you to set the image size and save the file in the JPEG format in one step. The downside is that you don't then have the opportunity to apply the Unsharp Mask filter before saving the image. For important images, I always set the size with Image Size, sharpen with Unsharp Mask, and then use Save for Web to save the file. But for casual work, feel free to save a few seconds and do everything with Save for Web.

Saving JPEG Files

Save images headed for the Web in the JPEG format; browsers and e-mail programs can't open TIFF or PSD files. Also go JPEG for pictures that you plan to use in multimedia presentations.

JPEG earned its status as the leading online photo format because it produces smaller files than TIFF, PSD, and many other formats. To shrink files, JPEG applies *compression,* a process that eliminates some image data.

Compression comes in two forms:

- *Lossless compression* dumps only redundant image data and so does no visible harm to picture quality. LZW compression, available when you save in the TIFF format, is a lossless compression scheme.
- *Lossy compression* is less discriminating and can lead to a loss of image detail. JPEG uses this type of compression.

Watch Out!

When you save a JPEG file, you can specify how much compression you want to apply. The greater the compression, the more your image quality suffers. An over-compressed photo has a blocky look and is littered with *artifacts*—color defects that are most noticeable in areas of flat color.

Figure 15.13 compares an image saved with minimum JPEG compression to one saved with maximum compression. The highly compressed version has a much smaller file size—always a goal for Web images—but the photo looks awful. Figure 15.14 shows a close-up segment of both examples.

Figure 15.13: Lightly compressed JPEGs (left) look fine; heavy compression destroys image quality (right).

Minimum compression, 154K

Maximum compression, 9K

Figure 15.14: Overly compressed images have a "tiled" look.

Minimum compression

Maximum compression

Remember

You may be able to soften the impact of JPEG artifacts by using the blurring techniques discussed in Chapter 13.

As the photographer, you'll have to decide how much quality you're willing to trade for smaller files. Fortunately, Photoshop provides a *JPEG optimization tool* that helps you find the right balance. Take advantage of it as follows:

1. With your image open, choose File | Save for Web to open the Save for Web dialog box, shown in Figure 15.15.

2. Click the 4-Up tab at the top of the dialog box.

This enables you to compare your original image with a JPEG version at three different compression settings. The top-left preview shows the original image. By default, the top-right preview is selected, which means it will reflect the settings you choose next.

Hand tool

Zoom tool

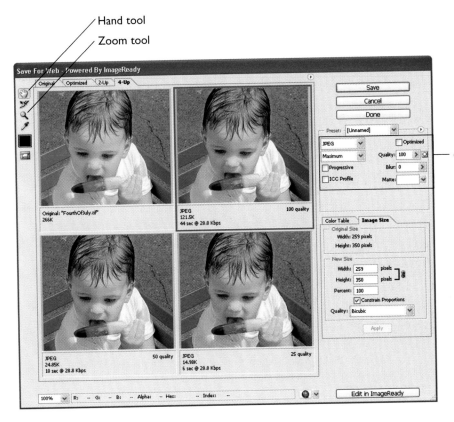

Compression options

Figure 15.15: Save for Web enables you to see how your image will appear at various compression amounts.

Format   Quality options

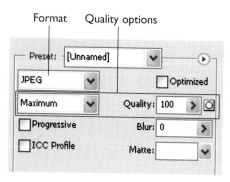

Figure 15.16: These options
control the file format and
compression amount.

3. Use the Zoom and Hand tools to adjust the area shown in the previews if needed.

Figure 15.15 labels these tools. Click a preview with the Zoom tool to zoom in; ALT-click (Windows) or OPTION-click (Mac) to zoom out. Drag in the preview with the Hand tool to scroll the image.

4. Choose JPEG from the Format menu.

Look for this menu in the area of the dialog box labeled Compression Options in Figure 15.15. An enlarged view appears in Figure 15.16.

5. Use the Quality settings to specify the compression amount.

Watch Out!

Pay attention here: The higher the Quality setting, the less compression you apply—because less compression means a better image. Quality settings range from 100 (least compression, largest files, best images) to 0 (maximum compression, smallest files, stinky images). Either specify an exact value using the Quality option or choose one of the quality ranges from the drop-down list to the left (Maximum is selected in Figure 15.16).

Ignore the little icon to the right of the Quality option. It enables you to use a mask to apply more or less compression to a specific area of an image. You probably won't affect file size much, and using two compression levels in the same image may create odd visual breaks.

6. Disable the other JPEG options.

- Turn off the Progressive, ICC Profile, and Optimized options, which can cause conflicts with some older browsers.
- The Blur option blurs the photo in a way that permits more compression. Unless you want a blurrier photo, leave the value at 0.
- The Matte option comes into play only if the bottom layer of your image contains transparent pixels. Transparent pixels will become the matte color that you select. If you choose None, they become white. Experienced Web designers sometimes set the matte color to match the Web page background so the areas of the photo that were transparent appear to be part of the background.

Click to open Preview menu

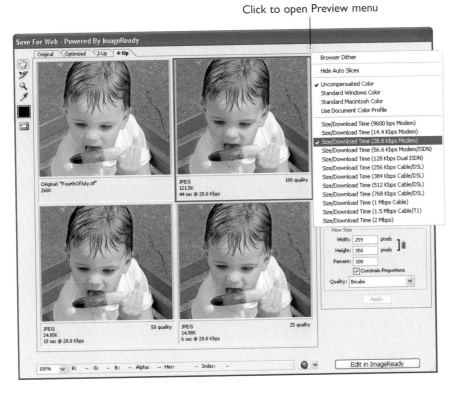

Figure 15.17: Select 28.8 Kbps to see how long your file will take to download over a slow dial-up modem.

7. **Open the Preview menu, labeled in Figure 15.17, and specify a modem speed.**

Underneath each preview, Photoshop shows you both the estimated file size and the download speed at the selected quality setting. Download speed is based on the option you select from the Preview menu. Choose 28.8 Kbps, as shown in the figure—this is the slowest speed at which most people access the Web today. Prepare images with this lowest common denominator in mind.

The color options on the menu enable you to preview the image as it will appear on Windows and Macintosh monitors. A better idea is to soft proof images before saving them, as discussed in Chapter 14, and use the Uncompensated Color option here. (The Use Document Color Profile option displays the file as it would be if you embedded a color profile, which I don't recommend for Web photos.)

8. **Compare the previews.**

After you specify the compression amount, Photoshop updates the previews. The top-right preview reflects your chosen compression settings. The other two previews show you how the image would appear at two lower-quality settings. To change the settings associated with any preview, click the preview and then adjust the Quality options.

Remember

Every time you edit and save a file in the JPEG format, it gets compressed again, resulting in more image damage. So never save works-in-progress in this format—always work in PSD. Save the JPEG version only when the file is finished and ready for its screen debut.

9. Click the preview that reflects the settings you want to use.

10. Click Save.

You're whisked to the Save Optimized As dialog box, a variation of the standard Save As dialog box. The dialog box design depends on your computer operating system; Figure 15.18 shows the Windows variety.

Figure 15.18: Select Images Only as the file type and stick with the Default Settings option.

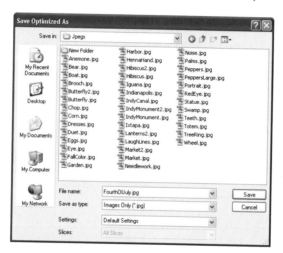

After naming the file and selecting the save location, set the Save as Type option to Images Only. Select Default Settings from the Settings drop-down list. (Other options here enable you to save an HTML file with or without the JPEG file. If you're an experienced Web designer, you may want to explore these features.)

Watch Out!

If you started out with a JPEG file, be sure to give this file a new name! Otherwise, you'll overwrite the original.

11. Click Save again.

Photoshop creates and saves the JPEG version of your file. The file does not appear on-screen; if you want to see it, open it in the usual way. Your original image remains open.

Time Saver

Using the controls on the Image Size tab of the dialog box, you can specify the pixel dimensions of the image at the same time you save the photo. (Refer to Figure 15.15.) As mentioned earlier, I don't recommend this option for important photos because you lose the chance to sharpen images after the resampling, but for quick projects, it's fine. Be sure to select Constrain Proportions and click Apply after you enter the new pixel dimensions. The Quality option here determines the resampling algorithm; see the preceding section for specifics.

Avoiding Save for Web Color Shifts

Take another look at Figure 15.17. Notice anything unusual? Colors in the original image (top-left preview) are slightly more intense than in the three JPEG previews. The issue has to do with the sRGB color profile, introduced in Chapter 14. This profile defines a spectrum of colors that supposedly can be reproduced in all Web browsers on all computer monitors.

Watch Out!

When you use another RGB profile as your working space—including the recommended working space, Adobe RGB—colors can sometimes shift when you use Save for Web. This occurs because Save for Web assumes that you're sending it an sRGB file, and sRGB offers a more limited color gamut than other RGB profiles.

If this color discrepancy disturbs you, you can usually get a little closer to your original colors by officially converting the image to the sRGB profile before you head to the Save for Web dialog box. Follow these steps:

1. **Save your image in the PSD format as a backup.**

2. **Choose Image | Mode | Convert to Profile.**

The dialog box shown in Figure 15.19 appears.

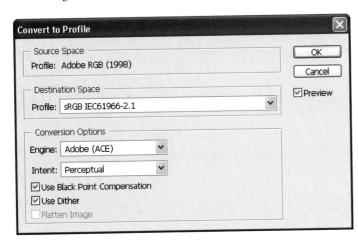

Figure 15.19: To reduce the color shifts that can happen with Save for Web, convert the image to the sRGB color space first.

3. **Select sRGB from the Profile drop-down list, as shown in the figure.**

4. **Set the Conversion Options.**

Set the Engine to Adobe (ACE) and select Perceptual as the Intent. Select the Use
Black Point Compensation and Use Dither boxes. If your image contains layers,
also select the Flatten Image box.

5. **Click OK.**

6. **Use Save for Web as outlined in the preceding section.**

7. **Close your PSD image without saving it.**

> **Watch Out!**
>
> The Convert to Profile command officially converts the file to the sRGB space. You
> want to make this change only for your Web image, not to the original. So don't save
> the original when closing it. As an alternative, choose Edit | Undo to undo the conver-
> sion without closing the image.

Going to sRGB from a larger color space usually involves some loss of color, but
you should be able to get Save for Web to respect your original colors more closely
using this method.

Creating an Online Gallery

For a quick way to create a nice online presentation of your work, check out the
Web Photo Gallery command. With this tool, you can create a simple Web page
such as the one shown in Figure 15.20.

You can choose from a number of design templates, all of which feature small
thumbnails that the viewer clicks to display a larger view of a single image.
You also can include your contact information and other details.

From a design standpoint, the available templates aren't terribly dynamic, but you
can put up a serviceable gallery in minutes. To try it out, follow these steps:

1. **Select the images for the gallery.**

| v.7 | ■ In Version 7, move all the images into a single folder. |

| CS | ■ In CS, select the image thumbnails in the File Browser. |

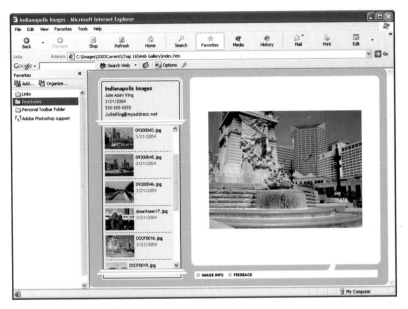

Figure 15.20: Use the Web Photo
Gallery command to produce an
online gallery in minutes.

2. Select the Web Photo Gallery command.

■ In Version 7, choose the command from the File | Automate submenu.

CS ■ In CS, choose the command from the Automate menu at the top of
the File Browser.

The dialog box shown in Figure 15.21 appears.

3. Choose a design template from the Styles drop-down list.

The little preview on the right side of the dialog box gives you an idea of what
each design looks like.

4. Enter your e-mail address if you want to include it on the
gallery page.

v.7 ## 5. Select the folder that contains the gallery images
(Version 7 only).

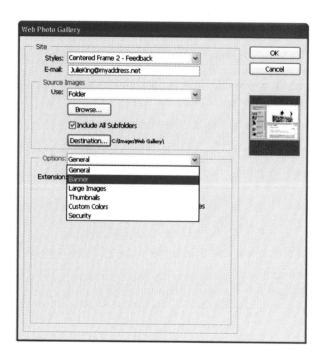

Figure 15.21: Click the Options drop-down list and select the design element you want to customize.

If the correct folder doesn't appear in the Use drop-down list, click the Browse button (Windows) or Choose button (Mac) to select the folder. If you choose Include All Subfolders, Photoshop also grabs any images contained in subfolders inside the main folder you select.

6. **Click the Destination button and choose a folder to store the files used to produce the gallery page.**

It's usually best to create a new folder to hold all the gallery components, which will include not only image files but the HTML files needed to display the gallery in a Web browser.

7. **Customize the layout by working through each category in the Options drop-down list.**

You see the list unfurled in Figure 15.21. When you select an item from the list, relevant options appear in the bottom half of the dialog box.

8. **Click OK.**

Photoshop begins processing and creating all the files needed to produce the Web page. When finished, it stores all the files in the folder you specified in Step 6 and displays the page in your default Web browser. Notice that the size of the gallery page is designed to allow for the browser itself to consume some of the horizontal and vertical screen space, as shown in Figure 15.20.

From here, you have to take control of getting the page to the Web. You don't necessarily need to run your own Web site, however. If you have an e-mail account, your service provider may make a small amount of personal Web space available to you; check their customer service information to find out how to post your page in that space.

INDEX

INTERNATIONAL CONTACT INFORMATION

AUSTRALIA
McGraw-Hill Book Company
Australia Pty. Ltd.
TEL +61-2-9900-1800
FAX +61-2-9878-8881
http://www.mcgraw-hill.com.au
books-it_sydney@mcgraw-hill.com

CANADA
McGraw-Hill Ryerson Ltd.
TEL +905-430-5000
FAX +905-430-5020
http://www.mcgraw-hill.ca

**GREECE, MIDDLE EAST, & AFRICA
(Excluding South Africa)**
McGraw-Hill Hellas
TEL +30-210-6560-990
TEL +30-210-6560-993
TEL +30-210-6560-994
FAX +30-210-6545-525

MEXICO (Also serving Latin America)
McGraw-Hill Interamericana Editores
S.A. de C.V.
TEL +525-1500-5108
FAX +525-117-1589
http://www.mcgraw-hill.com.mx
carlos_ruiz@mcgraw-hill.com

SINGAPORE (Serving Asia)
McGraw-Hill Book Company
TEL +65-6863-1580
FAX +65-6862-3354
http://www.mcgraw-hill.com.sg
mghasia@mcgraw-hill.com

SOUTH AFRICA
McGraw-Hill South Africa
TEL +27-11-622-7512
FAX +27-11-622-9045
robyn_swanepoel@mcgraw-hill.com

SPAIN
McGraw-Hill/
Interamericana de España, S.A.U.
TEL +34-91-180-3000
FAX +34-91-372-8513
http://www.mcgraw-hill.es
professional@mcgraw-hill.es

**UNITED KINGDOM, NORTHERN,
EASTERN, & CENTRAL EUROPE**
McGraw-Hill Education Europe
TEL +44-1-628-502500
FAX +44-1-628-770224
http://www.mcgraw-hill.co.uk
emea_queries@mcgraw-hill.com

ALL OTHER INQUIRIES Contact:
McGraw-Hill/Osborne
TEL +1-510-420-7700
FAX +1-510-420-7703
http://www.osborne.com
omg_international@mcgraw-hill.com